FAVORITE BRAND NAME™

VEGETARIAN COOKING

Publications International, Ltd.

Favorite Brand Name Recipes at www.fbnr.com

Front cover photography by Chris Cassidy Photography, Inc.

Pictured on the front cover *(clockwise from left):* Thin-Crust Whole Wheat Veggie Pizza *(page 144),* Black Bean Burgers *(page 154),* Grilled Vegetable Pasta Salad *(page 120),* Veggie-Pepper Bowls with Rice *(page 82)* and Cheese Polenta with Vegetable Medley *(page 220).*
Pictured on the jacket flaps: Eggplant Crêpes with Roasted Tomato Sauce *(page 218)* and Herb-Stuffed Tomatoes *(page 44).*
Pictured on the back cover *(clockwise from top):* Pepperonata *(page 334),* Minted Fruit Rice Salad *(page 102),* Cheese Blintzes *(page 186)* and Chilled Potato Cucumber Soup with Roasted Red Pepper Swirl *(page 60).*

ISBN-13: 978-1-4127-2960-4
ISBN-10: 1-4127-2960-2

Manufactured in China.

8 7 6 5 4 3 2 1

Microwave Cooking: Microwave ovens vary in wattage. Use the cooking times as guidelines and check for doneness before adding more time.

The HEALTHY CHOICE® recipes contained in this book have been tested by the manufacturers and have been carefully edited by the publisher. The publisher and the manufacturers cannot be held responsible for any ill effects caused by the errors in the recipes, or by spoiled ingredients, unsanitary conditions, incorrect preparation procedures or any other cause.

FAVORITE BRAND NAME™
VEGETARIAN
COOKING

VEGETARIAN BASICS

What is Vegetarianism?

By definition vegetarians eat no meat, poultry or seafood. They rely primarily on plants as sources for food. This doesn't mean that they consume only vegetables. A diet based on plants also includes grains and the foods made from grains—cereals, pastas and breads. Nuts, seeds, legumes and fruits round out the diet.

Vegetarians generally fall into one of three categories—vegans, ovo-lacto-vegetarians and lacto-vegetarians. Those who consume only food from plant sources are called vegans. They avoid meat, poultry, fish, eggs and dairy products. Ovo-lacto-vegetarians make up the largest group of American vegetarians and supplement their diets with both dairy products and eggs, but eat no meat, fish or poultry. Lacto-vegetarians consume dairy products but not eggs.

Health & Nutrition Concerns

The latest guidelines from the United States Department of Agriculture and the Department of Health and Human Services suggest that a healthful diet should include lots of grain-based foods, fruits and vegetables. These organizations and registered dietitians recommend reducing the consumption of animal-based foods in order to reduce the total fat, saturated fat and cholesterol in our diets. The vegetarian diet fits well with these recommendations.

For those who use dairy products and eggs, care must be exercised to limit the use of eggs and high-fat dairy products, such as cheese, butter, sour cream and cream. Substitute reduced-fat dairy products for these high-fat products whenever possible.

Protein is a necessary nutrient in our diets, but nutrition professionals believe that most adults who consume animal-based foods eat too much protein. A diet based primarily on plant sources can fulfill the body's protein requirements. Once you know the basics, it is easy to get enough protein.

Unlike animal products, plant foods generally do not contain complete proteins except rice, potatoes and soy beans. Plant foods contain certain amounts of complementary proteins that when consumed in combination with specific other complementary proteins become complete. Current thinking that as long as the right complementary proteins are consumed within the same day, adequate complete protein will be available to meet the body's needs. In other words, a diet rich in a variety of grains, seeds, nuts, legumes, fruits and vegetables can easily provide the components of complete proteins.

For quick reference, follow these basic combinations to form the most complete proteins:

Dairy Products + Grains = Complete Protein

Legumes + Seeds = Complete Protein

Legumes + Grains = Complete Protein

Of greater concern is meeting the body's need for vitamins D and B$_{12}$. The primary dietary source of vitamin D is fortified milk. Plants do not provide this essential vitamin. However, the body can make vitamin D when the skin is exposed to sunshine. With concerns about exposure to sunlight, obtaining enough vitamin D can be difficult for vegans. Getting an adequate amount of vitamin B$_{12}$ is more of a problem, because it is found naturally only in animal products and the body cannot make it. Consequently, vegans must rely on fortified foods, such as breakfast cereals and soy milk, or supplements for these two vitamins.

DRIED BEANS

Legumes, which include dried beans, peas and lentils, are a nutritional windfall. They provide a low-fat, low-sodium, cholesterol-free source of protein. They are also high in complex carbohydrates and fiber and are loaded with many vitamins and minerals, including iron and calcium.

Dried beans are readily available and are sold prepackaged or in bulk. Beans labeled as "quick-cooking" are presoaked and redried before packaging, making them quicker to prepare. However, their bite isn't as firm as regular dried beans.

Always rinse and sort through dried legumes before cooking them. Discard any foreign material, as well as any beans that are shriveled, discolored or cracked.

After sorting, most beans are rehydrated either by the overnight soaking method or the quick-soak method. This reduces cooking time, softens the beans and removes undigestible sugars that may cause flatulence. Split peas and lentils do not need to be soaked before cooking.

Overnight Soaking Method: If you are planning your meal a day in advance, the overnight soaking method is ideal for rehydrating beans. Place sorted dried beans in a large bowl or saucepan; cover them with 4 inches of water. Let stand at room temperature at least 8 hours, then rinse and drain.

Quick-Soak Method: When you do not have 8 hours to soak beans, the quick-soak method is an easy way to rehydrate beans. Place sorted dried beans in a large saucepan; cover them with 4 inches of water. Bring to a boil over high heat. Uncover pan; boil for 2 minutes. Remove pan from the heat; cover. Let stand 1 hour in water, then rinse and drain.

GUIDE TO COOKING DRIED BEANS

Bean	Amount	Water	Simmering Time	Yield
Black Beans	1 pound	8 cups	1½ hours	6 cups
Black-Eyed Peas	1 pound	8 cups	45–60 minutes	7 cups
Garbanzo Beans	1 pound	8 cups	1½–2½ hours	6¼ cups
Great Northern Beans	1 pound	8 cups	1–1½ hours	7 cups
Lentils	1 pound	8 cups	25–45 minutes	7 cups
Lima Beans	1 pound	8 cups	1–1½ hours	6½ cups
Navy Beans	1 pound	8 cups	1–1½ hours	7 cups
Red Kidney Beans	1 pound	8 cups	1–1½ hours	6⅔ cups
Split Peas	1 pound	8 cups	25–45 minutes	7 cups

Use the Guide to Cooking Dried Beans chart on page 5 as a handy reference when cooking dried beans. Measure the amount of water and beans specified into a large saucepan. Bring to a boil over medium-high heat. Reduce the heat to low. Cover; simmer for the time specified or until the beans are tender, stirring occasionally.

To test the doneness of dried beans, remove several beans from the saucepan. Gently squeeze the beans between your thumb and index finger. The beans are done when they are tender, but not mushy. When the beans are tender, remove them from the heat and immediately run them under cold running water to cool. Drain in a colander. If left in their cooking water, the beans continue to cook, loose their shape and may become mushy.

1 pound dried beans = 2½ to 3 cups uncooked = 6 to 7 cups cooked
1 (16-ounce) can beans = 1⅔ cups drained

Store dried beans in an airtight container at room temperature for up to one year or in the freezer indefinitely. Place cooked beans in an airtight container and store up to one week in the refrigerator or up to six months in the freezer.

GRAINS

Grains such as barley, bulgur, corn, oats, quinoa, rice, rye, wheat and wild rice are the edible seed kernels of cereal plants and grasses. They are excellent sources of inexpensive protein and complex carbohydrates and are important parts of a vegetarian diet.

Most grains undergo various processings before they are sold. Grains can be polished which removes the bran and germ from the kernel. Grains are also steamed to soften the kernels or cracked or ground which shortens cooking times.

Barley is a hardy grain that is available in several forms. Hulled barley has only the husk removed so that its bran and germ are intact. Scotch barley and barley grits have been further processed by grinding or cracking. The most common form of barley is pearled, meaning that it has been polished many times to remove the bran and most of the germ. Pearl barley is also available in a quick-cooking form.

Bulgur consists of wheat kernels that have been steamed, dried and crushed. It comes in coarse, medium and fine grinds and has a tender, chewy texture.

Cornmeal is corn kernels that have been ground. It comes in coarse, medium and fine grinds, as well as in yellow, white or blue colors. The color of the cornmeal is dependent on the type of corn that is ground.

GUIDE TO COOKING GRAINS

Grain	Amount	Water	Simmering Time	Yield
Arborio Rice	1 cup	1½ cups	20 minutes	2 cups
Barley, Pearl	1 cup	4 cups	45 minutes	3½ cups
Barley, Quick-Cooking	1 cup	1½ cups	10–12 minutes	2½ cups
Basmati Rice	1 cup	2½ cups	20 minutes	3 cups
Brown Rice	1 cup	2 cups	45 minutes	3 cups
Bulgur	1 cup	2 cups	15–20 minutes	2½ cups
Oats, Quick-Cooking	1 cup	2 cups	1 minute	2 cups
Oats, Regular	1 cup	2 cups	5–7 minutes	2 cups
White Rice	1 cup	2 cups	20 minutes	3 cups
Wild Rice	1 cup	2 cups	50 minutes	2⅔ cups

Oats must be processed before they can be eaten. They are cleaned, toasted and hulled to make oat groats. Groats are steamed and flattened into flakes to make regular rolled oats, often called old-fashioned oats. Further processing yields quick-cooking rolled oats. The more processed the oats, the less chewy the texture they have when cooked.

Quinoa was a staple of the ancient Incas who called it "the mother grain." It remains a very important part of South American cuisine. Often compared to couscous, it is tiny, bead-shaped and ivory colored. Quinoa cooks like rice, but in about half the time and can be used in any way suitable for rice. Its flavor is delicate and almost bland.

Pasta, Beans and Rice Varieties pictured at right: 1. Orzo pasta, 2. White basmati rice, 3. Instant white rice, 4. Arborio rice, 5. Wild rice, 6. Black beans, 7. Split peas, 8. Bulgur, 9. Couscous, 10. Cornmeal (polenta), 11. Black-eyed peas, 12. Garbanzo beans, 13. Lima beans, 14. Pinto beans, 15. Cannellini beans, 16. Great Northern beans, 17. Lentils, 18. Red kidney beans, 19. Elbow macaroni, 20. Rotini, 21. Angel hair pasta, 22. Ditalini, 23. Bow tie pasta, 24. Ravioli, 25. Radiatore, 26. Linguine, 27. Spinach fettuccine, 28. Fusilli, 29. Small shell pasta, 30. Lasagna noodles

Rice is a staple for more than half the world's population, making it one of the most popular grains. It is classified according to the length of its grains. Long-grain is the most common type of rice and is interchangeable with medium-grain rice. Short-grain rice contains more starch than long and medium grains, which makes the grains very sticky when cooked. There are many different varieties of rice that can be found in most large supermarkets.

• Arborio rice is an Italian-grown short-grain rice that has large, plump grains with a delicious nutty taste. Arborio rice is traditionally used for risotto dishes because its high starch content produces a creamy texture and it can absorb more liquid than regular or long-grain rice.

• Aromatic rice is a general term used to classify rices with fragrant, nutlike flavors and aromas. Basmati rice from India, jasmine rice from Thailand and Texmati rice from Texas are some of the more common aromatic rices.

• Brown rice is the least processed of all rice varieties. Only the hull is removed. The rice has a natural tan color due to the bran layers that are left on the grain. When cooked, brown rice has a nutty flavor and slightly chewy texture.

• White rice is also referred to as polished rice. It is completely milled to remove the hull and bran layers. Over 90% of milled rice in the United States is enriched with thiamin, riboflavin, niacin and iron. Do not rinse enriched rice before cooking because those nutrients will be lost. This rice has a mild, delicate flavor.

• Precooked (quick-cooking) rice is brown or white long-grain rice that has been cooked, rinsed and dried by a patented process. Precooked rice takes only minutes to prepare because it only needs to be rehydrated during preparation.

Wild rice has a chewy texture and earthy flavor. It is often classified as a rice, but it is actually the seed of an aquatic marsh grass native to Minnesota.

Use the Guide to Cooking Grains chart on page 6 as a handy reference when cooking grains. As a general rule, most uncooked grains expand two to three times their original size during cooking. Measure the amount of water specified into a medium saucepan. Bring to a boil over medium-high heat. Slowly add the grains and return to a boil. Reduce the heat to low. Cover; simmer for the time specified or until the grains are tender and most of the water has been absorbed.

Because of their tendency to become rancid, unpolished whole grains should be bought in small quantities and stored in the refrigerator in an airtight container. They will keep up to six months. Polished kernels stored in a cool, dry place in an airtight container will keep up to one year.

PASTA

Pasta is one of the most versatile, convenient and economical foods available. It is made from durum wheat, water and sometimes eggs and comes in over 150 shapes. Pasta provides an excellent source of complex carbohydrates and a good supply of iron, magnesium, thiamin, niacin and riboflavin.

For best results when cooking pasta, use plenty of rapidly boiling water. For 1 pound of pasta use 4 to 6 quarts water. Oil and salt are often added to the cooking water for flavor. However, they can be omitted without altering the final product, thus reducing added fat and salt in your diet. Gradually add the pasta, stirring gently until the water returns to a boil. Stirring prevents the pasta from sticking to the pan and allows it to cook more evenly.

Cooking times vary by the type and sometimes by the brand of pasta. Use the Guide to Cooking Dried Pasta chart below as a handy reference when cooking pasta. Begin checking for doneness at the minimum recommended time by removing a piece or strand of pasta and biting into it. If it's tender but still firm (al dente), it's done. Immediately drain pasta. Pasta should only be rinsed if it is to be used in a salad. Rinsing cools the pasta and washes away excess starch, which causes sticking. Pasta that is to be baked, such as lasagna noodles, should be slightly undercooked or it will be too soft after baking.

Dried, commercially prepared pasta can be stored indefinitely in an airtight container at room temperature.

VEGETABLES

Vegetables are an important part of all diets because they supply a wide variety of essential nutrients. They are rich in vitamins A and C as well as other vitamins, minerals and fiber.

However, cooking vegetables places these nutrients at risk of being lost. The greatest loss of nutrients occurs from placing a vegetable in water because many of the nutrients dissolve. High temperatures and long cooking times also cause nutritional loss. Use the Guide to Fresh Vegetables chart on pages 10 and 11 as a handy reference for cooking vegetables to the proper doneness. All vegetables should be cooked no longer than necessary to make them just tender and then removed quickly from heat source. The cooking times start when the water returns to a boil.

Steaming vs. Boiling

Even though steaming cooks with high temperatures, the vegetables cook quickly from the intense heat. Steaming also lessens the dissolving out of nutrients and flavors into the water because the vegetables are not submerged in water as they are when boiling, but sit above the water in a steaming rack. Delicate vegetables also benefit from steaming because they are above the rapidly boiling water and will remain intact.

Strong-flavored vegetables from the onion, cabbage and root families, such as garlic, broccoli and turnips, benefit from boiling because it lessens their strong taste and makes them more appealing. Use only enough water to cover the vegetables to minimize leaching of nutrients into the water and leave the vegetables uncovered to allow the flavors to escape. Always start root vegetables in cold water and bring to a boil. This allows the vegetables to cook throughout at an even rate.

Blanching is another way to cook vegetables. To blanch, vegetables are placed briefly in boiling water and then cooled quickly in cold water. It's perfect for removing the skin from tomatoes or brightening the color of raw vegetables to snack on.

GUIDE TO COOKING DRIED PASTA				
Pasta	**Amount**	**Water**	**Boiling Time**	**Yield**
Angel Hair	4 ounces	4 quarts	5-7 minutes	2 cups
Bow Ties	2 cups	4 quarts	10 minutes	2½ cups
Elbow Macaroni	2 cups	4 quarts	10 minutes	3 cups
Fettuccine	4 ounces	4 quarts	8–10 minutes	2 cups
Orzo	2 cups	4 quarts	5–8 minutes	4 cups
Spaghetti	4 ounces	4 quarts	10–12 minutes	2 cups

GUIDE TO FRESH VEGETABLES

Vegetable	Peak Season	Buying Tips	Yield of 1 pound	Steaming Time*	Boiling Time*
Asparagus	late February to mid-summer	• firm, smooth green stems • tightly closed tips • even green color	12–15 spears 3 cups chopped	8–10 minutes	4–6 minutes
Beans, green	May to September	• brightly colored, crisp beans • slenderness indicates tenderness	3½ cups whole 2¾ cups pieces	5–15 minutes	10–20 minutes
Broccoli	October to April	• firm stems • tightly packed dark green buds • tightly closed buds	2 cups chopped	florets: 5–6 minutes spears: 8–15 minutes	4–5 minutes 5–10 minutes
Brussels sprouts	October to April	• firm, heavy, compact sprouts • bright green color • small size indicates sweetness	4 cups raw 2½ cups cooked	6–12 minutes	5–10 minutes
Cabbage	year-round	• heavy, compact heads • bright-colored leaves	4–4½ cups shredded 2 cups cooked	shredded: 5–8 minutes wedges: 6–9 minutes	5–10 minutes 10–15 minutes
Carrots	year-round	• slender, firm and smooth • healthy reddish-orange color	3 cups chopped or sliced 2½ cups shredded	whole: 10–15 minutes slices: 4–5 minutes	15–20 minutes 5–10 minutes
Cauliflower	late fall to spring	• firm, heavy heads • compact florets • crisp, green leaves	1½ cups florets	whole: 15–20 minutes florets: 6–10 minutes	10–15 minutes 5–8 minutes
Corn	mid-July to early September	• soft, pliable outer husks • golden and soft silks	1 ear = ½ cup kernels	6–10 minutes	3–7 minutes
Eggplant	August and September	• firm, heavy and smooth • bright green, fresh stem • smaller size indicates sweetness and tenderness	3-4 cups chopped	5–6 minutes	5–10 minutes
Mushrooms	fall and winter	• firm and evenly colored • tightly closed caps	6 cups sliced	4–5 minutes	3–4 minutes

*Steaming and boiling times are based on 1 pound of vegetable.

GUIDE TO FRESH VEGETABLES, *continued*

Vegetable	Peak Season	Buying Tips	Yield of 1 pound	Steaming Time*	Boiling Time*
Onions	year-round	• dry, firm and heavy • mild scent	3 large or 4 medium 2–3 cups chopped	20–25 minutes	20–30 minutes
Peas	April to July	• small, plump, firm pods • shiny, bright green color	1 cup shelled peas	3–5 minutes	3 minutes
Peppers, bell	July to November	• firm, crisp and heavy • shiny, brightly colored skins • green, hard stems	1 large = 1 cup chopped 1¼ cups strips	2–4 minutes	4–5 minutes
Potatoes	year-round	• clean, firm and well shaped • smooth, dry skins free of sprouts	2–3 medium 3½ cups cooked, cut	whole: 12–30 minutes cut: 10–12 minutes	20–30 minutes 15–20 minutes
Spinach	year-round	• good colored, crisp leaves • narrow, tender stems	10–12 cups torn pieces 1 cup cooked	5–6 minutes	2–5 minutes
Squash, summer	summer	• small or medium in size • smooth, glossy unblemished skins • firm and heavy	3 medium 2½ cups chopped 1⅔ cups cooked	sliced: 3–6 minutes	5–10 minutes
Squash, winter	September to March	• hard, thick shells • heavy	1 cup cooked, mashed	sliced: 9–12 minutes	5–10 minutes
Tomatoes	mid-summer to September	• plump, firm and heavy • vibrant color and pleasant aroma	3 medium 8 plum 2 cups chopped	2–3 minutes	not recommended
Turnips	October to February	• firm and heavy • 2 inches in diameter • smooth, unblemished skin	2½ cups chopped	whole: 20–25 minutes cut: 12–15 minutes	15–20 minutes 5–8 minutes
Zucchini	July to September	• heavy, firm and well shaped • smooth, bright-colored skins • small size indicates tenderness	3 medium 2½ cups sliced	5–10 minutes	5–10 minutes

*Steaming and boiling times are based on 1 pound of vegetable.

PARTY–PLEASING APPETIZERS

Five-Layered Mexican Dip

½ cup low fat sour cream
½ cup GUILTLESS GOURMET®
   Salsa (mild, medium or hot)
1 jar (12.5 ounces) GUILTLESS
   GOURMET® Bean Dip
   (Black or Pinto, mild or spicy)
2 cups shredded lettuce
½ cup chopped tomato

¼ cup (1 ounce) shredded sharp
   Cheddar cheese
Chopped fresh cilantro and
   cilantro sprigs (optional)
1 large bag (7 ounces)
   GUILTLESS GOURMET®
   Baked Tortilla Chips (yellow,
   white or blue corn)

Mix together sour cream and salsa in small bowl. Spread bean dip in shallow glass bowl. Top with sour cream-salsa mixture, spreading to cover bean dip.* Just before serving, top with lettuce, tomato and cheese. Garnish with cilantro, if desired. Serve with tortilla chips.

Makes 8 servings

*Dip may be prepared to this point; cover and refrigerate up to 24 hours.

Five-Layered Mexican Dip

Hot Black Bean Dip

1 can (about 15 ounces) black
    beans, rinsed and drained
1 can (about 16 ounces) whole
    tomatoes, drained and
    chopped
1 canned chipotle chili in adobo
    sauce, drained and finely
    chopped*

1 teaspoon dried oregano leaves
1 cup (4 ounces) shredded
    reduced-fat Cheddar cheese
Tortilla chips

Place beans in medium bowl; mash with fork until smooth.

Place beans in heavy, small saucepan. Stir in tomatoes, chipotle and oregano. Cook over medium heat 5 minutes or until heated through, stirring occasionally. Remove saucepan from heat. Add cheese; stir constantly until cheese melts.

Pour bean dip into serving bowl. Serve hot with tortilla chips.   *Makes 8 servings*

*Chipotle chilies can sting and irritate the skin; wear rubber gloves when handling chilies and do not touch eyes.

Summer's Gold Medal Salsa

4 fresh ripe California nectarines
1 fresh ripe pear or apple
2 red bell peppers, seeded and
    chopped

3 tablespoons minced mild or hot
    fresh chile peppers
3 tablespoons minced onion
3 tablespoons fresh lime juice

Chop nectarines and pear. Mix all ingredients well, stirring to bring out some juices. Cover with plastic wrap; chill until ready to serve. May be made up to 4 hours ahead.

Makes 6 ($^{1}/_{2}$-cup) servings

Favorite recipe from **California Tree Fruit Agreement**

Hot Black Bean Dip

Nutty Broccoli Spread

Nutty Broccoli Spread

1 box (10 ounces) **BIRDS EYE®**
frozen Chopped Broccoli

4 ounces cream cheese

¼ cup grated Parmesan cheese

1 teaspoon dried basil

¼ cup walnuts

1 loaf frozen garlic bread

• Cook broccoli according to package directions; drain well.

• Preheat oven to 400°F. Place broccoli, cream cheese, Parmesan cheese and basil in food processor or blender; process until ingredients are mixed. *(Do not overmix.)* Add walnuts; process 3 to 5 seconds.

• Split garlic bread lengthwise. Spread broccoli mixture evenly over bread.

• Bake 10 to 15 minutes or until bread is toasted and broccoli mixture is heated through.

• Cut bread into bite-size pieces; serve hot.   *Makes about 2 cups spread*

Prep Time: 10 minutes   **Cook Time:** 10 to 15 minutes

Hummus Vegetable Dip

1 (16-ounce) can chick-peas, rinsed and well drained
5 tablespoons lemon juice
¼ cup water
¼ cup tahini (sesame seed paste)
2 tablespoons FILIPPO BERIO® Olive Oil
1 to 2 cloves garlic, sliced
¼ teaspoon ground cumin
Salt and freshly ground black pepper

Few drops hot pepper sauce (optional)
Additional lemon juice (optional)
Assorted cut-up fresh vegetables
Pita bread wedges
Oil-cured black olives (optional)
Additional FILIPPO BERIO® Olive Oil (optional)

In blender container or food processor, place chick-peas, 5 tablespoons lemon juice, water, tahini, 2 tablespoons olive oil, garlic and cumin; process until mixture is thick and creamy. Season to taste with salt, black pepper and hot pepper sauce, if desired. Adjust consistency with additional lemon juice or water, if desired. Transfer to serving bowl. Cover; refrigerate at least 1 hour before serving. Serve with vegetables and pita bread; garnish dip with olives and drizzle of additional olive oil, if desired.

Makes about 1¼ cups dip

Pimento Pepper Dip with Tortellini Kabobs

PIMENTO PEPPER DIP

1 small clove garlic, peeled
1 package (4 ounces) soft garlic
    and spice cheese spread
2 jars (4 ounces each) pimentos,
    rinsed, drained and dried

1 teaspoon balsamic, cider or wine
    vinegar

TORTELLINI KABOBS

1 to 1½ pounds spinach- or
    cheese-filled tortellini
2 tablespoons olive oil

1 tablespoon dried basil
Salt to taste

Mince garlic in food processor fitted with metal blade. Add cheese spread and process until puréed. Add pimentos and vinegar; process until smooth, about 1 minute. Transfer to medium bowl and refrigerate until 15 minutes before serving.

Cook tortellini according to package directions. Rinse with cold water and drain well. Place in large bowl and toss with olive oil, basil and salt to taste. Refrigerate.

Thread 2 tortellini on wooden picks and arrange on platter surrounding bowl of Pimento Pepper Dip.

Makes 12 to 14 servings

Note: Dip is best when made one day prior to serving and refrigerated overnight.

Favorite recipe from **Pimento Canners of America**

Zesty Spinach Dip

1 cup sour cream
¼ cup GREY POUPON® Dijon
   Mustard
1 (0.7-ounce) package Italian
   salad dressing mix
1 (10-ounce) package frozen
   chopped spinach, thawed and
   well drained

¼ cup finely grated carrot
2 tablespoons finely chopped red
   bell pepper
Hollowed green or red bell
   pepper cup, optional
Assorted vegetable crudités and
   crackers, for dipping

In medium bowl, blend sour cream, mustard and salad dressing mix. Stir in spinach, carrot and chopped bell pepper. Chill until serving time. If desired, spoon dip into green or red bell pepper cup. Serve with crudités and crackers. *Makes 2 cups*

Moroccan Spiced Hummus

2 cans (15½ ounces each) garbanzo
   beans, drained and rinsed
⅓ cup honey
¼ cup lemon juice
1 teaspoon minced garlic
1 teaspoon ground cumin

½ teaspoon salt
   Dash cayenne pepper
2 to 3 tablespoons chopped fresh
   cilantro or parsley
Toasted Pita Triangles (recipe
   follows) or crackers

Combine all ingredients except cilantro and Toasted Pita Triangles in food processor or blender. Process until smooth. Remove mixture to serving bowl. Stir in cilantro. Serve with Toasted Pita Triangles or crackers. *Makes 2½ cups dip*

Toasted Pita Triangles: Separate pita bread rounds into 2 circles each. Cut each circle into 6 or 8 triangles. Place on baking sheet. Bake at 400°F about 5 minutes or until crisp and lightly browned at edges.

Favorite recipe from **National Honey Board**

Fresh Garden Dip

1½ cups fat-free or reduced-fat
mayonnaise
1½ cups finely shredded DOLE®
Carrots
1 cup finely chopped DOLE®
Broccoli Florets

⅓ cup finely chopped DOLE®
Green Onions
2 teaspoons dill weed
¼ teaspoon garlic powder

• **Stir** together mayonnaise, carrots, broccoli, green onions, dill and garlic powder in medium bowl until blended.

• **Spoon** into serving bowl. Cover and chill 1 hour or overnight. Serve with Dole® Broccoli Florets, Cauliflower Florets and Peeled Mini Carrots. Garnish with fresh dill sprigs, if desired. Refrigerate any leftover dip in airtight container up to 1 week.

Makes 14 servings

Prep Time: 15 minutes   **Chill Time:** 1 hour

Hot Artichoke Spread

1 can (14 ounces) artichoke
hearts, drained, chopped
1 cup (4 ounces) KRAFT® 100%
Grated Parmesan Cheese

1 cup MIRACLE WHIP® Salad
Dressing or KRAFT® Real
Mayonnaise

• Heat oven to 350°F.

• Mix all ingredients; spoon into 9-inch pie plate or 2-cup casserole.

• Bake 20 minutes or until lightly browned. Garnish as desired. Serve with tortilla chips, crackers or party rye bread slices.

Makes about 2 cups

Top to bottom: **Fresh Garden Dip and Fiesta Quesadillas with Fruit Salsa** *(page 37)*

Ortega® Guacamole

2 medium ripe avocados, pitted,
    peeled and mashed
⅓ cup ORTEGA® Thick &
    Chunky Salsa, hot, medium
    or mild
¼ cup sour cream
2 tablespoons finely chopped onion

2 tablespoons chopped fresh
    cilantro
1 teaspoon lime juice
1 clove garlic, finely chopped
¼ teaspoon salt
    Tortilla chips

COMBINE avocados, salsa, sour cream, onion, cilantro, lime juice, garlic and salt in medium bowl. Cover; chill for at least 1 hour. Serve with chips.   *Makes 2 cups*

Tip: This all-time favorite dip can be used in tacos, burritos, tamales, chimichangas or combined with Ortega® Salsa for a spicy salad dressing.

Touchdown Taco Dip

1 (8-ounce) package cream cheese,
    softened
½ cup sour cream
½ cup ORTEGA® Mild, Medium
    or Hot Thick and Smooth
    Taco Sauce
1 teaspoon chili powder

¼ teaspoon ground red pepper
½ cup chopped cucumber
¼ cup sliced scallions
    Shredded lettuce, chopped
    tomato, sliced black olives,
    for garnish
MR. PHIPPS® Pretzel Chips

BEAT cream cheese and sour cream with electric mixer at medium speed until smooth. Stir in taco sauce, chili powder and red pepper. Fold in cucumber and scallions. Chill at least 1 hour. To serve, spoon dip into center of large round plate; top with lettuce, tomato and olives. Arrange pretzel chips around edge of dip. Serve with additional pretzel chips for dipping.   *Makes 2½ cups*

Ortega® Guacamole

Layered Avocado and Black Bean Dip

2 ripe medium avocados, pitted
  and peeled
¼ cup GREY POUPON® Dijon
  Mustard
2 tablespoons lime juice
¼ cup minced red onion
1 clove garlic, crushed
1 to 2 teaspoons liquid hot pepper
  seasoning
1 teaspoon chopped cilantro

1 (16-ounce) can black beans,
  rinsed and drained
½ cup sour cream
½ cup chopped tomato
  Shredded Cheddar cheese,
  sliced pitted ripe olives
  Additional sour cream, for
  garnish
  Tortilla chips

In electric blender container, combine avocados, mustard and lime juice until blended. Stir in onion, garlic, hot pepper seasoning and cilantro; set aside.

In medium bowl, mash black beans; combine with ½ cup sour cream. Spread black bean mixture on serving dish. Spread avocado mixture over bean layer. Top with tomato, cheese and olives. Garnish with additional sour cream. Serve with tortilla chips.

Makes 6 to 8 appetizer servings

Honey Nut Brie

¼ cup honey
¼ cup coarsely chopped pecans
1 tablespoon brandy (optional)

1 wheel (14 ounces) Brie cheese
  (about 5-inch diameter)

Combine honey, pecans and brandy, if desired, in small bowl. Place cheese on large round ovenproof platter or 9-inch pie plate. Bake in preheated 500°F oven 4 to 5 minutes or until cheese softens. Drizzle honey mixture over top of cheese. Bake 2 to 3 minutes longer or until topping is thoroughly heated. *Do not melt cheese.*

Makes 16 to 20 servings

Favorite recipe from **National Honey Board**

Grilled Vegetables with Olive Sauce

Grilled Vegetables with Olive Sauce

2 thawed frozen medium ears
    sweet corn, cut into 1-inch
    rounds
2 large yellow pattypan squash,
    coarsely chopped
1 medium zucchini, thinly sliced
    Vegetable oil

¼ cup butter or margarine
6 green olives with pimientos,
    finely chopped
1 tablespoon lemon juice
¼ teaspoon dried parsley
1 container (16 ounces) cottage
    cheese

Prepare barbecue grill for direct cooking.

Spray vegetable grilling grid with nonstick cooking spray. Place corn, squash and zucchini on prepared grid; brush with oil and season with salt and pepper to taste.

Grill, on covered grill, over hot coals 10 minutes or until crisp-tender, turning halfway through grilling time. Remove; keep warm.

Melt butter in small microwavable bowl on HIGH. Stir in olives, lemon juice and parsley.

Place vegetables on serving platter; drizzle with 2 tablespoons olive sauce. Serve with cottage cheese and remaining olive sauce. *Makes 4 servings*

Prep and Cook Time: 20 minutes

Southwestern Cheesecake

1 cup finely crushed tortilla chips
3 tablespoons butter or
    margarine, melted
2 (8-ounce) packages
    PHILADELPHIA BRAND®
    Cream Cheese, softened
2 eggs
1 (8-ounce) package KRAFT®
    Shredded Colby/Monterey
    Jack Cheese

1 (4-ounce) can chopped green
    chilies, drained
1 cup BREAKSTONE'S® or
    KNUDSEN® Sour Cream
1 cup chopped yellow or orange
    bell pepper
½ cup green onion slices
⅓ cup chopped tomatoes
¼ cup sliced pitted ripe olives

• Preheat oven to 325°F.

• Stir together chips and butter in small bowl; press onto bottom of 9-inch springform pan. Bake 15 minutes.

• Beat cream cheese and eggs in large mixing bowl at medium speed with electric mixer until well blended. Mix in shredded cheese and chilies; pour over crust. Bake 30 minutes.

• Spread sour cream over cheesecake. Loosen cake from rim of pan; cool before removing rim of pan. Chill.

• Top with remaining ingredients just before serving.

Makes 16 to 20 appetizer servings

Prep Time: 20 minutes plus chilling   **Cook Time:** 30 minutes

Hint: To make an attractive design on top of this cheesecake, cut three diamonds out of paper. Place on top of cheesecake. Place green onion slices around diamonds. Remove cutouts; fill in with bell peppers. Add a strip of tomatoes down the center. Garnish with olives.

Southwestern Cheesecake

Pesto Brie

Pesto Brie

2 tablespoons **GREY POUPON®**
Dijon Mustard
2 tablespoons **prepared pesto**
sauce
1 (8-ounce) **wheel Brie cheese**
2 tablespoons **PLANTERS®**
Walnuts, finely chopped

Chopped tomatoes and fresh
basil leaves, for garnish
Assorted crackers or
breadsticks

In small bowl, blend mustard and pesto; set aside. Cut cheese in half horizontally. Place bottom half on greased baking sheet, cut side up; spread with half the pesto mixture. Replace top of Brie, cut side down; spread with remaining pesto mixture and sprinkle with nuts.

Bake at 350°F for 3 to 4 minutes or until cheese is slightly softened. *Do not overbake.* Transfer to serving dish. Garnish with chopped tomatoes and basil leaves. Serve with assorted crackers or breadsticks. *Makes 6 to 8 appetizer servings*

Pesto Cheesecake

CRUST

1 cup fine dry bread crumbs
½ cup very finely chopped toasted
    pine nuts or walnuts

3 tablespoons melted butter or
    margarine

FILLING

2 cups (15 ounces) SARGENTO®
    Light Ricotta Cheese
½ cup half-and-half
2 tablespoons all-purpose flour
½ teaspoon salt

2 eggs
⅓ cup Homemade Pesto Sauce
    (recipe follows) or prepared
    pesto sauce

Preheat oven to 350°F. Lightly grease side of 8-inch springform pan.

Combine bread crumbs, nuts and butter in small bowl until well blended. Press evenly onto bottom of pan. Refrigerate until ready to use.

Combine ricotta cheese, half-and-half, flour and salt in medium bowl with electric mixer. Beat at medium speed until smooth. Add eggs, one at a time; beat until smooth. Pour into prepared crust. Drop teaspoonfuls pesto over cheese mixture. Gently swirl with knife for marbled effect.

Bake 45 minutes or until center is just set; turn off oven. Cool in oven with door open 30 minutes. Remove from oven. Cool completely on wire rack. Cut into thin slices before serving.

Makes 10 servings

Homemade Pesto Sauce: In food processor or blender, mince 1 clove garlic. Add ½ cup packed fresh basil leaves and 1 tablespoon toasted pine nuts or walnuts. Process until smooth, scraping down side of bowl once. With machine running, drizzle 2 tablespoons olive oil into bowl; process until smooth. Add ¼ cup (1 ounce) Sargento® Fancy Shredded Parmesan Cheese; process just until cheese is blended.

Lentil Patties with Coconut-Mango Relish

1¼ cups uncooked dried lentils,
  sorted and rinsed
Coconut-Mango Relish
  (page 31)
1 small onion, chopped
2 cloves garlic, minced
½ teaspoon cumin
¼ teaspoon salt

¼ teaspoon black pepper
⅛ teaspoon hot pepper sauce
1 small carrot, shredded
¼ cup all-purpose flour
1 egg
2 tablespoons chopped pitted
  black olives
Vegetable oil

Place lentils in 2-quart saucepan; cover with 2 inches water. Bring to a boil; reduce heat to low. Cover and simmer 30 to 40 minutes or until tender; drain. Spread lentils on baking sheet lined with paper towels. Let stand about 20 minutes or until lentils are cool and most of moisture has been absorbed. Meanwhile, prepare Coconut-Mango Relish; set aside.

Combine half of lentils, onion, garlic, cumin, salt, pepper and hot pepper sauce in food processor; process until just combined (mixture will be thick). Add carrot, flour, egg and olives. Process using on/off pulsing action until well blended; transfer to large bowl. Stir in remaining half of lentils with spoon.

Coat bottom of large skillet with oil. Heat over medium-high heat until very hot. Shape 2 rounded tablespoonfuls of lentil mixture into patty. Repeat with remaining lentil mixture. Cook patties over medium heat 6 to 7 minutes on each side until browned on both sides, adding additional oil if needed. Serve with Coconut-Mango Relish.

Makes 4 to 6 servings

Coconut-Mango Relish

½ cup shredded coconut
½ cup fresh cilantro
2 tablespoons fresh ginger

2 tablespoons fresh lemon juice
1 tablespoon water
½ cup chopped mango

Place all ingredients except mango in food processor; process until finely chopped. Stir in mango. Cover; refrigerate up to 4 hours before serving. *Makes ½ cup*

Sundried Tomato Cheese Ball

8 ounces cream cheese,* softened
1 cup shredded Cheddar cheese
   (4 ounces)
⅓ cup GREY POUPON®
   COUNTRY DIJON® Mustard
1 teaspoon dried basil leaves
1 clove garlic, crushed

½ teaspoon onion powder
¼ cup sundried tomatoes,** finely
   chopped
⅓ cup PLANTERS® Walnuts,
   toasted and chopped
Assorted crackers, breadsticks
   and bagel chips

In large bowl, with electric mixer at medium speed, mix cheeses, mustard, basil, garlic and onion powder until blended but not smooth. Stir in sundried tomatoes. Shape cheese mixture into a 5-inch ball; wrap and chill 1 hour. Roll cheese ball in chopped nuts. Wrap and chill until serving time.

Serve as a spread with assorted crackers, breadsticks and bagel chips.

Makes 1-pound cheese ball

Low-fat cream cheese may be substituted for regular cream cheese.

**If sundried tomatoes are very dry, soften in warm water for 15 minutes. Drain before using.*

Falafel with Garlic Tahini Sauce

¾ cup uncooked dried garbanzo
   beans, sorted and rinsed
½ cup uncooked bulgur
   Garlic Tahini Sauce (page 33)
1½ cups coarsely crumbled whole
   wheat bread
½ cup water
¼ cup fresh lemon juice

3 tablespoons chopped fresh
   cilantro
2 cloves garlic, minced
1 teaspoon ground cumin
½ teaspoon salt
½ teaspoon crushed red pepper
   Vegetable oil

To quick-soak beans, place in medium saucepan; cover with 4 inches water. Bring to a boil and cook 2 minutes. Remove from heat; cover. Let stand 1 hour; rinse and drain. Place in saucepan and cover with 4 cups water. Bring to a boil; reduce heat to low. Cover; simmer 2 hours or until tender. Rinse; drain and set aside. Meanwhile, prepare bulgur according to package directions; set aside. Prepare Garlic Tahini Sauce; set aside.

Place bread in small baking pan. Pour ½ cup water over bread and let stand 15 minutes or until water is absorbed. Squeeze water from bread.

Place beans, lemon juice, cilantro, garlic, cumin, salt and red pepper in food processor; process until smooth. Add bread and bulgur to food processor; process until combined. Shape bean mixture into 1½-inch balls. Place on baking sheet lined with waxed paper. Dry at room temperature 1 hour.

Heat 2 to 3 inches oil in large heavy skillet over medium-high heat. Carefully add falafel to skillet; cook 3 to 3½ minutes until golden brown. Remove falafel with slotted spoon and place on paper towels to drain. Serve with Garlic Tahini Sauce.

Makes 8 to 10 servings

Falafel with Garlic Tahini Sauce

Garlic Tahini Sauce

½ cup plain yogurt
¼ cup tahini*
3 tablespoons water
2 tablespoons fresh lemon juice

1 clove garlic, minced
½ teaspoon cumin
Salt and black pepper to taste

Combine all ingredients in small bowl. Stir with wire whisk until well blended. Cover; refrigerate 1 hour.

Makes about 1 cup

*Tahini is a thick paste made from ground sesame seed and is used in Middle Eastern cooking.

Spicy Empanadas

1 can (8¾ ounces) garbanzo
   beans, drained
1 teaspoon vegetable oil
¼ cup minced fresh onion
2 tablespoons minced green bell
   pepper
¼ teaspoon LAWRY'S® Garlic
   Powder with Parsley
2 tablespoons currants
2 tablespoons chopped pitted ripe
   olives

1 package (1 ounce) LAWRY'S®
   Taco Spices & Seasonings
1 teaspoon lemon juice
¼ cup (1 ounce) shredded
   Monterey Jack cheese
   All-purpose flour
1 sheet frozen puff pastry, thawed
1 egg yolk, beaten

Preheat oven to 400°F. In food processor or blender, place garbanzo beans. Pulse 30 seconds to chop finely; set aside. In large skillet, heat oil. Add onion, bell pepper and Garlic Powder with Parsley; sauté 3 to 4 minutes or until vegetables are crisp-tender. Add beans, currants, olives, Taco Spices & Seasonings and lemon juice; cook until mixture thickens, stirring occasionally. Remove from heat; stir in cheese. On lightly floured surface, roll out pastry sheet to approximately 18×10-inch rectangle; cut out six to eight (4-inch) circles. Spoon equal amounts of filling onto half of each circle; fold pastry over to form half circle. Press edges together with fork to seal. Place empanadas on greased baking sheet; brush with egg yolk. Bake 18 to 20 minutes or until golden brown. Garnish as desired. *Makes 6 to 8 empanadas*

Presentation: Great with salsa, sour cream and peeled avocado slices.

Hint: Double recipe for more appetizers.

Spicy Empanadas

Bruschetta Dijon

Bruschetta Dijon

¼ cup olive oil, divided
1 clove garlic, minced
18 (¼-inch-thick) slices French
    bread
1½ cups chopped eggplant
½ cup chopped onion
½ cup diced red, yellow or green
    bell pepper

1 cup chopped tomato
¼ cup GREY POUPON®
    COUNTRY DIJON® Mustard
¼ cup chopped pitted ripe olives
1 teaspoon dried oregano leaves
2 tablespoons grated Parmesan
    cheese
Chopped parsley, for garnish

Combine 2 tablespoons oil and garlic. Arrange bread slices on baking sheets; brush tops with oil mixture. Set aside.

In large skillet, over medium heat, sauté eggplant, onion and bell pepper in remaining 2 tablespoons oil until tender. Stir in tomato; cook for 2 minutes. Add mustard, olives and oregano; heat through.

Broil bread slices for 1 minute or until golden. Top each toasted bread slice with about 1 tablespoon vegetable mixture. Sprinkle with Parmesan cheese; garnish with parsley. Serve warm.

Makes 18 appetizers

Fiesta Quesadillas with Fruit Salsa

1 can (11 ounces) DOLE®
    Mandarin Oranges, drained
    and finely chopped
1 tablespoon chopped fresh
    cilantro or parsley
1 tablespoon lime juice
4 (8-inch) whole wheat or flour
    tortillas

¾ cup (3 ounces) shredded low fat
    Monterey Jack, mozzarella or
    Cheddar cheese
⅔ cup finely chopped DOLE®
    Pitted Dates or Pitted Prunes
⅓ cup crumbled feta cheese
2 tablespoons chopped DOLE®
    Green Onion

• **Combine** mandarin oranges, cilantro and lime juice in small bowl for salsa; set aside.

• **Place** 2 tortillas on large baking sheet. Sprinkle half of shredded cheese, dates, feta cheese and green onion over each tortilla to within ½ inch of edge; top with remaining tortillas.

• **Bake** at 375°F 5 to 8 minutes or until hot. Cut each quesadilla into 6 wedges.

• **Drain** salsa just before serving, if desired; serve over warm quesadillas. Garnish with fresh cilantro sprigs, if desired.

Makes 6 servings

Prep Time: 15 minutes   **Bake Time:** 8 minutes

Quesadillas with Texas Sweet Onions

1 large (14 to 16 ounces) Texas
    SPRINGSWEET® or Texas
    1015 SUPERSWEET® Onion,
    thinly sliced
1 tablespoon butter or margarine
6 (8-inch) flour tortillas
2 cups (8 ounces) shredded
    Monterey Jack or sharp
    Cheddar cheese

4 ounces feta cheese, crumbled
    (optional)
Pineapple Onion Salsa (recipe
    follows)
Sour cream

In medium skillet, sauté onion in butter until golden brown. Divide evenly among
3 tortillas and top with Monterey Jack cheese and feta cheese, if desired. Top with
remaining 3 tortillas. Place on barbecue grill over medium-hot coals or in large skillet
over medium heat; cook until lightly browned on bottom. Carefully turn and lightly
brown other side. Remove from grill or skillet and cut into wedges. Serve with
Pineapple Onion Salsa and sour cream. *Makes 6 appetizer servings*

Pineapple Onion Salsa

1 cup chopped Texas
    SPRINGSWEET® or Texas
    1015 SUPERSWEET® Onions
1 cup chopped red and/or green
    bell peppers

1 cup chopped pineapple
2 teaspoons chopped fresh cilantro
    Salt to taste

Combine all ingredients in medium bowl; stir well. Cover and refrigerate several hours
to let flavors blend. *Makes 3 cups*

Bruschetta al Pomodoro with Two Cheeses

1 loaf (1 pound) country Italian
    bread, cut diagonally into
    12 (1-inch) slices
2 teaspoons minced garlic
⅓ cup extra virgin olive oil
¼ teaspoon crushed red pepper
    flakes
4 large ripe plum tomatoes, thinly
    sliced crosswise
1 medium-size red onion, slivered
⅓ cup slivered fresh basil leaves *or*
    1 tablespoon dried basil

Red wine vinegar
½ cup (2 ounces) shredded
    ALPINE LACE® Fat Free
    Pasteurized Process Skim
    Milk Cheese Product—For
    Mozzarella Lovers
¼ cup (1 ounce) shredded ALPINE
    LACE® Fat Free Pasteurized
    Process Skim Milk Cheese
    Product—For Parmesan
    Lovers

1. Preheat the broiler. Place the bread slices in a single layer on baking sheet and toast both sides until golden brown. Immediately rub one side of each bread slice with garlic.

2. In a small saucepan, heat oil and red pepper flakes over medium heat until warm. Brush top of each slice with oil.

3. Top each bruschetta with 2 or 3 tomato slices, then add a few slivers of onion and basil. Sprinkle each with a little vinegar.

4. Sprinkle bruschetta with mozzarella and Parmesan. Broil 6 inches from heat for 4 minutes or until cheese is bubbly.

Makes 12 servings

Sesame-Onion Twists

2 tablespoons butter or margarine
1½ cups finely chopped onions
¼ teaspoon paprika
Nonstick cooking spray

1 loaf (16 ounces) frozen bread
dough, thawed
1 egg, beaten
1 tablespoon sesame seeds

1. Grease large baking sheet; set aside. Melt butter in medium skillet over medium heat until foamy. Add onions and paprika; cook until onions are tender, stirring occasionally. Remove from heat.

2. Spray work surface with nonstick cooking spray. Roll thawed bread dough into 14×12-inch rectangle.

3. Spread onion mixture on one side of dough. Fold dough over onion mixture to make 14×6-inch rectangle.

4. Pinch 14-inch side of dough to seal. Cut dough into 14 strips, each 6×1 inches.

5. Gently twist dough strip two times and place on prepared sheet. Press both ends of strip down on cookie sheet. Repeat with remaining strips.

6. Cover with towel. Let twists rise in warm place about 40 minutes or until doubled in bulk. Brush with egg; sprinkle with sesame seeds.

7. Preheat oven to 375°F. Bake 15 to 18 minutes or until golden brown. Serve immediately.

Makes 14 twists

Sesame-Onion Twists

Roasted Vegetable Cheese Crispies

12 ounces shredded JARLSBERG LITE™ Cheese
1½ teaspoons dried thyme, crumbled
½ teaspoon dry mustard
½ teaspoon finely ground black pepper
1 large peeled potato

½ small peeled turnip
2 to 3 medium peeled carrots
8 to 10 small (or 4 to 5 large) peeled, thinly sliced shallots or other mild-flavored onion
6 large cloves garlic, minced
½ cup broth or water

Preheat oven to 425°F. Line 17×11-inch baking pan with foil. Coat with nonstick cooking spray.

Combine cheese, thyme, mustard and pepper in bowl and mix well; set aside.

Using slicing side of grater (or slicing disk of food processor), cut potato, turnip and carrots in nearly paper-thin slices. Mix vegetables with shallots and garlic and spread on bottom of baking pan.

Cover with cheese mixture; drizzle with broth. Bake 40 minutes. Cut into squares and serve hot or warm. Vegetables should be crispy on bottom, soft in middle and cheese should be crispy on top. *Makes 72 bite-size appetizer snack squares*

South-of-the-Border Quiche Squares

South-of-the-Border Quiche Squares

1 (8-ounce) package refrigerated
    crescent dinner roll dough
1½ cups (6 ounces) shredded
    Monterey Jack and Colby
    cheese blend
½ cup diced green chiles
½ cup chopped onion
4 eggs, beaten

1 cup milk
⅓ cup GREY POUPON®
    COUNTRY DIJON® Mustard
1 tablespoon chopped cilantro or
    parsley
½ teaspoon chili powder
    Chopped tomato and yellow and
    green bell peppers, for garnish

Unroll dough and press perforations together. Press dough on bottom and 1 inch up sides of greased 13×9×2-inch baking pan. Bake crust at 375°F for 5 to 8 minutes or until lightly golden. Remove from oven; sprinkle with half the cheese. Top with chiles, onion and remaining cheese.

In medium bowl, blend eggs, milk, mustard, cilantro and chili powder. Pour mixture evenly over cheese layer. Bake at 375°F for 25 to 30 minutes or until set. Cool 5 minutes. Garnish with tomato and bell peppers; cut into 2-inch squares. Serve hot.

Makes 24 appetizers

Herb-Stuffed Tomatoes

15 cherry tomatoes
½ cup 1% low-fat cottage cheese
1 tablespoon thinly sliced green
 onion
1 teaspoon chopped fresh chervil
 or ¼ teaspoon dried chervil
 leaves, crushed

½ teaspoon chopped fresh dill or
 ⅛ teaspoon dried dill weed
⅛ teaspoon lemon pepper

Cut thin slice off top of each tomato. Scoop out pulp with small spoon; discard pulp.
Invert tomatoes on paper towels to drain.

Combine cottage cheese, green onion, chervil, dill and lemon pepper in small bowl.
Spoon into tomatoes. Serve at once or cover and refrigerate up to 8 hours.

Makes 15 stuffed tomatoes

Gilroy Bruschetta

1 French bread baguette, sliced
 into ¼-inch slices
6 to 8 ripe Roma tomatoes,
 chopped
½ cup shredded Romano cheese
4 tablespoons olive oil

2 tablespoons chopped fresh basil
3 cloves CHRISTOPHER
 RANCH Garlic, finely
 chopped
Salt and pepper to taste

Toast bread slices on both sides in broiler until golden. Set aside. Combine tomatoes,
cheese, oil, basil and garlic. Spread spoonful of mixture on each bread slice and serve.

Makes about 6 servings

Herb-Stuffed Tomatoes

Mozzarella and Vegetable Marinara

MOZZARELLA AND VEGETABLES

3 eggs
1¾ cups CONTADINA® Seasoned
  Bread Crumbs
1 pound mozzarella cheese, cut
  into ¼-inch strips
1 medium zucchini, cut into
  ¼-inch strips (about 1 cup)

1 medium red or green bell
  pepper, cut into ¼-inch strips
  (about 1 cup)
Olive or vegetable oil

MARINARA SAUCE

1 tablespoon olive or vegetable oil
½ cup chopped onion
1 clove garlic, minced
2 cups (15-ounce can)
  CONTADINA® Tomato Sauce

1 tablespoon chopped fresh basil
  or 1 teaspoon dried basil
  leaves, crushed
⅛ teaspoon crushed red pepper
  flakes

For Mozzarella and Vegetables: In shallow dish, beat eggs. In separate shallow dish, place bread crumbs. Dip cheese and vegetables into eggs; coat with bread crumbs. Repeat dipping into eggs and crumbs to coat again. Add enough oil to medium skillet to cover bottom to 1-inch depth. Heat oil. Add coated cheese and vegetables, a few pieces at a time, to hot oil; cook until golden brown. Remove from oil with slotted spoon. Drain on paper towels. Repeat with remaining cheese and vegetables. Serve with Marinara Sauce.

For Marinara Sauce: In small saucepan, heat oil. Add onion and garlic; sauté for 1 minute. Stir in tomato sauce, basil and red pepper flakes. Bring to a boil. Reduce heat to low; simmer, uncovered, for 10 minutes, stirring occasionally. Serve warm.

Makes 12 servings

Black Bean Tortilla Pinwheels

1 (8-ounce) package cream cheese,
    softened
1 cup sour cream
1 cup (4 ounces) shredded
    Wisconsin Monterey Jack
    cheese
¼ cup chopped, well-drained
    pimento-stuffed green olives

¼ cup chopped red onion
½ teaspoon seasoned salt
⅛ teaspoon garlic powder
1 (15-ounce) can black beans,
    drained
5 (10-inch) flour tortillas
    Salsa

Combine cream cheese and sour cream; mix well. Stir in Monterey Jack cheese, olives, onion and seasonings. Chill 2 hours.

Purée beans in food processor or blender. Spread each tortilla with thin layer of beans. Spread cream cheese mixture over beans. Roll up tightly; chill. Cut into ¾-inch slices. Serve with salsa.

Makes 12 to 16 servings

Favorite recipe from **Wisconsin Milk Marketing Board**

Italian Tomato Bread

3½ cups (two 14.5-ounce cans)
    CONTADINA® Pasta Ready
    Chunky Tomatoes with Three
    Cheeses, drained
¼ cup sliced green onions

1 loaf (1 pound) Italian or French
    bread
1½ cups (6 ounces) shredded
    mozzarella cheese

In medium bowl, combine tomatoes and green onions. Cut bread in half lengthwise. Scoop out ½-inch layer of bread to within 1 inch of side crusts; reserve removed bread for another use. Spoon tomato mixture equally into bread shells; top with cheese. Place on ungreased baking sheet. Bake in preheated 450°F. oven for 5 to 8 minutes or until heated through and cheese is melted. Cut diagonally into 1-inch-thick slices.

Makes about 24 appetizers

Cold Asparagus with Lemon-Mustard Dressing

12 fresh asparagus spears	1 tablespoon fresh lemon juice
2 tablespoons fat-free mayonnaise	1 teaspoon grated lemon peel,
1 tablespoon sweet brown mustard	divided

1. Steam asparagus until crisp-tender and bright green; immediately drain and run under cold water. Cover and refrigerate until chilled.

2. Combine mayonnaise, mustard and lemon juice in small bowl; blend well. Stir in $\frac{1}{2}$ teaspoon lemon peel; set aside.

3. Divide asparagus between 2 plates. Spoon 2 tablespoons dressing over top of each serving; sprinkle each with $\frac{1}{4}$ teaspoon lemon peel. Garnish with carrot strips and edible flowers, such as pansies, violets or nasturtiums, if desired.

Makes 2 appetizer servings

Ortega® Snack Mix

3 cups lightly salted peanuts	1 package (1¼ ounces) ORTEGA®
3 cups corn chips	Taco Seasoning Mix
3 cups spoon-size shredded wheat	¼ cup (½ stick) butter or
2 cups lightly salted pretzels	margarine, melted

COMBINE peanuts, corn chips, shredded wheat, pretzels, taco seasoning mix and butter in large bowl. Toss well to coat. *Makes about 20 servings*

Tip: This is a great party mix or snack for lunches. Store in airtight plastic container or resealable plastic food storage bag.

Cold Asparagus with Lemon-Mustard Dressing

SATISFYING SOUPS, STEWS & CHILIS

Gazpacho

3 cups tomato juice
4 tomatoes, chopped
1 green bell pepper, chopped
1 cucumber, chopped
1 cup chopped celery
1 cup chopped green onions
3 tablespoons red wine vinegar
2 tablespoons FILIPPO BERIO®
   Olive Oil

1 tablespoon chopped fresh
   parsley
1 to 2 teaspoons salt
1 clove garlic, finely minced
   Freshly ground black pepper or
    hot pepper sauce

In large bowl, combine tomato juice, tomatoes, bell pepper, cucumber, celery, green onions, vinegar, olive oil, parsley, salt and garlic. Cover; refrigerate several hours or overnight before serving. Season to taste with black pepper or hot pepper sauce. Serve cold. *Makes 10 to 12 servings*

Gazpacho

Wild Rice Soup

Wild Rice Soup

½ cup lentils
3 cups water
1 package (6 ounces) long grain
    and wild rice blend
1 can (14½ ounces) vegetable
    broth

1 package (10 ounces) frozen
    mixed vegetables
1 cup skim milk
½ cup (2 ounces) reduced-fat
    processed American cheese,
    cut into pieces

1. Rinse and sort lentils, discarding any debris or blemished lentils. Combine lentils and water in small saucepan. Bring to a boil; reduce heat to low. Simmer, covered, 5 minutes. Let stand, covered, 1 hour. Drain and rinse lentils.

2. Cook rice according to package directions in medium saucepan. Add lentils and remaining ingredients. Bring to a boil; reduce heat to low. Simmer, uncovered, 20 minutes. Garnish as desired.

Makes 6 servings

Indian Corn Stew

½ cup chopped onion
1 clove garlic, minced
2 tablespoons butter or margarine
6 medium tomatoes (about
    2 pounds), peeled, cored and
    cut into eighths *or* 1 can
    (28 ounces) tomatoes,
    undrained
2 cups CORN CHEX® brand
    cereal
2½ teaspoons sugar*

2 teaspoons seasoned salt
1 teaspoon oregano leaves,
    crushed
1 bay leaf
2 ears corn, shucked and cut into
    fourths
2 small zucchini, sliced ¼ inch
    thick (1½ cups)
1 small green pepper, cut into
    large pieces (1 cup)

In large saucepan sauté onion and garlic in butter about 5 minutes or until tender. Add tomatoes, Chex®, sugar and seasonings. Stir to break up tomatoes. Heat to a boil. Reduce heat; cover and simmer 10 minutes, stirring frequently.

Stir in remaining vegetables. Return to a boil; cover and simmer 15 to 20 minutes or until tender, stirring occasionally. Remove bay leaf before serving.

Makes 8 servings (about 7 cups)

When using canned tomatoes, reduce sugar to 2 teaspoons.

Navy Vegetable Soup with Tortilla Crisps

1 cup dried navy beans, sorted
   and rinsed
3 cups water
1 teaspoon salt, divided
1 pound leeks (about 2), cut into
   ½-inch pieces
¾ pound unpeeled new potatoes
2 cups sliced button mushrooms
1½ cups thinly sliced carrots

6 cups Vegetable Stock (page 74)
1½ teaspoons dried thyme leaves
1 bay leaf
½ teaspoon ground black pepper
2 corn tortillas (6-inch diameter)
2 teaspoons olive oil
¼ teaspoon garlic salt
2 medium tomatoes, seeded and
   chopped

Place beans in large saucepan. Add water. Bring to a boil over high heat. Cover and remove from heat. Let stand 30 minutes. Return to a boil over high heat. Reduce heat to low. Cover and simmer 30 minutes; stir in ½ teaspoon salt. Cover and simmer 1 hour more; drain.

Add leeks, potatoes, mushrooms, carrots, stock, thyme, bay leaf, remaining ½ teaspoon salt and pepper to Dutch oven. Bring to a boil over high heat. Reduce heat to low. Cover and simmer 25 minutes. Add beans and cook 5 minutes. Remove bay leaf; discard.

Meanwhile, preheat oven to 425°F. Brush tortillas on both sides with oil; sprinkle top of each with garlic salt. Cut into ¼-inch-wide strips. Arrange on baking sheet; bake 10 to 12 minutes or until crisp. Cool. Ladle soup into shallow soup bowls; sprinkle evenly with tomatoes and tortilla crisps. *Makes 8 (1¼-cup) servings*

Navy Vegetable Soup with Tortilla Crisps

Olive-Bean Chili

3 tablespoons molasses
1½ teaspoons dry mustard
1½ teaspoons soy sauce
2 teaspoons olive oil
2 medium carrots, cut diagonally
 into ¼-inch slices
1 large onion, chopped
1 tablespoon chili powder
3 large tomatoes (1½ pounds),
 chopped

1 (15-ounce) can pinto beans,
 drained
1 (15-ounce) can kidney beans,
 drained
¾ cup California ripe olives, sliced
½ cup plain nonfat yogurt
 Crushed red pepper flakes

Combine molasses, mustard and soy sauce; set aside. Heat oil in large skillet; add carrots, onion, chili powder and ¼ cup water. Cook, covered, about 4 minutes or until carrots are almost tender. Uncover and cook, stirring, until liquid has evaporated. Add molasses mixture with tomatoes, pinto beans, kidney beans and olives. Cook, stirring gently, about 5 minutes or until mixture is hot and tomatoes are soft. Ladle chili into bowls; top with yogurt. Sprinkle with pepper flakes to taste. *Makes 4 servings*

Prep Time: About 15 minutes **Cook Time:** About 10 minutes

Favorite recipe from **California Olive Industry**

Pasta e Fagioli

10 ounces (1¼ cups) dry navy or
    cranberry beans, sorted and
    rinsed
3¾ cups cold water
⅔ cup plus 3 tablespoons vegetable
    oil, divided
1 bay leaf
2 to 3 cloves garlic
1½ teaspoons salt
3 carrots, diced

2 ribs celery, sliced
1 large onion, chopped
1 to 2 cloves garlic, crushed
1 teaspoon dried oregano leaves,
    crumbled
½ teaspoon dried basil leaves,
    crumbled
Pepper
6 to 7 tomatoes, peeled, chunked
8 ounces shell-shaped pasta

1. Place beans in Dutch oven; add cold water. Soak beans at room temperature 6 to 8 hours or overnight.

2. Add ⅔ cup oil, bay leaf, whole garlic cloves and salt to soaked beans. Simmer gently until beans are tender, 2 to 3 hours, stirring occasionally. Drain beans; reserve 1½ cups cooking liquid. Remove and discard bay leaf and garlic.

3. Heat 3 tablespoons oil in large skillet. Add carrots, celery and onion; cook until soft. Add crushed garlic and seasonings; simmer 30 minutes. Add tomatoes; cook 10 minutes.

4. Cook pasta in boiling water until just tender; drain. Combine beans, vegetables, pasta and reserved cooking liquid. Cover; simmer 10 minutes, stirring occasionally.

5. Garnish with chopped fresh parsley; serve with grated Parmesan cheese.

Makes 6 to 8 servings

Favorite recipe from **Michigan Bean Commission**

Hearty Lentil Stew

2 tablespoons olive or
    vegetable oil
3 medium carrots, sliced
3 ribs celery, sliced
1 cup lentils
3 cups water, divided
1 envelope LIPTON® Recipe
    Secrets® Savory Herb with
    Garlic Soup Mix

1 tablespoon cider vinegar or red
    wine vinegar
Hot cooked brown rice,
    couscous or pasta

In 3-quart saucepan, heat oil over medium heat and cook carrots and celery, stirring occasionally, 3 minutes. Add lentils and cook 1 minute. Stir in 2 cups water. Bring to a boil over high heat. Reduce heat to low and simmer covered, stirring occasionally, 25 minutes. Stir in Savory Herb with Garlic Soup Mix blended with remaining 1 cup water. Simmer covered additional 10 minutes or until lentils are tender. Stir in vinegar. Serve over hot rice.

Makes about 4 servings

• Also terrific with Lipton® Recipe Secrets® Onion-Mushroom or Onion Soup Mix.

Creamy Vegetable Bisque

1 bag (16 ounces) BIRDS EYE®
    frozen Broccoli Cuts
2 teaspoons butter or margarine
⅓ cup chopped celery or onion (or
    a combination)

1 can (10¾ ounces) cream of
    celery soup
1¼ cups milk or water
1 tablespoon chopped parsley

• Cook broccoli according to package directions. Melt butter in saucepan. Add celery; cook and stir 3 to 5 minutes. Blend in broccoli, soup, milk and parsley; cook over medium heat 4 to 5 minutes.

Makes 4 to 6 servings

Prep Time: 2 to 3 minutes   **Cook Time:** 8 to 10 minutes

Vegetarian Chili

Vegetarian Chili

1 tablespoon vegetable oil	1 can (28 ounces) peeled whole
2 cloves garlic, finely chopped	tomatoes
1½ cups thinly sliced mushrooms	⅔ cup frozen baby lima beans
⅔ cup chopped red onion	½ cup rinsed, drained canned
⅔ cup chopped red bell pepper	Great Northern beans
2 teaspoons chili powder	3 tablespoons nonfat sour cream
¼ teaspoon ground cumin	3 tablespoons shredded reduced-
⅛ teaspoon ground red pepper	fat Cheddar cheese
⅛ teaspoon dried oregano leaves	

1. Heat oil in large nonstick saucepan over medium-high heat until hot. Add garlic. Cook and stir 3 minutes. Add mushrooms, onion and bell pepper. Cook 5 minutes, stirring occasionally. Add chili powder, cumin, ground red pepper and oregano. Cook and stir 1 minute. Add tomatoes and beans. Reduce heat to medium-low. Simmer 15 minutes, stirring occasionally.

2. Top servings evenly with sour cream and cheese. *Makes 4 servings*

Chilled Potato Cucumber Soup with Roasted Red Pepper Swirl

1 large cucumber, peeled and
   seeded
1 cup chopped leeks
1 cup cubed, peeled red potatoes
1½ cups canned vegetable broth
1 cup water
1 teaspoon ground cumin

1 cup buttermilk
½ teaspoon salt
¼ teaspoon ground white pepper
Roasted Red Pepper Swirl
  (recipe follows)
Fresh chives for garnish

Cut cucumber halves into quarters; cut crosswise into ½-inch pieces. Combine cucumber, leeks, potatoes, broth, water and cumin in large saucepan. Bring to a boil over high heat. Reduce heat to low. Cover and simmer 20 minutes or until vegetables are tender. Cool.

Process cucumber mixture in food processor in batches until smooth. Pour into large bowl. Stir in buttermilk, salt and pepper. Cover; refrigerate until cold.

Just before serving, prepare Roasted Red Pepper Swirl. Ladle soup into bowls; spoon Roasted Red Pepper Swirl into soup and swirl with knife. Garnish, if desired.

Makes 6 servings

Roasted Red Pepper Swirl

3 cups diced red bell peppers
1 small dried hot red chili, seeded
   and torn

½ cup boiling water
1 clove garlic, sliced
2 teaspoons white wine vinegar

Preheat oven to 400°F. Spray nonstick baking sheet with cooking spray. Place bell peppers and chili on prepared baking sheet. Bake 30 minutes or until bell pepper is browned on edges, stirring after 15 minutes. Process peppers, chili, boiling water, garlic and vinegar in food processor until smooth.

Makes ¾ cup

Chilled Potato Cucumber Soup with Roasted Red Pepper Swirl

Hearty Vegetable Gumbo

Nonstick cooking spray
½ cup chopped onion
½ cup chopped green bell pepper
¼ cup chopped celery
2 cloves garlic, minced
2 cans (about 14 ounces each)
　no-salt-added stewed
　tomatoes, undrained
2 cups no-salt-added tomato juice
1 can (15 ounces) red beans,
　drained and rinsed

1 tablespoon chopped fresh
　parsley
¼ teaspoon dried oregano leaves
¼ teaspoon hot pepper sauce
2 bay leaves
1½ cups quick-cooking brown rice
1 package (10 ounces) frozen
　chopped okra, thawed

1. Spray 4-quart Dutch oven with cooking spray; heat over medium heat until hot. Add onion, bell pepper, celery and garlic. Cook and stir 3 minutes or until crisp-tender.

2. Add stewed tomatoes, juice, beans, parsley, oregano, pepper sauce and bay leaves. Bring to a boil over high heat. Add rice. Reduce heat to medium-low. Simmer, covered, 15 minutes or until rice is tender.

3. Add okra; simmer, covered, 5 minutes more or until okra is tender. Remove bay leaves; discard. Garnish as desired. *Makes 4 (2-cup) servings*

Cold Cucumber Soup

1 cucumber, peeled
1 cup low-fat buttermilk
2 tablespoons red onion, finely
　chopped

1 teaspoon dried mint flakes
1 teaspoon sugar
Dash hot pepper sauce

Process all ingredients in food processor until smooth. Serve immediately or chill in refrigerator until serving. *Makes 2 servings*

Favorite recipe from **The Sugar Association, Inc.**

Hearty Vegetable Gumbo

Greens, White Bean and Barley Soup

½ pound carrots, peeled
2 tablespoons olive oil
1½ cups chopped onions
2 cloves garlic, minced
1½ cups sliced button mushrooms
6 cups Vegetable Stock (page 74)
2 cups cooked barley
1 can (16 ounces) Great Northern
    beans, drained and rinsed
2 bay leaves

1 teaspoon sugar
1 teaspoon dried thyme leaves
1½ pounds collard greens, washed,
    stemmed and chopped (about
    7 cups)
1 tablespoon white wine vinegar
    Hot pepper sauce
    Red bell pepper strips for
    garnish

Cut carrots lengthwise into quarters; cut crosswise into ¼-inch pieces. Heat oil in Dutch oven over medium heat until hot. Add carrots, onions and garlic; cook and stir 3 minutes. Add mushrooms; cook and stir 5 minutes or until tender.

Add stock, barley, beans, bay leaves, sugar and thyme. Bring to a boil over high heat. Reduce heat to low. Cover and simmer 5 minutes. Add greens; simmer 10 minutes. Remove bay leaves; discard. Stir in vinegar. Season to taste with pepper sauce. Garnish, if desired.

Makes 8 (1¼-cup) servings

Black Bean Soup

¼ cup mild salsa
1 (16-ounce) can black beans
2 cups water

1 cup cherry tomatoes, tops
    removed
1½ teaspoons ground cumin
1 teaspoon sugar

Strain salsa discarding chunks. Drain and rinse beans; reserve 1 tablespoon black beans. Process all ingredients in food processor or blender until smooth. Stir in reserved black beans; chill until serving.

Makes 4 servings

Favorite recipe from **The Sugar Association, Inc.**

Greens, White Bean and Barley Soup

Santa Fe Wild Rice Soup

2 cups frozen or fresh corn
    kernels
⅓ cup diced onion
⅓ cup diced carrot
3 (14-ounce) cans vegetable broth,
    divided
2 cups cooked California wild rice
1 (4-ounce) can chopped green
    chiles
1 teaspoon chili powder

1 teaspoon ground cumin
½ teaspoon dried oregano,
    crumbled
⅛ teaspoon cayenne pepper (or to
    taste)
1 tablespoon coarsely chopped
    cilantro leaves
Fresh Tomato Salsa (recipe
    follows)

In large saucepan over medium heat, combine corn, onion, carrot and 1 can broth and bring to a boil. Reduce heat and simmer 10 to 15 minutes or until onion is tender. Stir in remaining 2 cans broth, wild rice, green chiles, chili powder, cumin, oregano and cayenne. Simmer, uncovered, about 5 minutes or until heated through. Sprinkle with cilantro. Top each bowl with heaping tablespoon of Fresh Tomato Salsa.

Makes 4 servings

Fresh Tomato Salsa

2 medium tomatoes, seeded and
    diced
⅓ cup chopped green onions
¼ cup chopped cilantro leaves

1 teaspoon lime juice or red wine
    vinegar
Salt to taste

Combine all ingredients in medium bowl. Taste to adjust seasonings.

Favorite recipe from **California Wild Rice**

Totally Veggie Vegetarian Soup

10 cups vegetable stock, divided
3 tablespoons Chef Paul
 Prudhomme's VEGETABLE
 MAGIC®
1 large onion, peeled and cut into
 8 to 10 wedges, divided
1 large potato, peeled, cut into
 1-inch rounds, and quartered,
 divided
2 large carrots, scrubbed, cut
 lengthwise in half, then into
 1-inch pieces, divided
½ small green cabbage, cut into 4
 or 5 wedges, divided

1 large red bell pepper, cut into
 1-inch pieces, divided
1 large yellow bell pepper, cut into
 1-inch pieces, divided
1 medium-size turnip, scrubbed
 and cut into 10 wedges,
 divided
1 medium-size rutabaga, peeled
 and cut into 10 wedges,
 divided
4 ribs bok choy, cut into 1-inch
 diagonal pieces, divided
2 cups apple juice

Place heavy 10-quart stockpot over high heat and add 6 cups stock. Bring to a full boil; add Vegetable Magic® and one-fourth of each vegetable. Cook until vegetables are tender, about 14 to 16 minutes. Strain cooked vegetables, reserving broth; transfer to food processor. Process vegetables, adding a little of reserved broth if necessary, until they are puréed, about 2 to 3 minutes.

Return puréed mixture to stockpot, adding remaining 4 cups stock and apple juice. Mix and bring to a boil. Add remaining vegetables and return mixture to a boil over high heat. Reduce heat to medium; cover and simmer until vegetables are fork-tender, about 25 to 30 minutes.

Makes 20 cups

Garden Fresh Gazpacho

SOUP BASE

4 large tomatoes (about 2 pounds)
1 large cucumber, peeled and seeded
½ *each* red and green bell pepper, seeded
½ red onion
3 cloves garlic
2 tablespoons minced fresh basil leaves

¼ cup FRANK'S® Original REDHOT® Cayenne Pepper Sauce
¼ cup red wine vinegar
3 tablespoons olive oil
1 teaspoon salt

GARNISH

2 cups chopped vegetables, such as tomatoes, bell peppers, cucumber and/or green onions

Coarsely chop Soup Base vegetables; place vegetables and remaining Soup Base ingredients in food processor or blender. Cover and process until smooth. (If necessary, process vegetables in batches.) Transfer soup to large glass bowl. Stir in chopped vegetables, leaving some to sprinkle on top for garnish if desired. Cover and refrigerate 1 hour before serving. Divide among 6 individual serving bowls. Sprinkle with remaining garnish.

Makes 6 servings (about 6 cups)

Prep Time: 30 minutes   **Chill Time:** 1 hour

Tip: Soup may be prepared up to 2 days before serving.

Garden Fresh Gazpacho

Chunky Vegetable Chili

Chunky Vegetable Chili

2 tablespoons vegetable oil	1½ cups water
1 medium onion, chopped	1 cup frozen corn
2 ribs celery, diced	1 can (6 ounces) tomato paste
1 carrot, diced	1 can (4 ounces) diced mild green
3 cloves garlic, minced	chiles, undrained
2 cans (about 15 ounces each)	1 tablespoon chili powder
Great Northern beans, rinsed	2 teaspoons dried oregano leaves
and drained	1 teaspoon salt

1. Heat oil in large skillet over medium-high heat until hot. Add onion, celery, carrot and garlic; cook 5 minutes or until vegetables are tender, stirring occasionally.

2. Stir beans, 1½ cups water, corn, tomato paste, chiles, chili powder, oregano and salt into skillet. Reduce heat to medium-low. Simmer 20 minutes, stirring occasionally. Garnish with cilantro, if desired. *Makes 8 servings*

Ravioli Stew

2 tablespoons olive or
   vegetable oil
1 medium onion, chopped
2 medium carrots, diced
2 ribs celery, diced
1 medium green bell pepper,
   chopped
1 clove garlic, finely chopped*
1 can (15 to 19 ounces) red kidney
   beans, rinsed and drained

4 plum tomatoes, chopped
1 envelope LIPTON® Recipe
   Secrets® Golden Herb with
   Lemon Soup Mix
2½ cups water
1 package (8 or 10 ounces)
   refrigerated cheese ravioli

In Dutch oven or 6-quart saucepot, heat oil over medium heat and cook onion, carrots, celery, green pepper and garlic, stirring occasionally, 5 minutes or until tender. Stir in beans, tomatoes and Golden Herb with Lemon Soup Mix blended with water. Bring to a boil over high heat. Stir in ravioli. Reduce heat to medium and cook, stirring gently, 5 minutes or until ravioli are tender. Serve, if desired, with grated Parmesan cheese.

Makes about 4 (2-cup) servings

If using Lipton® Recipe Secrets® Savory Herb with Garlic Soup Mix, omit garlic.

• Also terrific with Lipton® Recipe Secrets® Savory Herb with Garlic Soup Mix.

Double Pea Soup

1 tablespoon vegetable oil
1 large white onion, finely
    chopped
3 cloves garlic, finely chopped
2 cups dried split peas
1 bay leaf

1 teaspoon ground mustard
1½ cups frozen green peas
1 teaspoon salt
¼ teaspoon ground black pepper
    Nonfat sour cream (optional)

1. Heat oil in large saucepan or Dutch oven over medium-high heat until hot. Add onion; cook 5 minutes or until onion is tender, stirring occasionally. Add garlic; cook and stir 2 minutes.

2. Stir 2 cups water, split peas, bay leaf and mustard into saucepan. Bring to a boil over high heat. Cover; reduce heat to medium-low. Simmer 45 minutes or until split peas are tender, stirring occasionally.

3. Stir green peas, salt and pepper into saucepan; cover. Cook 10 minutes or until green peas are tender. Remove bay leaf; discard. Blend using hand-held blender until smooth or process small batches in blender or food processor until smooth.

4. Top each serving with sour cream before serving. Garnish as desired.

Makes 6 servings

Note: If a smoky flavor is desired, a chipotle chili can be added during the last 5 minutes of cooking.

Double Pea Soup

Vegetable Stock

2 medium onions
2 tablespoons vegetable oil
2 leeks, cleaned
3 ribs celery, cut into 2-inch pieces
8 cups cold water
6 medium carrots, cut into 1-inch
   pieces
1 turnip, peeled, cut into chunks
   (optional)

2 cloves garlic, peeled and crushed
4 parsley sprigs
1 teaspoon dried thyme leaves,
   crushed
¼ teaspoon ground black pepper
2 bay leaves

Trim tops and roots from onions, leaving most of dried outer skin intact; cut into wedges.

Heat oil in stockpot or 5-quart Dutch oven over medium-high heat until hot. Add onions, leeks and celery; cook and stir 5 minutes or until vegetables are limp but not brown. Add water, carrots, turnip, garlic, parsley, thyme, pepper and bay leaves. Bring to a boil over high heat. Reduce heat to medium-low; simmer, uncovered, 1½ hours. Remove from heat. Cool slightly and strain through large sieve or colander to remove vegetables and herbs. Press vegetables lightly with slotted spoon to remove excess liquid; discard vegetables.

Use immediately or refrigerate stock in tightly covered container up to 2 days or freeze stock in batches in freezer containers for several months. *Makes about 7 cups stock*

Cool Italian Tomato Soup

Cool Italian Tomato Soup

1¾ cups (14.5-ounce can)
    CONTADINA® Pasta
    Ready Chunky Tomatoes
    with Crushed Red Pepper,
    undrained
2 cups tomato juice
½ cup half-and-half

2 tablespoons lemon juice
1 large cucumber, peeled, diced
    (about 2 cups)
1 medium green bell pepper, diced
    (about ½ cup)
Chopped fresh basil (optional)
Croutons (optional)

In blender container, place tomatoes with juice, tomato juice, half-and-half and lemon juice; blend until smooth. Pour into large bowl or soup tureen; stir in cucumber and bell pepper. Sprinkle with basil and croutons just before serving, if desired.

Makes 6 cups

75

Jamaican Black Bean Stew

2 cups uncooked brown rice
2 pounds sweet potatoes
3 pounds butternut squash
1 large onion, coarsely chopped
1 can (about 14 ounces) vegetable
 broth
3 cloves garlic, minced
1 tablespoon curry powder
1½ teaspoons allspice

½ teaspoon ground red pepper
¼ teaspoon salt
2 cans (15 ounces each) black
 beans, drained and rinsed
½ cup raisins
3 tablespoons fresh lime juice
1 cup diced tomato
1 cup diced, peeled cucumber

1. Prepare rice according to package directions. Peel potatoes; cut into ¾-inch chunks to measure 4 cups. Peel squash; remove seeds. Cut into ¾-inch cubes to measure 5 cups.

2. Combine potatoes, squash, onion, broth, garlic, curry powder, allspice, pepper and salt in Dutch oven. Bring to a boil; reduce heat to low. Simmer, covered, 5 minutes. Add beans and raisins. Simmer 5 minutes or just until sweet potatoes and squash are tender and beans are hot. Remove from heat; stir in lime juice.

3. Serve stew over brown rice; top with tomato and cucumber. Garnish with lime peel.

Makes 8 servings

Jamaican Black Bean Stew

Vegetable-Bean Chowder

Vegetable-Bean Chowder

Nonstick cooking spray
½ cup chopped onion
½ cup chopped celery
2 cups water
½ teaspoon salt
2 cups cubed, peeled potatoes
1 cup carrot slices

1 can (15 ounces) cream-style corn
1 can (15 ounces) cannellini beans
   drained and rinsed
¼ teaspoon dried tarragon leaves
¼ teaspoon ground black pepper
2 cups 1% low-fat milk
2 tablespoons cornstarch

1. Spray 4-quart Dutch oven or large saucepan with cooking spray; heat over medium heat until hot. Add onion and celery. Cook and stir 3 minutes or until crisp-tender.

2. Add water and salt. Bring to a boil over high heat. Add potatoes and carrot. Reduce heat to medium-low. Simmer, covered, 10 minutes or until potatoes and carrot are tender. Stir in corn, beans, tarragon and pepper. Simmer, covered, 10 minutes or until heated through.

3. Stir milk into cornstarch in medium bowl until smooth. Stir into vegetable mixture. Simmer, uncovered, until thickened. Garnish as desired. *Makes 5 (1½-cup) servings*

Roasted Winter Vegetable Soup

1 small or ½ medium acorn
   squash, halved
2 medium tomatoes
1 medium onion, unpeeled
1 green bell pepper, halved
1 red bell pepper, halved
2 small red potatoes
3 cloves garlic, unpeeled

1½ cups tomato juice
½ cup water
4 teaspoons vegetable oil
1 tablespoon red wine vinegar
¼ teaspoon ground black pepper
¾ cup chopped fresh cilantro
4 tablespoons nonfat sour cream

1. Preheat oven to 400°F. Spray baking sheet with nonstick cooking spray. Place acorn squash, tomatoes, onion, bell peppers, potatoes and garlic on baking sheet. Bake 40 minutes, removing garlic and tomatoes after 10 minutes. Let stand 15 minutes or until cool enough to handle.

2. Peel vegetables and garlic; discard skins. Coarsely chop vegetables. Combine half of chopped vegetables, tomato juice, ½ cup water, oil and vinegar in food processor or blender; process until smooth.

3. Combine puréed vegetables, remaining chopped vegetables and black pepper in large saucepan. Bring to a simmer over medium-high heat. Simmer 5 minutes or until heated through, stirring constantly. Top servings evenly with cilantro and sour cream.

Makes 4 servings

VEGETABLE, GRAIN & BEAN SALADS

Easy Greek Salad

6 leaves romaine lettuce, washed
   and torn into 1½-inch pieces
1 cucumber, peeled and sliced
1 tomato, chopped
½ cup sliced red onion
1 ounce feta cheese, crumbled
   (about ⅓ cup)

2 tablespoons extra-virgin olive oil
2 tablespoons lemon juice
1 teaspoon dried oregano leaves
½ teaspoon salt

1. Combine lettuce, cucumber, tomato, onion and cheese in large serving bowl.

2. Whisk together oil, lemon juice, oregano and salt in small bowl. Pour over lettuce mixture; toss until coated. Serve immediately. *Makes 6 servings*

Prep Time: 10 minutes

Easy Greek Salad

Veggie-Pepper Bowls with Rice

8 medium green bell peppers,
halved and seeded
3 cups cooked long-grain white
rice
1 package (10 ounces) frozen peas
and carrots

1 cup whole kernel corn
½ cup chopped green onions
1¾ cups ORTEGA® Salsa, any
variety, divided
1½ cups 4-cheese Mexican blend,
divided

PREHEAT oven to 375°F.

PLACE bell peppers in microwave-safe dish with 3 tablespoons water. Cover with plastic wrap. Microwave on HIGH (100%) for 4 to 5 minutes or until slightly tender. Drain.

COMBINE rice, peas and carrots, corn, green onions, ¾ cup salsa and 1 cup cheese in large bowl. Fill each pepper with about ½ cup rice mixture. Place peppers in ungreased 13×9-inch baking dish; top with remaining salsa and cheese.

BAKE, covered, for 20 to 25 minutes. Uncover; bake for additional 5 minutes or until heated through and cheese is melted.   *Makes 8 servings*

Veggie-Pepper Bowls with Rice

Winter Pear and Stilton Salad

⅓ cup extra-virgin olive oil
1½ tablespoons sherry wine vinegar
    or white wine vinegar
4 teaspoons honey
1 tablespoon Dijon mustard
¼ teaspoon salt
5 cups packed torn assorted
    gourmet mixed salad greens
    (about 3 ounces), such as
    oakleaf, frisée, watercress,
    radicchio, arugula or escarole

2 cups packed torn Boston or bibb
    lettuce leaves
    (about 1½ ounces)
2 ripe Bosc, Bartlett or Anjou
    pears, cored, quartered and
    cut into ½-inch pieces
    Lemon juice
1½ cups (6 ounces) crumbled Stilton
    or Gorgonzola cheese
    Freshly ground black pepper

Place oil, vinegar, honey, mustard and salt in small bowl. Whisk until combined. Cover and refrigerate up to 2 days.

Combine all salad greens in large bowl. To help prevent discoloration, brush pear pieces with lemon juice, if desired. Add pears, cheese and dressing to salad mixture. Toss lightly to coat; sprinkle with pepper.

Makes 6 to 8 servings

Creamy Dijon Coleslaw

½ cup GREY POUPON®
    COUNTRY DIJON® Mustard
½ cup prepared ranch, creamy
    Italian or blue cheese salad
    dressing
2 tablespoons chopped parsley

½ teaspoon celery seed
3 cups shredded green cabbage
2 cups shredded red cabbage
1 cup shredded carrots
½ cup chopped onion
⅓ cup chopped red bell pepper

In small bowl, blend mustard, salad dressing, parsley and celery seed; set aside.

In large bowl, combine green and red cabbages, carrots, onion and bell pepper. Add mustard mixture, tossing to coat well. Chill at least 1 hour before serving.

Makes about 5 cups

Winter Pear and Stilton Salad

Wisconsin Provolone and Sweet Pepper Slaw

Wisconsin Provolone and Sweet Pepper Slaw

3 cups shredded green cabbage
2 cups (8 ounces) cubed Wisconsin
  Provolone cheese
1 cup shredded red cabbage

1 cup coarsely chopped assorted
  bell peppers (red, yellow,
  green and orange)
⅓ cup sliced green onions
¾ cup bottled Caesar dressing

In large bowl, combine all ingredients; mix well. Cover; refrigerate 1 hour to blend flavors. Toss before serving.

Makes 6 to 8 servings

Favorite recipe from **Wisconsin Milk Marketing Board**

Chinese Spinach Toss

3 to 4 cups fresh bean sprouts *or*
2 cans (16 ounces each) bean
sprouts, well drained
⅓ cup honey
⅓ cup white wine or rice vinegar
2 tablespoons vegetable oil
2 teaspoons soy sauce

1 to 2 teaspoons grated fresh
gingerroot
6 cups washed and torn fresh
spinach
1 cup diced peeled jicama
1 cup crisp Chinese noodles

Place bean sprouts in large glass or ceramic bowl. Combine honey, vinegar, oil, soy sauce and gingerroot in small bowl; pour over bean sprouts. Cover and refrigerate at least 1 hour, tossing occasionally. Just before serving, add spinach and jicama; toss gently to coat. Top each serving with noodles. *Makes 6 servings*

Favorite recipe from **National Honey Board**

Mediterranean Montrachet® Salad

1 head Boston lettuce, washed,
drained, dried and separated
10 new potatoes, quartered, grilled,
cooled
3 cups blanched young green
beans, cooled
4 medium tomatoes, cut into
eighths
1 red bell pepper, peeled, seeded
and julienned

1 yellow bell pepper, peeled,
seeded and julienned
1 cup vinaigrette dressing
3 tablespoons coarsely chopped
fresh basil
2 packages (3.5 ounces each)
MONTRACHET®, cut into
4 slices

Divide lettuce among 6 plates. Divide remaining vegetables among each plate. Drizzle each plate with vinaigrette. Garnish with fresh basil and Montrachet® slices. Serve at room temperature. *Makes 6 servings*

Spring Mushroom Asparagus Salad

1½ pounds fresh asparagus spears, trimmed
⅓ cup frozen orange juice concentrate, thawed
¼ cup vegetable oil
2 tablespoons red wine vinegar
1 teaspoon salt
⅛ teaspoon ground black pepper
1 pound fresh white mushrooms, sliced (about 5 cups)
Lettuce leaves
1½ cups cherry tomato quarters

Bring large saucepan filled halfway with water to a boil; add asparagus. Boil until bright green and firm, about 2 minutes; drain. Place asparagus in cold water about 5 minutes or until cool; drain. Transfer asparagus to glass baking dish.

In small bowl, whisk together orange juice concentrate, 2 tablespoons water, oil, vinegar, salt and black pepper; set aside (can be prepared up to 24 hours ahead). Add mushrooms to baking dish. Whisk orange juice mixture and pour over asparagus and mushrooms; stir gently to coat. On 6 serving plates lined with lettuce, arrange mushrooms, dividing evenly; arrange asparagus spears in a spoke pattern (this can be done up to 2 hours ahead, covered and refrigerated). Just before serving, sprinkle cherry tomatoes over salad; drizzle with remaining orange juice mixture from baking dish.

Makes 6 servings

Favorite recipe from **Mushroom Council**

Fennel with Black Olive Dressing

1¼ pounds (about 2 medium-size heads) fennel
⅓ cup lemon juice
¼ cup olive or salad oil
⅔ cup pitted California ripe olives, coarsely chopped
Salt and pepper

Trim stems and root end from fennel; core. Reserve feathery wisps of fennel for garnish, if desired. Slice fennel crosswise into ¼-inch-thick pieces. In 4- to 5-quart pan, bring 3 to 4 quarts water to a boil over high heat. Add fennel and cook, uncovered, just until tender to bite, about 5 minutes. Drain; immerse fennel in ice water until cold. Drain well again. In small bowl, beat lemon juice and oil; stir in olives and add salt and pepper to taste. To serve, divide fennel among 6 salad plates and spoon dressing over fennel. Garnish with reserved feathery wisps of fennel, if desired. *Makes 6 servings*

Prep Time: 10 minutes   **Cook Time:** About 5 minutes

Favorite recipe from **California Olive Industry**

Rio Grande Valley Marinated Onion Salad

1 large (14 to 16 ounces) Texas SPRINGSWEET® or Texas 1015 SUPERSWEET® Onion, thinly sliced and separated into rings
1½ pounds ripe tomatoes, sliced
1 cucumber, peeled and sliced
½ cup vegetable oil
¼ cup wine vinegar

1 teaspoon Dijon mustard
½ teaspoon salt
¼ teaspoon sugar
¼ teaspoon black pepper
¼ cup sliced fresh basil leaves
Shaved fresh Parmesan cheese or crumbled blue cheese, optional

Place *half* of onion rings in large, shallow casserole. Layer tomatoes and cucumber over onion and top with *remaining* onion rings. In small bowl, combine oil, vinegar, mustard, salt, sugar and pepper; whisk well to blend. Pour over vegetables. Top with fresh basil. Cover and let marinate several hours in refrigerator. Top with cheese before serving, if desired. *Makes 8 to 10 servings*

Roasted Pepper and Avocado Salad

2 red bell peppers
2 orange bell peppers
2 yellow bell peppers
2 ripe avocados, halved, pitted
   and peeled
3 shallots, thinly sliced
¼ cup FILIPPO BERIO® Extra
   Virgin Olive Oil

1 clove garlic, crushed
Finely grated peel and juice of
   1 lemon
Salt and freshly ground black
   pepper

Place bell peppers on baking sheet. Broil, 4 to 5 inches from heat, 5 minutes on each side or until entire surface of each bell pepper is blistered and blackened slightly. Place bell peppers in paper bag. Close bag; cool 15 to 20 minutes. Cut around cores of bell peppers; twist and remove. Cut bell peppers lengthwise in half. Peel off skin with paring knife; rinse under cold water to remove seeds. Slice bell peppers into ½-inch-thick strips; place in shallow dish.

Cut avocados into ¼-inch-thick slices; add to bell peppers. Sprinkle with shallots.

In small bowl, whisk together olive oil, garlic, lemon peel and juice. Pour over bell pepper mixture. Cover; refrigerate at least 1 hour before serving. Season to taste with salt and black pepper. *Makes 6 servings*

Roasted Pepper and Avocado Salad

Mozzarella & Tomato with Lemon Dijon Dressing

Mozzarella & Tomato with Lemon Dijon Dressing

⅓ cup olive oil
¼ cup GREY POUPON®
    COUNTRY DIJON®
    Mustard*
2 tablespoons lemon juice
2 teaspoons finely chopped fresh
    basil leaves
½ teaspoon sugar

3 medium tomatoes, sliced
6 ounces fresh mozzarella cheese,
    sliced
2 cups mixed salad greens
¼ cup coarsely chopped pitted ripe
    olives
Chopped fresh basil leaves

In small bowl, whisk oil, mustard, lemon juice, basil and sugar; set aside. Arrange tomato and cheese slices over salad greens on serving platter. Top with chopped olives and basil leaves; garnish as desired. Drizzle with prepared dressing before serving.

Makes 6 appetizer servings

Grey Poupon® Peppercorn Mustard may be substituted for Country Dijon® Mustard.

Festive Pepper Medley à la Grecque

1 green bell pepper, thinly sliced
1 yellow bell pepper, thinly sliced
1 red bell pepper, thinly sliced
3 tablespoons olive oil
1 tablespoon water
2 teaspoons balsamic vinegar
1 tablespoon chopped fresh
oregano *or* 1 teaspoon dried
oregano

Salt and pepper, to taste
¾ cup chopped walnuts
¼ cup olives (Greek or niçoise)
¼ cup crumbled feta cheese
(optional)

Arrange bell peppers on microwave-safe serving platter. Combine oil, water, vinegar, oregano, salt and black pepper; pour over peppers. Sprinkle with walnuts. Microwave on HIGH 5 minutes. Top with olives and feta. Serve warm or at room temperature. Garnish with radicchio or spinach leaves, if desired. *Makes 4 to 6 servings*

Favorite recipe from **Walnut Marketing Board**

Thai Pasta Salad with Peanut Sauce

¼ cup evaporated skim milk
4½ teaspoons creamy peanut butter
4½ teaspoons finely chopped red
onion
1 teaspoon lemon juice
¾ teaspoon brown sugar
½ teaspoon reduced-sodium soy
sauce

⅛ teaspoon crushed red pepper
½ teaspoon finely chopped fresh
ginger
1 cup hot cooked whole wheat
spaghetti
2 teaspoons finely chopped green
onion

Combine milk, peanut butter, red onion, lemon juice, sugar, soy sauce and red pepper in medium saucepan. Bring to a boil over high heat, stirring constantly. Boil 2 minutes, stirring constantly. Reduce heat to medium-low. Add ginger; blend well. Add spaghetti; toss to coat. Top with green onion. Serve immediately. *Makes 2 servings*

Gourmet Deli Potato & Pea Salad

1½ pounds new potatoes, scrubbed
and quartered
1 cup water
¾ teaspoon salt, divided
½ pound sugar snap peas or snow
peas, trimmed
⅓ cup reduced fat mayonnaise

⅓ cup plain nonfat yogurt
3 tablespoons FRENCH'S® Dijon
Mustard
⅓ cup finely chopped red onion
2 tablespoons minced fresh dill *or*
2 teaspoons dried dill weed
1 clove garlic, minced

Place potatoes, water and ½ *teaspoon* salt in 3-quart microwave-safe baking dish. Cover and microwave on HIGH 15 minutes or until potatoes are tender, stirring once. Add peas. Cover and microwave on HIGH 3 minutes or until peas are crisp-tender. Rinse with cold water and drain. Cool completely.

Combine mayonnaise, yogurt, mustard, onion, dill, garlic and remaining ¼ *teaspoon* salt in large bowl; mix well. Add potatoes and peas; toss to coat evenly. Cover and refrigerate 1 hour before serving. Garnish as desired.   *Makes 6 side-dish servings*

Prep Time: 15 minutes   **Cook Time:** 18 minutes   **Chill Time:** 1 hour

Gourmet Deli Potato & Pea Salad

Mediterranean Pasta Salad

2 ounces uncooked bow tie pasta
1 cup canned garbanzo beans
    (chick-peas), rinsed and
    drained
1 cup cooked canned artichoke
    hearts, rinsed, drained and
    quartered
¾ cup sliced zucchini, halved

¼ cup chopped red onion
3 tablespoons lemon juice
2 tablespoons olive oil
½ teaspoon Italian seasoning
⅛ teaspoon ground black pepper
⅛ teaspoon garlic powder
2 tablespoons crumbled feta
    cheese

1. Cook pasta according to package directions, omitting salt. Rinse with cool water; drain. Cool.

2. Combine pasta, beans, artichoke hearts, zucchini and onion in large bowl.

3. Combine lemon juice, oil, Italian seasoning, pepper and garlic powder in small bowl until well blended. Drizzle over pasta mixture; toss to coat. Top with cheese before serving. Serve on lettuce leaves, if desired. *Makes 6 servings*

Fresh Orange-Pasta Salad

Grated peel of ½ SUNKIST®
    Orange
Juice of 1 SUNKIST® Orange
    (⅓ cup)
3 tablespoons olive or vegetable
    oil
2 teaspoons chopped fresh dill *or*
    ½ teaspoon dried dill weed
¼ teaspoon seasoned salt

2 cups curly or spiral macaroni,
    cooked and drained
2 SUNKIST® Oranges, peeled and
    cut into half-cartwheel slices
2 cups broccoli flowerets, cooked
    and drained
½ cup sliced celery
¼ cup sliced green onions

In large bowl, combine orange peel and juice, oil, dill and seasoned salt. Add remaining ingredients; toss gently. Cover and chill; stir occasionally. *Makes 6 servings*

Mediterranean Pasta Salad

Taco Salad

Taco Salad

3 ounces uncooked radiatore
  pasta, cooked
½ cup frozen corn, thawed
½ cup chopped seeded tomato
1 can (4 ounces) diced mild green
  chiles, drained
¼ cup chopped onion

2 tablespoons sliced ripe olives
2 tablespoons chopped fresh
  cilantro
½ cup mild or medium chunky
  salsa
½ teaspoon chili powder

Combine pasta, corn, tomato, chiles, onion, olives and cilantro in large bowl. Combine salsa and chili powder in small bowl until well blended. Pour over pasta mixture; toss to coat. Cover; refrigerate 2 hours.   *Makes 6 servings*

Pasta Salad with Hummus Dressing

8 ounces uncooked rigatoni, penne
   or pasta twists
3 tablespoons sesame seeds
   (optional)
1 (16-ounce) can chick-peas,
   rinsed and well drained
¼ cup water
¼ cup FILIPPO BERIO® Olive Oil
   Juice of 1½ lemons
3 cloves garlic, peeled
½ teaspoon ground cumin

¼ teaspoon chili powder
1 bunch green onions, trimmed,
   halved and sliced
½ green bell pepper, seeded and
   chopped
1 tablespoon chopped fresh Italian
   parsley
6 tablespoons mayonnaise
   Salt and freshly ground black
   pepper
   Ripe and green olive slivers

Preheat oven to 300°F. Cook pasta according to package directions until al dente (tender but still firm). Drain. Meanwhile, place sesame seeds, if desired, in shallow pan; toast in oven until lightly browned, stirring occasionally.

In blender container or food processor, combine chick-peas, water, olive oil, lemon juice, garlic, cumin and chili powder; process until mixture forms a creamy paste. Transfer mixture to large bowl. Add green onions, bell pepper and parsley; mix well. Add hot pasta; toss until lightly coated with dressing. Cover; refrigerate 30 minutes. Stir in mayonnaise. Season to taste with salt and black pepper. Sprinkle with sesame seeds; top with olives. *Makes 4 servings*

Roasted Corn & Wild Rice Salad

½ cup uncooked wild rice
1½ cups fresh whole kernel corn
(about 3 medium ears)
½ cup diced seeded tomato
½ cup finely chopped yellow or
green bell pepper
⅓ cup minced fresh cilantro

2 tablespoons minced seeded
jalapeño peppers* (optional)
2 tablespoons fresh lime juice
2 tablespoons prepared honey
mustard
1 tablespoon olive oil
½ teaspoon ground cumin

1. Place 1½ cups water in small saucepan; bring to a boil over high heat. Stir in wild rice; cover. Reduce heat to medium-low. Simmer 40 minutes or until rice is just tender but still firm to the bite. Drain rice; discard liquid.

2. Preheat oven to 400°F. Spray baking sheet with nonstick cooking spray.

3. Spread corn evenly over prepared baking sheet. Bake 20 to 25 minutes or until corn is lightly browned, stirring after 15 minutes.

4. Combine rice, corn, tomato, bell pepper, cilantro and jalapeños in large bowl. Combine lime juice, honey mustard, oil and cumin in small bowl until well blended. Drizzle over rice mixture; toss to coat. Cover; refrigerate 2 hours. Serve on lettuce leaves, if desired.
Makes 6 servings

*Jalapeño peppers can sting and irritate the skin; wear rubber gloves when handling peppers and do not touch eyes.

Roasted Corn & Wild Rice Salad

Minted Fruit Rice Salad

⅔ cup DOLE® Pineapple Orange Juice or Mandarin Tangerine Juice
⅓ cup water
1 cup uncooked instant rice
1 can (11 ounces) DOLE® Mandarin Oranges, drained

1 can (8 ounces) DOLE® Crushed Pineapple
½ cup chopped cucumber
⅓ cup chopped DOLE® Red Onion
3 tablespoons chopped fresh mint

• **Combine** juice and water in medium saucepan. Bring to boil. Stir in rice. Remove from heat; cover. Let stand 10 minutes.

• **Stir** together rice, mandarin oranges, undrained pineapple, cucumber, onion and mint in medium serving bowl. Serve at room temperature or chilled. Garnish with fresh mint leaves, if desired.   *Makes 4 servings*

Prep Time: 5 minutes   **Cook Time:** 15 minutes

Wild Rice Waldorf Salad

2 cups cooked wild rice, chilled (⅔ cup uncooked)
2 large red apples, unpeeled and diced (Fireside, Cortland or Regent)

1 tablespoon lemon juice
2 tablespoons packed brown sugar
2 ribs celery, sliced
½ cup plain nonfat yogurt
¼ cup low-fat mayonnaise

Toss apples with lemon juice and brown sugar. Stir in celery and wild rice. Blend yogurt and mayonnaise. Toss with salad ingredients. Chill.   *Makes 6 servings*

Favorite recipe from **Minnesota Cultivated Wild Rice Council**

Minted Fruit Rice Salad

Santa Fe Black Beans & Rice Salad

Santa Fe Black Beans & Rice Salad

½ cup GREY POUPON® Dijon
    Mustard
2 tablespoons REGINA® White
    Wine Vinegar
2 tablespoons olive oil
1 tablespoon chopped cilantro
1½ teaspoons liquid hot pepper
    seasoning
½ teaspoon chili powder

¼ teaspoon ground cumin
3 cups cooked long grain and wild
    rice
1 (15-ounce) can black beans,
    rinsed and drained
1 cup chopped tomato
1 cup canned corn
⅓ cup chopped red onion
¼ cup diced green chiles

In small bowl, blend mustard, vinegar, oil, cilantro, hot pepper seasoning, chili powder and cumin; set aside.

In large bowl, combine rice, beans, tomato, corn, onion and chiles. Add mustard mixture, tossing to coat well. Chill at least 1 hour before serving. Garnish as desired.

Makes 6 cups

Greek Rice Salad

1 package (7.2 ounces)
   RICE-A-RONI® Rice Pilaf
1 cup chopped cucumber
1 cup crumbled feta cheese or
   cubed brick or Monterey
   Jack cheese
¼ cup chopped parsley

⅓ cup olive oil or vegetable oil
3 tablespoons red wine vinegar or
   lemon juice
1 clove garlic, minced
2 teaspoons dried oregano leaves
   or dried mint
1 large tomato, chopped

1. Prepare Rice-A-Roni® Mix as package directs. Cool 10 minutes.

2. In large bowl, combine prepared Rice-A-Roni®, cucumber, cheese and parsley.

3. Combine oil, vinegar, garlic and oregano. Pour over rice mixture; toss. Cover; chill 4 hours or overnight. Stir in tomato just before serving. *Makes 5 servings*

Serving Suggestion: Serve with 1 cup plain yogurt, topped with a little honey per serving.

Western-Style Bean Salad

1¾ cups (16-ounce jar) ORTEGA®
   Thick & Chunky Salsa, hot,
   medium or mild or Garden
   Style Salsa, medium or mild
1¾ cups (15-ounce can) black
   beans, rinsed, drained

1 cup whole kernel corn
½ cup quartered, sliced red onion
¼ cup chopped fresh cilantro or
   parsley
1 tablespoon lime juice
½ teaspoon ground cumin

COMBINE salsa, beans, corn, onion, cilantro, lime juice and cumin in large bowl. Cover; chill for at least 2 hours.

SERVE as a side dish or in a tossed green salad. *Makes 8 servings*

Confetti Wild Rice Salad

1 package (6 ounces) white and
   wild rice mix
1 *each* red and yellow bell pepper,
   seeded and chopped
¼ cup finely chopped red onion
¼ cup minced fresh parsley
¼ cup minced fresh basil leaves
⅓ cup FRENCH'S® Dijon Mustard
¼ cup olive oil
¼ cup red wine vinegar

Prepare rice according to package directions; cool. Place rice in large bowl. Add peppers, onion, parsley and basil. Combine mustard, oil and vinegar in small bowl; mix well. Pour over rice and vegetables; toss well to coat evenly. Cover and refrigerate 1 hour before serving. Garnish as desired.   *Makes 8 side-dish servings*

Prep Time: 20 minutes   **Cook Time:** 20 minutes   **Chill Time:** 1 hour

Golden Touch Tabbouleh Salad

½ cup bulgur
¾ cup boiling water
2 large plum tomatoes, seeded,
   chopped
4 large red radishes, shredded
½ cup chopped fresh parsley
¼ cup golden raisins
3 to 4 tablespoons finely chopped
   fresh mint leaves
¼ cup light olive oil
¼ cup fresh lemon juice
1 clove garlic, minced
1 teaspoon curry powder
¼ teaspoon ground cumin
¼ teaspoon ground cinnamon
1½ cups (6 ounces) SARGENTO®
   Fancy Shredded Cheddar
   Cheese
½ cup chopped peanuts

In medium bowl, soak bulgur in boiling water 30 minutes. Add tomatoes, radishes, parsley, raisins and mint; toss. Combine oil, lemon juice, garlic, curry powder, cumin and cinnamon; mix well. Add to bulgur; toss well. Cover; refrigerate at least 30 minutes. Just before serving, stir in Cheddar cheese; sprinkle with peanuts.

Makes 6 to 8 servings

Confetti Wild Rice Salad

Pearls o' Barley Salad

2 cups water
½ cup QUAKER® Scotch Brand
    Pearled Barley*
⅛ teaspoon salt (optional)
½ cup (2 ounces) cubed Swiss
    cheese
½ medium cucumber, cut into
    matchstick pieces
⅓ cup sliced celery
⅓ cup sliced green onions
¼ cup finely chopped fresh parsley

¼ cup sliced green olives
¼ cup Italian salad dressing
¼ teaspoon dried oregano leaves,
    crumbled
⅛ to ¼ teaspoon ground red
    pepper
  Fresh spinach leaves, rinsed,
    trimmed
2 to 3 tablespoons dry roasted
    sunflower kernels

Bring water to a boil; stir in barley and salt. Cover and reduce heat. Simmer 45 to 50 minutes or until tender. Remove from heat; let stand 5 minutes.

In large bowl, combine barley with remaining ingredients except spinach leaves and sunflower kernels. Marinate several hours or overnight. Serve on large platter or individual plates lined with spinach leaves. Sprinkle with sunflower kernels. Garnish with tomato wedges, if desired. *Makes 8 servings*

Quick Method: *Use ⅔ cup Quaker® Scotch Brand Quick Pearled Barley; decrease simmer time to 10 to 12 minutes. Proceed as directed.*

Dicey Tomato, Bean and Walnut Salad

1 medium cucumber, peeled,
   sliced and quartered
1 (14.5-ounce) can FRANK'S or
   SNOWFLOSS Original Style
   Diced Tomatoes, well drained
½ cup walnut pieces
1 small clove garlic
3 tablespoons cold water
1 tablespoon red wine vinegar

Salt and black pepper to taste
Cayenne pepper (optional)
2 tablespoons chopped parsley
2 tablespoons chopped cilantro
   (optional)
1 tablespoon finely chopped onion
1 (15½-ounce) can light or dark
   red kidney beans, drained
Lettuce leaves

1. Salt cucumbers in bowl to draw out some water.

2. Drain diced tomatoes on paper towels to absorb excess moisture.

3. In food processor or blender, process walnuts and garlic into a paste. Stir in water and vinegar. Add salt, black pepper and cayenne to taste.

4. Mix in parsley, cilantro and onion, if desired.

5. Pat cucumbers dry and add to mixture.

6. Add beans and tomatoes to mixture; mix well. Serve on a bed of lettuce.

Makes 4 servings

Prep Time: 15 minutes

Bean Salad with Bulgur

¾ cup uncooked dried red kidney
beans, sorted and rinsed
¾ cup uncooked dried pinto beans,
sorted and rinsed
8 ounces fresh green beans, cut
into 2-inch pieces
½ cup uncooked bulgur
⅓ cup vegetable oil

1 tablespoon dark sesame oil
6 green onions with tops, chopped
2 tablespoons minced fresh ginger
3 cloves garlic, minced
¼ teaspoon crushed red pepper
3 tablespoons soy sauce
2 tablespoons white wine vinegar
½ teaspoon sugar

Soak kidney and pinto beans overnight in cold water; rinse and drain. Place in large saucepan and cover with 6 cups water. Bring to a boil; reduce heat to low. Cover and simmer 1 hour or until tender. Rinse; drain and set aside. Meanwhile, place green beans in 2-quart saucepan; cover with water. Bring to a boil over medium-high heat. Reduce heat to low; simmer, covered, 5 to 6 minutes until beans are crisp-tender. Rinse; drain and set aside.

Combine bulgur and 1 cup water in 1-quart saucepan. Bring to a boil over medium heat. Reduce heat to low; simmer, covered, 15 minutes or until water is absorbed and bulgur is fluffy.

Combine green beans, bulgur, kidney and pinto beans in large bowl.

Heat vegetable oil and sesame oil in large skillet over medium heat. Add onions, ginger, garlic and crushed red pepper. Cook and stir about 3 minutes or until onions are tender. Remove from heat. Stir in soy sauce, vinegar and sugar. Pour oil mixture into bean mixture; mix well. Cover; refrigerate 2 to 3 hours. Garnish, if desired.

Makes 6 to 8 servings

Bean Salad with Bulgur

Confetti Barley Salad

4 cups water
1 cup dry pearl barley
⅓ cup GREY POUPON® Dijon
   Mustard
⅓ cup olive oil
¼ cup REGINA® Red Wine
   Vinegar
2 tablespoons chopped parsley
2 teaspoons chopped fresh
   rosemary leaves *or* ½
   teaspoon dried rosemary
   leaves

2 teaspoons grated orange peel
1 teaspoon sugar
1½ cups diced red, green or yellow
   bell peppers
½ cup sliced green onions
½ cup sliced pitted ripe olives
   Fresh rosemary and orange and
   tomato slices, for garnish

In 3-quart saucepan, over medium-high heat, heat water and barley to a boil; reduce heat. Cover; simmer for 45 to 55 minutes or until tender. Drain and cool.

In small bowl, whisk mustard, oil, vinegar, parsley, rosemary, orange peel and sugar until blended; set aside.

In large bowl, combine barley, bell peppers, green onions and olives. Stir in mustard dressing, tossing to coat well. Chill several hours to blend flavors. To serve, spoon barley mixture onto serving platter; garnish with rosemary and orange and tomato slices.

Makes 6 to 8 servings

Confetti Barley Salad

Southwestern Bean and Corn Salad

1 can (about 15 ounces) pinto
   beans, rinsed and drained
1 cup fresh (about 2 ears) or
   thawed frozen whole kernel
   corn
1 red bell pepper, finely chopped
4 green onions, finely chopped

2 tablespoons cider vinegar
2 tablespoons honey
½ teaspoon salt
½ teaspoon ground mustard
½ teaspoon ground cumin
⅛ teaspoon cayenne pepper

1. Combine beans, corn, bell pepper and onions in large bowl.

2. Blend vinegar and honey in small bowl until smooth. Stir in salt, mustard, cumin and cayenne pepper. Drizzle over bean mixture; toss to coat. Cover; refrigerate 2 hours. Serve on lettuce leaves, if desired. *Makes 4 servings*

Mediterranean Couscous

1 (10-ounce) package couscous
⅓ cup GREY POUPON®
   COUNTRY DIJON® Mustard
¼ cup lemon juice
¼ cup chopped parsley
3 tablespoons chopped fresh mint
1 tablespoon grated lemon peel
1 clove garlic, minced

⅔ cup olive oil
1 (7-ounce) jar roasted red
   peppers, drained and
   chopped
4 ounces feta cheese, diced
½ cup chopped pitted ripe olives
   Sliced tomatoes and cucumbers,
   for garnish

Prepare couscous according to package directions; cool.

In small bowl, whisk mustard, lemon juice, parsley, mint, lemon peel and garlic until blended. Whisk in oil.

In large bowl, combine couscous, peppers, cheese and olives; add mustard mixture, tossing to coat well. Chill at least 1 hour. To serve, arrange couscous mixture on serving plate; garnish with tomato and cucumber slices. *Makes 6 servings*

Southwestern Bean and Corn Salad

French Lentil Salad

¼ cup chopped walnuts
1½ cups dried lentils, rinsed, sorted
and drained*
4 green onions, finely chopped
3 tablespoons balsamic vinegar
2 tablespoons chopped fresh
parsley

1 tablespoon olive oil
¾ teaspoon salt
½ teaspoon dried thyme leaves
¼ teaspoon ground black pepper

1. Preheat oven to 375°F.

2. Spread walnuts in even layer over baking sheet. Bake 5 minutes or until lightly browned. Remove from oven. Cool completely on baking sheet.

3. Combine 2 quarts water and lentils in large saucepan; bring to a boil over high heat. Cover; reduce heat to medium-low. Simmer 30 minutes or until lentils are tender, stirring occasionally. Drain lentils; discard liquid.

4. Combine lentils, onions, vinegar, parsley, oil, salt, thyme and pepper in large bowl. Cover; refrigerate 1 hour or until cool.

5. Serve on lettuce leaves, if desired. Top with walnuts before serving. Garnish as desired.   *Makes 4 servings*

*Packages of dried lentils may contain grit and tiny stones. Therefore, thoroughly rinse lentils. Then sort through and discard grit or any unusual looking pieces.

French Lentil Salad

Glorious Garbanzo Salad

5 cups cooked low-sodium
garbanzo beans, well drained
3 medium-sized tomatoes, diced
⅓ cup chopped toasted* California
walnuts
¼ cup chopped parsley
¼ cup chopped green onions

½ cup nonfat cottage cheese
3 tablespoons wine vinegar
1 tablespoon olive oil
1 clove garlic, minced
1 teaspoon salt
½ teaspoon freshly ground black
pepper

Rinse beans under running water, then drain well again. Place in medium bowl. Add tomatoes, walnuts, parsley and green onions; set aside.

In small bowl, whisk together cottage cheese, vinegar, oil, garlic, salt and pepper. Pour over salad ingredients and toss to combine. Chill before serving, tossing occasionally. Season with additional pepper and vinegar, if necessary. *Makes 8 servings*

Toasting walnuts is optional.

Favorite recipe from **Walnut Marketing Board**

Papaya-Kiwifruit Salad with Orange Dressing

1 papaya
4 kiwifruit
6 tablespoons frozen orange juice
concentrate, thawed

3 tablespoons honey
1 cup sour cream
1 tablespoon grated orange peel
1 tablespoon grated lime peel

1. Peel and remove seeds from papaya. Slice lengthwise into thin slices.

2. Peel kiwifruit and cut crosswise into thin slices. Arrange papaya and kiwifruit on 4 salad plates.

3. Combine orange juice concentrate and honey in small bowl. Stir in sour cream. Spoon dressing over salads; sprinkle with peels. *Makes 4 servings*

Tuscan Summer Salad

1 small loaf coarse day-old Italian bread
¼ cup olive oil
3 tablespoons balsamic vinegar
1 clove garlic, crushed
1 teaspoon salt
1 teaspoon TABASCO® pepper sauce
3 large ripe tomatoes, cut into large chunks
1 large red onion, cut in half and sliced

1 large cucumber, cut into large chunks
1 large red bell pepper, seeded and cut into large pieces
1 large yellow bell pepper, seeded and cut into large pieces
1 cup arugula leaves
½ cup chopped fresh basil leaves
½ cup sliced black olives
1 tablespoon capers

Tear bread into large pieces to make about 4 cups. In large bowl, combine olive oil, balsamic vinegar, garlic, salt and TABASCO® sauce. Add remaining ingredients; toss to mix well. Let mixture stand 30 minutes before serving. *Makes 4 servings*

Grilled Vegetable Pasta Salad

1 tablespoon plus 1 teaspoon olive oil, divided

1 tablespoon plus 2 teaspoons fresh lemon juice, divided

1 tablespoon plus 1 teaspoon Dijon mustard

1 tablespoon capers, rinsed and drained (optional)

2 teaspoons minced fresh tarragon

2 yellow Grilled Bell Peppers (recipe follows)

2 small green zucchini (about 8 ounces), halved lengthwise

½ pint cherry tomatoes

6 ounces uncooked rotini, cooked and drained

2 tablespoons grated Parmesan cheese

1. Prepare wooden or bamboo skewers by soaking in water 20 to 30 minutes to keep from burning. To make dressing, whisk together 1 tablespoon oil, 1 tablespoon lemon juice and mustard. Stir in capers, if desired, and tarragon; set aside.

2. Prepare Grilled Bell Peppers. Combine remaining 1 teaspoon oil and 2 teaspoons lemon juice in small bowl. Brush onto zucchini and tomatoes. Grill zucchini on covered grill over medium coals 10 to 13 minutes or until grillmarked and tender, basting and turning once. To grill cherry tomatoes, thread tomatoes onto prepared skewers. Grill on covered grill over medium coals 5 minutes or until blistered and browned, basting and turning once.

3. Stir dressing into pasta in large bowl. Dice peppers and add to pasta. Slice zucchini crosswise into ½-inch pieces and add to pasta along with tomatoes. Sprinkle with Parmesan and gently stir to combine. Garnish as desired. *Makes 6 servings*

Grilled Bell Pepper

1 bell pepper (any color), stemmed, seeded and halved

Grill bell pepper halves, skin side down, on covered grill over medium to hot coals 15 to 25 minutes or until skin is charred, without turning. Remove from grill and place in plastic bag until cool enough to handle, about 10 minutes. Remove skin with paring knife and discard.

Grilled Vegetable Pasta Salad

Cool Summer Gazpacho Salad

1 DOLE® Fresh Pineapple
2 cups chopped tomatoes, drained
1 large cucumber, halved
    lengthwise and thinly sliced
¼ cup chopped DOLE® Green
    Onions

¼ cup red wine vinegar
4 teaspoons olive or vegetable oil
½ teaspoon dried basil leaves,
    crushed

• **Twist** crown from pineapple. Cut pineapple lengthwise into quarters. Remove fruit from shell; core and chop fruit. Drain.

• **Stir** pineapple, tomatoes, cucumber, green onions, vinegar, oil and basil in large serving bowl; cover and chill 1 hour or overnight. Stir before serving.

Makes 10 servings

Prep Time: 20 minutes   **Chill Time:** 1 hour

Cool Fruit and Vegetable Salad with Hot Tomato Dipping Sauce

2 medium tomatoes
¼ cup olive oil
2 tablespoons red wine vinegar
¾ teaspoon TABASCO® pepper
    sauce
3 sprigs cilantro
¼ teaspoon salt

1 small head green leaf lettuce
4 large honeydew melon slices
1 large orange, peeled and sliced
1 medium cucumber, thinly sliced
1 red bell pepper, cut into thin
    strips
3 green onions

In food processor or blender combine tomatoes, olive oil, vinegar, TABASCO® sauce, cilantro and salt. Process until mixture is smooth. Refrigerate until ready to serve.

Arrange lettuce leaves on large serving platter; top with melon, orange, cucumber, red pepper and green onions. Serve salad with dipping sauce.   *Makes 6 servings*

Cool Summer Gazpacho Salad

Honey Dijon Fruit Salad

½ cup prepared HIDDEN
    VALLEY RANCH® Honey
    Dijon Ranch Creamy
    Dressing
½ cup low-fat pineapple-flavored
    yogurt
¼ cup finely chopped fresh
    pineapple or drained canned
    crushed pineapple

1 teaspoon grated lemon peel
1 teaspoon lemon juice
4 cups assorted fresh fruit
    (grapes, berries, sliced apples,
    pears or bananas)
Lettuce leaves

Combine dressing, yogurt, pineapple, lemon peel and lemon juice in medium bowl. Arrange fruit on lettuce-lined serving plate or 4 individual plates. Serve dressing with salad.

Makes 4 servings

Apple-Nut Slaw

½ head green cabbage, shredded
1 cup shredded red cabbage
1 cup toasted walnuts*
2 red apples, sliced

1½ cups prepared HIDDEN
    VALLEY RANCH® Reduced
    Calorie or Low Fat Original
    Ranch® salad dressing

Combine all ingredients in large bowl; toss gently to coat. Cover and refrigerate until ready to serve.

Makes 4 to 6 servings

To toast walnuts, spread in a single layer on baking sheet. Toast in preheated 375°F oven 8 to 10 minutes until very lightly browned.

Top to bottom: **Honey Dijon Fruit Salad and Apple-Nut Slaw**

SANDWICHES, PIZZAS & MORE

Eggplant & Pepper Cheese Sandwiches

1 (8-ounce) eggplant, cut into
   18 slices
   Salt and pepper, to taste
⅓ cup GREY POUPON®
   COUNTRY DIJON® Mustard
¼ cup olive oil
2 tablespoons REGINA® Red
   Wine Vinegar

¾ teaspoon dried oregano leaves
1 clove garlic, crushed
6 (4-inch) pieces French bread,
   cut in half
1 (7-ounce) jar roasted red
   peppers, cut into strips
1½ cups shredded mozzarella
   cheese (6 ounces)

Place eggplant slices on greased baking sheet, overlapping slightly. Sprinkle lightly with salt and pepper. Bake at 400°F for 10 to 12 minutes or until tender.

Blend mustard, oil, vinegar, oregano and garlic. Brush eggplant slices with ¼ cup mustard mixture; broil eggplant for 1 minute.

Brush cut sides of French bread with remaining mustard mixture. Layer 3 slices eggplant, a few red pepper strips and ¼ cup cheese on each bread bottom. Place on broiler pan with roll tops, cut-sides up; broil until cheese melts. Close sandwiches with bread tops and serve immediately; garnish as desired. *Makes 6 sandwiches*

Eggplant & Pepper Cheese Sandwiches

Vegetarian Burger

Vegetarian Burgers

½ cup A.1.® Steak Sauce, divided
¼ cup plain yogurt
⅔ cup slivered almonds
⅔ cup salted peanuts
⅔ cup sunflower kernels
½ cup chopped green bell pepper

¼ cup chopped onion
1 clove garlic, minced
1 tablespoon red wine vinegar
4 (5-inch) pita breads, halved
4 lettuce leaves
4 tomato slices

In small bowl, combine ¼ cup steak sauce and yogurt; set aside. In food processor or blender, process almonds, peanuts, sunflower kernels, green pepper, onion and garlic until coarsely chopped. With motor running, slowly add remaining steak sauce and vinegar until blended; shape mixture into 4 patties. Grill burgers over medium heat for 1½ minutes on each side or until heated through, turning once. Split open top edge of each pita bread. Layer lettuce, burger, tomato slice and 2 tablespoons prepared sauce in each pita bread half. Serve immediately.

Makes 4 servings

Grilled Vegetable Sandwiches

2 pounds assorted fresh
    vegetables*
1 envelope LIPTON® Recipe
    Secrets® Onion Soup Mix
⅓ cup olive or vegetable oil
2 tablespoons balsamic vinegar or
    red wine vinegar

½ teaspoon dried basil leaves,
    crushed
4 (8-inch) pita breads, warmed
1 cup (4 ounces) shredded
    Montrachet, mozzarella,
    Jarlsberg, Monterey Jack or
    Cheddar cheese

In bottom of broiler pan, with rack removed, arrange vegetables. Stir in Onion Soup Mix blended with oil, vinegar and basil, tossing until evenly coated. Broil vegetables until tender. To serve, cut 1-inch strip off each pita. Fill evenly with vegetables and sprinkle with cheese. Garnish, if desired, with shredded lettuce and sliced tomato.

Makes about 4 servings

Use any of the following, sliced: red, green or yellow bell peppers, mushrooms, zucchini or eggplant.

•Also terrific with Lipton® Recipe Secrets® Savory Herb with Garlic, Golden Herb with Lemon, Fiesta Herb with Red Pepper or Golden Onion Soup Mix.

Meatless Sloppy Joes

Nonstick cooking spray
2 cups thinly sliced onions
2 cups chopped green bell peppers
2 cloves garlic, finely chopped
2 tablespoons ketchup
1 tablespoon mustard

1 can (about 15 ounces) kidney
  beans, mashed
1 can (8 ounces) tomato sauce
1 teaspoon chili powder
  Cider vinegar
2 sandwich rolls, halved

1. Spray large nonstick skillet with cooking spray; heat over medium heat until hot. Add onions, peppers and garlic. Cook and stir 5 minutes or until vegetables are tender. Stir in ketchup and mustard.

2. Add beans, sauce and chili powder. Reduce heat to medium-low. Cook 5 minutes or until thickened, stirring frequently and adding up to ⅓ cup vinegar if dry. Top sandwich roll halves evenly with bean mixture. *Makes 4 servings*

BelGioioso® Asiago and Sweet Pepper Sandwiches

2 tablespoons olive oil
1 red bell pepper, sliced into strips
1 yellow bell pepper, sliced into
  strips
1 medium onion, thinly sliced
1 teaspoon dried thyme

Hot pepper sauce
Salt and pepper to taste
4 ounces BELGIOIOSO® Asiago,
  thinly sliced
4 long sandwich buns, sliced open
  lengthwise

Heat olive oil in large skillet. Add red and yellow bell peppers and cook over medium heat about 6 minutes. Add onion and cook until vegetables are softened. Stir in thyme, hot pepper sauce, salt and pepper to taste.

Layer Asiago cheese on bottom half of buns and top with vegetable mixture. Serve immediately. *Makes 4 servings*

Meatless Sloppy Joe

California Veggie Rolls

1 package (8 ounces) cream
   cheese, softened
½ teaspoon LAWRY'S® Garlic
   Powder with Parsley
½ teaspoon LAWRY'S® Lemon
   Pepper
6 large or 12 regular-size flour
   tortillas

1 large bunch fresh spinach
   leaves, cleaned and stems
   removed
1½ cups (6 ounces) shredded
   Cheddar cheese
1½ cups shredded carrots
   Fresh salsa

In small bowl, blend together cream cheese, Garlic Powder with Parsley and Lemon
Pepper. On each flour tortilla, spread a layer of cream cheese mixture. Layer spinach
leaves, Cheddar cheese and carrots over cream cheese mixture. Roll up tortillas. Slice
each tortilla into 1½-inch pieces. Serve with salsa.   *Makes 3 dozen*

Egg Salad Sandwiches

1 cup EGG BEATERS® Healthy
   Real Egg Product, hard-
   cooked and chopped
¼ cup chopped celery
¼ cup chopped onion
2 tablespoons fat-free mayonnaise

12 slices whole wheat bread,
   divided
6 lettuce leaves
1 large tomato, cut into 6 thin
   slices

In small bowl, combine hard-cooked Egg Beaters®, celery, onion and mayonnaise. On
each of 6 bread slices, place lettuce leaf and tomato slice; top each with about ¼ cup egg
salad and remaining bread slice.   *Makes 6 servings*

Prep Time: 20 minutes

California Veggie Rolls

Huevos Ranchwich

¼ cup EGG BEATERS® Healthy
Real Egg Product
1 teaspoon diced green chiles
1 whole wheat hamburger roll,
split and toasted

1 tablespoon thick and chunky
salsa, heated
1 tablespoon shredded reduced-
fat Cheddar and Monterey
Jack cheese blend

On lightly greased griddle or skillet, pour Egg Beaters® into lightly greased 4-inch egg ring or biscuit cutter. Sprinkle with chiles. Cook 2 to 3 minutes or until bottom of egg patty is set. Remove egg ring and turn egg patty over. Cook 1 to 2 minutes longer or until done.

To serve, place egg patty on bottom of roll. Top with salsa, cheese and roll top.

Makes 1 sandwich

Prep Time: 10 minutes   **Cook Time:** 5 minutes

Cheese Vegetable Pita Pockets

½ cup (4 ounces) SARGENTO®
Light Ricotta Cheese
1 tablespoon milk
1 tablespoon Dijon mustard
¾ cup broccoli flowerets
½ red bell pepper, diced
1 small carrot, shredded
⅓ cup chopped fresh mushrooms

2 tablespoons thinly sliced green
onions
1 cup (4 ounces) SARGENTO®
Classic Shredded Mild
Cheddar Cheese
4 (6-inch) pita pocket breads
4 red leaf lettuce leaves

In medium bowl, combine ricotta cheese, milk and mustard; stir until smooth. Add broccoli, red pepper, carrot, mushrooms, green onions and Cheddar cheese; mix lightly. With sharp knife, slice end from each pita and open to form pocket. Line each pocket with lettuce leaf. Spoon vegetable mixture evenly into each pita pocket.

Makes 4 sandwiches

Berry, Cucumber and Brie Baguette

1 package (6 ounces) Wisconsin
   Brie cheese, rind removed
   and cut into cubes
1/3 cup bottled cucumber ranch
   dressing
1 loaf (16 ounces) sourdough,
   French or Italian bread
Lettuce leaves

1 1/2 cups raspberries and sliced
   strawberries
1 cup sliced cucumber
12 thin slices assorted cheeses,
   such as Wisconsin Fontina,
   Havarti, Swiss or Colby
   cheese
1/3 cup chopped pecans

In medium bowl, combine Brie and dressing; mix to coat. Slice bread in half horizontally. Hollow out bottom half, leaving 3/4-inch shell. Spread Brie mixture on bottom. Top with lettuce, berries, cucumber, cheese and pecans. Top with bread; secure with long wooden picks. Slice into individual servings. Serve immediately or pack ingredients in containers to assemble later. *Makes 6 to 8 servings*

Favorite recipe from **Wisconsin Milk Marketing Board**

Cherry-Veggie Roll-Ups

1 package (3 ounces) cream
   cheese, softened
1 tablespoon finely chopped chives
1 teaspoon lemon juice
1/8 teaspoon coarsely ground black
   pepper

4 (7-inch) flour tortillas
1 cup chopped Northwest fresh
   sweet cherries
1 medium cucumber, thinly sliced
1 cup alfalfa sprouts
4 lettuce leaves

Combine cream cheese, chives, lemon juice and pepper; mix well. Spread each of 4 tortillas with cream cheese mixture. Top with cherries, cucumber, sprouts and lettuce; roll up tortillas. *Makes 4 servings*

Prep Time: 15 minutes

Favorite recipe from **Northwest Cherry Growers**

Hummus Pita Sandwiches

2 tablespoons sesame seeds
1 can (15 ounces) chick-peas
1 to 2 cloves garlic
¼ cup loosely packed parsley
    sprigs
3 tablespoons fresh lemon juice
1 tablespoon olive oil
¼ teaspoon coarsely ground black
    pepper

4 pita breads
2 tomatoes, thinly sliced
1 cucumber, sliced
1 cup alfalfa sprouts, rinsed and
    drained
2 tablespoons crumbled feta
    cheese

1. Toast sesame seeds in small nonstick skillet over medium heat until lightly browned, stirring frequently. Remove from skillet and cool. Drain chick-peas; reserve liquid.

2. Place garlic in food processor. Process until minced. Add chick-peas, parsley, lemon juice, olive oil and pepper. Process until almost smooth, scraping sides of bowl once. If mixture is very thick, add 1 to 2 tablespoons reserved chick-pea liquid. Pour hummus into medium bowl. Stir in sesame seeds.

3. Cut pita breads in half. Spread about 3 tablespoons hummus in each pita bread half. Divide tomatoes, cucumber slices and alfalfa sprouts evenly among pita breads. Sprinkle with feta cheese.   *Makes 4 servings*

Hummus Pita Sandwiches

Middle Eastern Vegetable Grain Burgers

⅓ cup uncooked dried red lentils,
    sorted and rinsed
¼ cup uncooked brown or basmati
    rice
1 tablespoon olive oil
1 pound fresh mushrooms, sliced
1 medium onion, chopped
¾ cup grated Parmesan cheese
½ cup walnut halves, finely
    chopped

¼ cup chopped fresh cilantro
2 large eggs
½ teaspoon ground black pepper
6 toasted sesame seed buns or
    toasted pita bread halves
Mayonnaise
Sliced red onion
Shredded lettuce
Sliced tomatoes

Place lentils in medium saucepan; cover with 1 inch water. Bring to a boil; reduce heat to low. Simmer, covered, 25 to 35 minutes until tender. Rinse; drain and set aside. Meanwhile, cook rice according to package directions; set aside.

Heat oil in heavy, large skillet over medium heat. Add mushrooms and chopped onion. Cook and stir 20 to 25 minutes until mushrooms are brown. Combine mushroom mixture, cheese, walnuts, lentils, rice, cilantro, eggs and pepper in large bowl; mix well. Cover; chill.

Preheat broiler. Grease 15×10-inch jelly-roll pan with oil. Shape lentil mixture into 6 (½-inch-thick) patties. Arrange patties on prepared pan. Broil, 4 inches from heat, 3 to 4 minutes on each side or until golden brown, turning once. Serve on buns with mayonnaise, red onion, lettuce and tomatoes. *Makes 6 servings*

Spinach and Tomato Tofu Toss

Spinach and Tomato Tofu Toss

Nonstick cooking spray
¾ cup chopped onion
1 teaspoon chopped garlic
1 package (10 ounces) extra-firm
    tofu, drained and cut into
    ½-inch cubes
2 teaspoons soy sauce

¼ teaspoon ground black pepper
¼ pound washed spinach leaves,
    divided
4 whole wheat pitas, cut in half
2 large ripe tomatoes, chopped
¾ cup chopped red bell pepper

1. Spray large nonstick skillet with cooking spray; heat over medium heat until hot. Add onion and garlic. Cook and stir 2 minutes or until onion is crisp-tender.

2. Add tofu, soy sauce and black pepper to skillet; toss until well combined. Cook over medium heat 3 to 4 minutes or until heated through. Remove from heat and cool slightly.

3. Set aside 8 whole spinach leaves; tear remaining leaves into bite-size pieces. Line pita halves with whole spinach leaves. Add tomatoes, torn spinach and bell pepper to tofu mixture; toss to combine. Fill pita halves with tofu mixture. Serve immediately.

Makes 4 servings

Meatless Muffaletta Sandwich

1 (12-inch) loaf French- or
    Italian-style bread, unsliced
½ cup LAWRY'S® Classic Red
    Wine Vinaigrette with
    Cabernet Sauvignon Dressing
½ cup mayonnaise
2 teaspoons capers
1 ripe avocado, peeled, pitted and
    sliced
½ cup sliced green Spanish olives

1 can (2¼ ounces) sliced pitted
    ripe olives, drained
4 ounces sliced Swiss cheese
    Fresh basil leaves
4 Roma tomatoes, sliced, *or*
    4 ounces roasted red pepper
    slices
3 thin slices red onion, separated
    into rings

Slice bread horizontally. Hollow out each loaf, leaving ¾-inch shell. (Tear removed bread into crumbs; freeze for another use.) Set bread shells aside. In food processor or blender, place Classic Red Wine Vinaigrette with Cabernet Sauvignon Dressing, mayonnaise and capers; process until well blended. Spread vinaigrette mixture evenly onto insides of shells. Into bottom bread shell, evenly layer remaining ingredients. Cover with top half of bread; press bread halves together firmly. Wrap tightly in plastic wrap; refrigerate 30 minutes.

Makes 4 servings

Presentation: Unwrap loaf; slice into four 3-inch portions. Flavors are best when sandwich is served at room temperature. For crispier crust, place uncut loaf in 225°F oven. Bake 15 to 20 minutes. Remove from oven. Cut and fill loaf as directed.

Note: If desired, rinse olives in cold water to reduce saltiness.

Meatless Muffaletta Sandwich

Veggie Sandwich

Veggie Sandwiches

¼ cup reduced-fat mayonnaise
1 clove garlic, minced
⅛ teaspoon dried marjoram leaves
⅛ teaspoon dried tarragon leaves
8 slices Savory Summertime Oat
    Bread (page 198) or whole-
    grain bread
8 green leaf lettuce leaves

1 large tomato, thinly sliced
1 small cucumber, thinly sliced
4 slices reduced-fat Cheddar
    cheese slices
1 medium red onion, thinly sliced
    and separated into rings
½ cup alfalfa sprouts

1. To prepare mayonnaise spread, combine mayonnaise, garlic, marjoram and tarragon in small bowl. Refrigerate until ready to use.

2. To assemble sandwiches, spread each of 4 bread slices with 1 tablespoon mayonnaise spread. Divide lettuce, tomato, cucumber, cheese, onion and sprouts among bread slices. Top with remaining bread. Cut sandwiches into halves and serve immediately.

Makes 4 sandwiches

142

Vegetable and Pecan Burgers

½ cup chopped onion
1 tablespoon minced garlic
1 tablespoon olive oil
1 package (8 ounces) mushrooms, sliced
½ cup toasted pecans
3 cups KELLOGG'S® RICE KRISPIES® cereal

1 cup cooked brown rice
1 cup shredded carrots
¼ cup finely chopped green pepper
½ teaspoon salt
¼ teaspoon black pepper
⅛ teaspoon cayenne pepper
2 egg whites

1. In 12-inch nonstick skillet, over medium heat, sauté onion and garlic in oil 2 minutes. Add mushrooms and sauté 4 minutes longer or until mushrooms are just tender. Remove from heat.

2. Coarsely chop pecans in food processor, using metal blade. Add Kellogg's® Rice Krispies® cereal, rice, carrots, green pepper, seasonings and mushroom mixture. Process using on/off pulsing action about 15 seconds or until mixture is mealy consistency. Remove to mixing bowl and stir in egg whites. Divide mixture into 6 portions, about ½ cup each, and shape into patties. Place on baking sheet coated with vegetable cooking spray.

3. Broil, 6 inches from heat, about 5 minutes per side or until browned. Serve hot on buns with lettuce and tomato or with chutney.   *Makes 6 burgers*

Prep Time: 35 minutes   **Broil Time:** 10 minutes

Thin-Crust Whole Wheat Veggie Pizza

¾ to 1 cup all-purpose flour, divided
½ cup whole wheat flour
1 teaspoon rapid-rise active dry yeast
1½ teaspoons dried basil, divided
¼ teaspoon salt
1 tablespoon olive oil
1 clove garlic, minced
½ cup very warm water (120° to 130°F)
1 teaspoon yellow cornmeal

½ cup no-salt-added tomato sauce
1 cup thinly sliced mushrooms
½ cup thinly sliced zucchini
⅓ cup chopped green onions
1 large roasted red bell pepper,* cut lengthwise into thin strips *or* ¾ cup sliced, drained, bottled roasted red peppers
1 cup (4 ounces) shredded part-skim mozzarella cheese
¼ teaspoon red pepper flakes

1. Combine ½ cup all-purpose flour, whole wheat flour, yeast, 1 teaspoon basil and salt. Blend oil and garlic in small cup; stir into flour mixture with water. Stir in ¼ cup all-purpose flour until soft, slightly sticky dough forms. Knead dough on lightly floured surface about 5 minutes, adding remaining ¼ cup all-purpose flour as needed to make smooth and elastic dough. Shape dough into a ball. Cover; let rest 10 minutes.

2. Place oven rack in lowest position; preheat oven to 400°F. Spray 12-inch pizza pan or baking sheet with nonstick cooking spray; sprinkle with cornmeal. Roll dough into large circle on lightly floured surface. Transfer to prepared pan, stretching dough to edge of pan. (Too much rolling makes crust heavy and dense; stretching dough to fit pan is best.)

3. Combine tomato sauce and remaining ½ teaspoon basil in small bowl; spread evenly over crust. Top with mushrooms, zucchini, green onions, roasted pepper and mozzarella; sprinkle with red pepper flakes. Bake 20 to 25 minutes or until crust is golden brown and cheese is melted. *Makes 4 servings*

*To roast pepper, cut pepper lengthwise into halves; remove stem, membrane and seeds. Broil 3 inches from heat, skin side up, until skin is blackened and blistered. Place halves in small resealable food storage bag. Seal; set aside 15 minutes. Remove pepper from bag. Peel off skin; drain on paper towel.

Thin-Crust Whole Wheat Veggie Pizza

Grilled Cheese 'n' Tomato Sandwiches

8 slices whole wheat bread,
  divided
6 ounces part-skim mozzarella
  cheese, cut into 4 slices
1 large tomato, cut into 8 thin
  slices
⅓ cup yellow cornmeal
2 tablespoons grated Parmesan
  cheese

1 teaspoon dried basil leaves
½ cup EGG BEATERS® Healthy
  Real Egg Product
¼ cup skim milk
2 tablespoons margarine, divided
1 cup low-salt tomato sauce,
  heated

On each of 4 bread slices, place 1 cheese slice and 2 tomato slices; top with remaining bread slices. Combine cornmeal, Parmesan cheese and basil on waxed paper. In shallow bowl, combine Egg Beaters® and milk. Melt 1 tablespoon margarine on large nonstick griddle or skillet. Dip sandwiches in egg mixture; coat with cornmeal mixture. Transfer 2 sandwiches to griddle. Cook sandwiches for 3 minutes on each side or until golden. Repeat using remaining margarine and sandwiches. Cut sandwiches in half; serve warm with tomato sauce for dipping.

Makes 4 servings

Prep Time: 20 minutes   **Cook Time:** 14 minutes

Grilled Cheese 'n' Tomato Sandwich

Speedy Garden Roll-Ups

Chick-Pea Spread (recipe
follows)
4 (6-inch) flour tortillas
½ cup shredded carrot

½ cup shredded red cabbage
½ cup (2 ounces) shredded
reduced-fat Cheddar cheese
4 washed red leaf lettuce leaves

1. Prepare Chick-Pea Spread; set aside.

2. Spread each tortilla with ¼ cup Chick-Pea Spread to about ½ inch from edge. Sprinkle evenly with 2 tablespoons *each* carrot, cabbage and cheese. Top with 1 lettuce leaf.

3. Roll up tortillas jelly-roll fashion. Seal with additional Chick-Pea Spread.

4. Serve immediately or wrap tightly with plastic wrap and refrigerate up to 4 hours.

Makes 4 servings

Chick-Pea Spread

1 can (about 15 ounces) chick-
peas, drained and rinsed
¼ cup fat-free cream cheese
1 tablespoon finely chopped onion
1 tablespoon chopped cilantro

2 teaspoons lemon juice
2 cloves garlic
½ teaspoon dark sesame oil
⅛ teaspoon ground black pepper

1. Combine chick-peas, cream cheese, onion, cilantro, lemon juice, garlic, sesame oil and pepper in food processor; process until smooth.

Speedy Garden Roll-Ups

Mediterranean Pita Sandwich

Mediterranean Pita Sandwiches

1 cup plain nonfat yogurt
1 tablespoon chopped fresh
   cilantro
2 cloves garlic, minced
1 teaspoon lemon juice
1½ cups thinly sliced cucumbers,
   cut into halves
1 can (15 ounces) chick-peas,
   drained and rinsed

1 can (14 ounces) artichoke
   hearts, drained, rinsed and
   coarsely chopped
½ cup shredded carrots
½ cup chopped green onions
4 whole wheat pitas, cut into
   halves

1. Combine yogurt, cilantro, garlic and lemon juice in a small bowl.

2. Combine cucumbers, chick-peas, artichoke hearts, carrots and green onions in medium bowl. Stir in yogurt mixture until well blended.

3. Divide cucumber mixture among pita halves. Garnish as desired.

Makes 4 servings

Vegetable Calzones

1 loaf (1 pound) frozen bread
dough
1 package (10 ounces) frozen
chopped broccoli, thawed and
well drained
1 cup (8 ounces) SARGENTO®
Light Ricotta Cheese
1 cup (4 ounces) SARGENTO®
Classic Shredded Mozzarella
Cheese

1 clove garlic, minced
¼ teaspoon white pepper
1 egg beaten with 1 tablespoon
water
1 jar (16 ounces) spaghetti sauce,
heated (optional)
SARGENTO® Grated Parmesan
Cheese (optional)

Thaw bread dough; let rise according to package directions. Combine broccoli, ricotta
and mozzarella cheeses, garlic and pepper. Punch down bread dough; turn out onto
lightly floured surface. Divide into 4 equal pieces. One at a time, roll out each piece into
8-inch circle. Place about ¼ cup cheese mixture on half of circle, leaving 1-inch border.
Fold dough over to cover filling, forming semi-circle; press and crimp edges with fork
tines to seal. Brush with egg mixture. Place on greased baking sheet; bake at 350°F
30 minutes or until brown and puffed. Transfer to rack; cool 10 minutes. Top with hot
spaghetti sauce and Parmesan cheese.   *Makes 4 servings*

Greek Pizza

¼ cup olive oil
2 cups chopped onions
3 cloves garlic, minced
3 packages (10 ounces each) frozen chopped spinach, thawed, squeezed dry
½ cup chopped fresh basil
2 tablespoons chopped fresh oregano
2 tablespoons lemon juice
1 teaspoon pepper

10 sheets ATHENS® or APOLLO® Fillo Dough, thawed according to package directions
⅓ cup butter, melted
4 cups (1 pound) shredded mozzarella cheese, divided
3 medium tomatoes, thinly sliced
1 cup Italian-style dry bread crumbs
1 cup (4 ounces) crumbled feta cheese

In large skillet, heat oil over medium heat; add onions and garlic. Cook and stir 5 minutes or until onions are translucent. Add spinach; cook and stir until all excess moisture has evaporated. Add basil, oregano, lemon juice and pepper. Mix well. Cool slightly.

Carefully unroll fillo sheets onto smooth, dry surface. Cover fillo completely with plastic wrap; cover with damp towel. When handling fillo, remove fillo sheets, one at a time, replacing plastic wrap and damp towel over remainder each time.

Brush each sheet of fillo dough with butter. Place length of fillo sheets across width of 13×9-inch baking pan. Layer and brush 2 fillo sheets, side by side, so that entire pan is covered. Repeat with remaining fillo. Roll overlapping fillo onto itself at corners, then pan edges to form "pizza crust." Brush with butter.

Spread spinach mixture on prepared fillo sheets. Top spinach with 3 cups mozzarella. Dredge tomatoes in bread crumbs and arrange on top of mozzarella. Top with remaining 1 cup mozzarella and feta cheese.

Bake in preheated 400°F oven 25 to 30 minutes or until golden brown.

Makes 12 servings

Vegetable Pizza

Vegetable Pizza

2 to 3 cups BIRDS EYE® frozen
    Farm Fresh Mixtures
    Broccoli, Red Peppers,
    Onions and Mushrooms
1 Italian bread shell or pizza
    crust, about 12 inches

1 to 1½ cups shredded mozzarella
    cheese, divided
Dried oregano, basil or Italian
    seasoning

• Preheat oven according to directions on pizza crust package.

• Rinse vegetables in colander under warm water. Drain well; pat with paper towel to remove excess moisture.

• Spread crust with half the cheese and all the vegetables. Sprinkle with herbs; top with remaining cheese.

• Follow baking directions on pizza crust package; bake until hot and bubbly.

Makes 3 to 4 servings

Prep Time: 5 minutes   **Cook Time:** 15 minutes

Black Bean Burgers

2 cans (about 15 ounces each) black beans, rinsed and drained, divided
¾ cup plain dry bread crumbs
⅔ cup green onion tops
2 egg whites
¼ cup chopped fresh basil
2 teaspoons onion powder
2 teaspoons dried oregano
1 teaspoon baking powder
1 teaspoon ground cumin
1 teaspoon black pepper, or more to taste
½ teaspoon salt
¾ cup corn
¾ cup chopped roasted red pepper
Nonstick cooking spray
6 whole wheat hamburger buns
Salsa (optional)
Avocado slices (optional)

1. Place half the beans in bowl of food processor fitted with metal blade. Add bread crumbs, green onions, egg whites, basil, onion powder, oregano, baking powder, cumin, black pepper and salt. Pulse 30 to 40 seconds until mixture begins to hold together. Fold in remaining beans, corn and roasted red pepper. Let sit 20 minutes at room temperature for flavors to develop.

2. Preheat oven to 350°F. Line baking sheet with parchment paper.

3. Shape mixture into 6 patties (about ½ cup each). Place patties on prepared baking sheet. Spray tops with nonstick cooking spray. Bake 18 to 20 minutes or until patties are firm. Serve between buns topped with salsa and avocado slices, if desired.

Makes 6 burgers

Tip: Cooked burgers can be wrapped up and frozen to save for grilling season. Just grill burgers on a medium hot grid until heated through.

Black Bean Burger

Mediterranean Pita Pizza

Mediterranean Pita Pizza

2 tablespoons olive oil
2½ cups (8 ounces) diced, peeled
    eggplant
1 cup sliced zucchini (1 small)
1 cup sliced fresh mushrooms
¼ cup chopped green bell pepper
¼ cup chopped onion
1 clove garlic, minced
1 cup (half of 15-ounce can)
    CONTADINA® Pizza Sauce

½ cup sliced ripe olives
¼ teaspoon salt
⅛ teaspoon crushed red pepper
    flakes
6 (6-inch) pita breads
1½ cups (6 ounces) shredded
    mozzarella or fontina cheese

Heat oil in large skillet over medium-high heat. Add eggplant, zucchini, mushrooms, bell pepper, onion and garlic; sauté for 4 to 5 minutes or until vegetables are tender.

Stir in pizza sauce, olives, salt and red pepper flakes; bring to a boil. Reduce heat to low; simmer, uncovered, for 5 minutes.

Toast both sides of pita breads under broiler. Spoon *½ cup* vegetable mixture onto each pita bread; sprinkle with cheese.

Broil until cheese is melted.
Makes 6 servings

Stuffed Pizza Pie

Refrigerated pastry for double
    crust 10-inch pie
5 eggs, lightly beaten
2 cups (15-ounce container)
    ricotta cheese
1 cup (4 ounces) grated Parmesan
    cheese
¼ cup chopped onion
2 tablespoons chopped fresh
    parsley *or* 2 teaspoons dried
    parsley flakes

1 large clove garlic, minced
1¾ cups (15-ounce can)
    CONTADINA® Pizza Sauce
1 teaspoon Italian herb seasoning
½ pound thinly sliced mozzarella
    cheese, divided
½ cup sliced pitted ripe olives,
    drained
1 small green bell pepper, cut into
    strips

Divide pastry in half. On lightly floured surface, roll out *half* of pastry to 12-inch circle; place on bottom and up side of 10-inch deep-dish pie plate. Roll out *remaining* pastry to 12-inch circle; cover and set aside. In medium bowl, combine eggs, ricotta cheese, Parmesan cheese, onion, parsley and garlic. In small bowl, combine pizza sauce and Italian seasoning. Spread *half* of ricotta cheese mixture onto bottom of pie shell; cover with layers of *half* of sauce, mozzarella cheese, olives and bell pepper strips. Repeat layers. Top with remaining pie crust; flute edges. Cut slits into top crust to allow steam to escape. Bake in preheated 425°F. oven for 40 to 45 minutes or until crust is lightly browned. Let stand for 20 minutes before cutting into slices to serve.　*Makes 8 servings*

Mexican Deep Dish Pizza

Thick Pizza Crust (page 165)
Nonstick cooking spray
½ small onion, diced
1 teaspoon chili powder
½ teaspoon ground cumin
¼ teaspoon ground cinnamon
1 can (15 ounces) 50%-less-
  sodium black beans, rinsed
  and drained
½ can (4 ounces) diced green
  chilies (optional)
1 cup (4 ounces) shredded
  reduced-fat Cheddar cheese,
  divided

¾ cup diced tomatoes
½ cup frozen corn, thawed
½ green bell pepper, diced
½ can (2¼ ounces) sliced black
  olives, drained
½ teaspoon olive oil
  Salsa (optional)
  Reduced-fat sour cream
  (optional)

Prepare Thick Pizza Crust. Preheat oven to 500°F.

Spray 2- to 3-quart saucepan with cooking spray. Place over medium heat. Add onion, chili powder, cumin, cinnamon and 1 tablespoon water; stir. Cover and cook 3 to 4 minutes. Stir in beans and chilies, if desired. Transfer ½ of bean mixture to food processor; process until almost smooth.

Spread puréed bean mixture over prepared crust up to thick edge. Top with ½ cup cheese, remaining bean mixture, tomatoes, corn, bell pepper and olives. Top with remaining ½ cup cheese. Bake 10 to 12 minutes or until crust is deep golden. Brush crust edge with olive oil. Garnish with cilantro, if desired. Cut into 8 wedges. Serve with salsa and sour cream, if desired.   *Makes 4 servings*

Mexican Deep Dish Pizza

Salad Pizza

Whole Wheat Crust (recipe
follows)
¼ cup balsamic vinegar
1 tablespoon Dijon mustard
1 tablespoon minced shallot
1 clove garlic, minced
1 teaspoon sugar
½ teaspoon dried basil leaves
½ teaspoon dried oregano leaves
½ teaspoon black pepper
2 tablespoons olive oil

¾ cup (3 ounces) reduced-fat part-
skim mozzarella cheese or
reduced-fat Swiss cheese
2 tablespoons grated Parmesan
cheese
4 cups assorted gourmet mixed
salad greens, washed and torn
½ cup cherry tomato halves
½ cup sliced red onion
¼ cup chopped yellow bell pepper

Prepare Whole Wheat Crust. Preheat oven to 450°F.

Combine balsamic vinegar, mustard, shallot, garlic, sugar, basil, oregano and black pepper in small bowl; whisk to combine. Gradually whisk in olive oil.

Sprinkle cheeses on prepared crust. Bake 10 to 15 minutes or until crust is golden brown and cheese is melted.

Meanwhile, combine salad greens, tomatoes, onion and bell pepper in large bowl. Pour vinegar mixture over top; toss to combine.

Remove crust from oven and top with salad mixture. Cut into 8 wedges; serve immediately.

Makes 8 servings

Whole Wheat Crust

1¼ cups warm water (110° to
115°F)
2 tablespoons honey or sugar
1 package (¼ ounce) active dry
yeast

2 to 2½ cups all-purpose flour,
divided
1 cup whole wheat flour
¼ teaspoon salt (optional)
1 tablespoon cornmeal

Salad Pizza

Combine water and honey in small bowl; stir to dissolve honey. Sprinkle yeast on top; stir to combine. Let stand 5 minutes until foamy.

Combine 2 cups all-purpose flour, whole wheat flour and salt, if desired, in large bowl. Stir in yeast mixture. Mix until mixture forms soft dough. Remove dough to lightly floured surface. Knead 5 to 10 minutes, adding remaining ½ cup all-purpose flour, if necessary, until dough is smooth and elastic.

Place dough in large bowl coated with nonstick cooking spray. Turn dough in bowl so top is coated with cooking spray; cover with towel or plastic wrap. Let rise in warm place about 1½ hours or until doubled in bulk. Punch down dough and pat into disk. Gently stretch dough into 14- to 15-inch circle.

Spray 14-inch pizza pan with cooking spray; sprinkle with cornmeal. Press dough into pan. Follow topping and baking directions for individual recipes.

Makes 1 thick 14-inch crust

161

Vegetable Pizza with Oat Bran Crust

1 cup QUAKER® Oat Bran hot
  cereal, uncooked
1 cup all-purpose flour
1 teaspoon baking powder
¾ cup skim milk
3 tablespoons vegetable oil
1 tablespoon QUAKER® Oat Bran
  hot cereal, uncooked
1 can (8 ounces) low-sodium
  tomato sauce
1 cup sliced mushrooms (about
  3 ounces)

1 medium green, red or yellow
  bell pepper, or combination,
  cut into rings
½ cup chopped onion
1¼ cups (5 ounces) shredded part-
  skim mozzarella cheese
½ teaspoon dried oregano
  leaves, crumbled or Italian
  seasoning, crumbled

Combine 1 cup oat bran, flour and baking powder. Add milk and oil; mix well. Let stand 10 minutes.

Heat oven to 425°F. Lightly spray 12-inch round pizza pan with vegetable oil cooking spray or oil lightly. Sprinkle with 1 tablespoon oat bran. With lightly oiled fingers, pat dough out evenly; shape edge to form rim. Bake 18 to 20 minutes. Spread sauce evenly over partially baked crust. Top with vegetables; sprinkle with cheese and oregano. Bake an additional 12 to 15 minutes or until golden brown. Cut into 8 wedges.

Makes 4 servings

Artichoke Heart, Olive and Goat Cheese Pizza

Thick Pizza Crust* (page 165)
2 teaspoons olive oil
2 teaspoons minced fresh
    rosemary leaves *or* 1 teaspoon
    dried rosemary leaves
3 cloves garlic, minced
½ cup (2 ounces) shredded
    reduced-fat Monterey Jack
    cheese, divided

1 jar (14 ounces) water-packed
    artichoke hearts, drained and
    quartered
3 oil-packed sun-dried tomatoes,
    drained and cut into slices
2½ ounces soft ripe goat cheese,
    such as Montrachet, sliced or
    crumbled
10 kalamata olives, pitted and
    halved (about ¼ cup)

Prepare Thick Pizza Crust.

Preheat oven to 500°F. Brush surface of prepared crust with olive oil. Sprinkle with rosemary and garlic; brush again to coat with oil. Bake about 4 minutes or until crust begins to turn golden.

Sprinkle with ¼ cup Monterey Jack cheese, leaving 1-inch border. Top with artichokes, tomatoes, goat cheese and olives. Sprinkle with remaining ¼ cup Monterey Jack cheese. Return to oven and bake 3 to 4 minutes more or until crust is deep golden and Monterey Jack cheese is melted. Cut into 8 wedges. *Makes 4 servings*

*Omit 10 to 20 minute rising once dough is in pizza pan. Do not prick crust with fork or bake 4 to 5 minutes before adding toppings.

Three-Pepper Pizza

Three-Pepper Pizza

1 cup (half of 14.5-ounce can)
　　CONTADINA® Chunky Pizza
　　Sauce with Three Cheeses
1 (12-inch) pizza crust
1½ cups (6 ounces) shredded
　　mozzarella cheese, divided
½ *each:* red, green and yellow bell
　　peppers, sliced into thin rings

2 tablespoons shredded Parmesan
　　cheese
1 tablespoon chopped fresh basil
　　or 1 teaspoon dried basil
　　leaves, crushed

Spread pizza sauce onto crust to within 1 inch of edge. Sprinkle with *1 cup* mozzarella cheese, bell peppers, *remaining* mozzarella cheese and Parmesan cheese. Bake according to pizza crust package directions or until crust is crisp and cheese is melted. Sprinkle with basil.

Makes 8 servings

164

Thick Pizza Crust

¾ cup warm water (110° to 115°F)
1 teaspoon sugar
½ of ¼-ounce package rapid-rise
   yeast or active dry yeast

2½ cups all-purpose or bread flour
½ teaspoon salt
1 tablespoon cornmeal (optional)

Combine water and sugar in small bowl; stir to dissolve sugar. Sprinkle yeast on top; stir to combine. Let stand 5 minutes until foamy.

Combine flour and salt in large bowl. Stir in yeast mixture. Mix until mixture forms soft dough. Remove dough to lightly floured surface. Knead dough 5 minutes or until smooth and elastic, adding additional flour as needed. Place in bowl coated with nonstick cooking spray. Turn dough in bowl so top is coated with cooking spray; cover with towel or plastic wrap. Let rise in warm place 30 minutes or until doubled in bulk.

Punch dough down; place on lightly floured surface and knead 2 minutes or until smooth. Pat dough into flat disk about 8 to 9 inches in diameter. Let rest 2 to 3 minutes. Pat and gently stretch dough from edges until dough seems to not stretch anymore. Let rest 2 to 3 minutes. Continue patting and stretching until dough is 12 to 14 inches in diameter. Spray 12- to 14-inch pizza pan with nonstick cooking spray; sprinkle with cornmeal, if desired. Press dough into pan. Cover with towel and let stand in warm place 10 to 20 minutes or until slightly puffed.

Preheat oven to 500°F. Prick crust with fork at 2-inch intervals. Bake 4 to 5 minutes or until top is dry but not yet golden. Remove from oven. Follow topping and baking directions for individual recipes, baking pizza on bottom rack of oven.

Makes 1 thick 12-inch crust

ANYTIME BREAKFAST FAVORITES

Breakfast Burritos with Tomato-Basil Topping

1 large tomato, diced
2 teaspoons finely chopped basil
    or ½ teaspoon dried basil
    leaves
1 medium potato, peeled and
    shredded (about 1 cup)
¼ cup chopped onion

2 teaspoons margarine
1 cup EGG BEATERS® Healthy
    Real Egg Product
⅛ teaspoon ground black pepper
4 (8-inch) flour tortillas, warmed
⅓ cup shredded reduced-fat
    Cheddar cheese

In small bowl, combine tomato and basil; set aside.

In large nonstick skillet, over medium heat, sauté potato and onion in margarine until tender. Pour Egg Beaters® into skillet; sprinkle with pepper. Cook, stirring occasionally until mixture is set.

Divide egg mixture evenly between tortillas; top with cheese. Fold tortillas over egg mixture. Top with tomato mixture.   *Makes 4 servings*

Prep Time: 15 minutes   **Cook Time:** 25 minutes

Breakfast Burritos with Tomato-Basil Topping

Triple-Decker Vegetable Omelet

1 cup finely chopped broccoli
½ cup diced red bell pepper
½ cup shredded carrot
⅓ cup sliced green onions
1 clove garlic, minced
2½ teaspoons margarine, divided
¾ cup low fat cottage cheese
　(1% milkfat), divided
1 tablespoon plain dry bread
　crumbs

1 tablespoon grated Parmesan
　cheese
½ teaspoon Italian seasoning
1½ cups EGG BEATERS® Healthy
　Real Egg Product, divided
⅓ cup chopped tomato
　Chopped fresh parsley, for
　garnish

In 8-inch nonstick skillet, over medium-high heat, sauté broccoli, bell pepper, carrot, green onions and garlic in 1 teaspoon margarine until tender. Remove from skillet; stir in ½ cup cottage cheese. Keep warm. Combine bread crumbs, Parmesan cheese and Italian seasoning; set aside.

In same skillet, over medium heat, melt ½ teaspoon margarine. Pour ½ cup Egg Beaters® into skillet. Cook, lifting edges to allow uncooked portion to flow underneath. When almost set, slide unfolded omelet onto ovenproof serving platter. Top with half each of the vegetable mixture and bread crumb mixture; set aside.

Prepare 2 more omelets with remaining Egg Beaters® and margarine. Layer 1 omelet onto serving platter over vegetable and bread crumb mixture; top with remaining vegetable mixture and bread crumb mixture. Layer with remaining omelet. Top omelet with remaining cottage cheese and tomato. Bake at 425°F for 5 to 7 minutes or until heated through. Garnish with parsley. Cut into wedges to serve.　*Makes 4 servings*

Prep Time: 20 minutes　**Cook Time:** 30 minutes

Triple-Decker Vegetable Omelet

Roasted Red Pepper Omelet

Nonstick cooking spray
¼ cup chopped green onions
¼ cup sliced fresh mushrooms
½ cup GUILTLESS GOURMET®
   Roasted Red Pepper Salsa
8 egg whites, at room temperature
4 egg yolks

⅓ cup skim milk
1 tablespoon reduced-calorie
   mayonnaise
¼ teaspoon coarsely ground black
   pepper
¼ cup GUILTLESS GOURMET®
   Nacho Dip (mild or spicy)

Preheat oven to 350°F. Coat large nonstick skillet with cooking spray; heat over medium-high heat until hot. Add onions and mushrooms; cook and stir until tender. Stir in salsa; remove from heat and set aside.

Beat egg whites in large bowl with electric mixer on high speed until stiff peaks form; set aside. Combine egg yolks, milk, mayonnaise and pepper in another large bowl; blend well. Fold egg whites into egg yolk mixture. Coat 8-inch *ovenproof* omelet pan or heavy skillet with cooking spray; heat over medium heat until hot. Pour egg mixture into skillet; gently smooth surface. Reduce heat to medium-low; cook 5 minutes or until puffy and light brown on bottom, gently lifting omelet at edge to judge color. *Do not stir.*

Place in oven; bake 10 minutes or until knife inserted in center comes out clean. Spoon reserved vegetable mixture over half the omelet; drop small spoonfuls nacho dip onto vegetable mixture. Loosen omelet with spatula; fold omelet in half. Gently slide onto warm serving platter. Serve hot.

Makes 4 servings

Cheesy Salsa Omelet

Cheesy Salsa Omelet

1 cup egg substitute
1 tablespoon skim milk
  Nonstick cooking spray
¼ cup sliced fresh mushrooms
¼ cup chopped green onions

¼ cup GUILTLESS GOURMET®
  Nacho Dip (mild or spicy)
¼ cup GUILTLESS GOURMET®
  Salsa (mild, medium or hot)

Combine egg substitute and milk in small bowl; beat well. Coat medium nonstick skillet with cooking spray; heat over medium-high heat until hot. Add mushrooms and onions; cook and stir 2 to 3 minutes or until vegetables are softened. Remove vegetables from skillet; set aside.

Add egg mixture to same skillet; cook over low heat until egg mixture sets, gently lifting edge with spatula to allow uncooked egg to flow under cooked portion. *Do not stir.* Top with reserved vegetable mixture. Drop spoonfuls nacho dip over vegetable mixture. Cover tightly; let stand 3 to 5 minutes. Fold omelet in half. Gently slide onto warm serving platter. Serve with salsa.

Makes 2 servings

Pita in the Morning

Pita in the Morning

1 teaspoon butter or margarine
2 eggs, lightly beaten
¼ teaspoon salt
   Dash pepper
1 whole wheat pita bread,
   cut in half

¼ cup alfalfa sprouts
2 tablespoons shredded Cheddar
   cheese
2 tablespoons chopped tomato
   Avocado slices (optional)

1. Melt butter at HIGH 30 seconds in microwavable 1-quart casserole.

2. Season eggs with salt and pepper. Add eggs to casserole. Microwave at HIGH 1½ to 2½ minutes, stirring once. Do not overcook; eggs should be soft with no liquid remaining.

3. Open pita to make pockets. Arrange sprouts in pockets. Divide cheese and eggs evenly between pockets. Top with tomato and avocado slices.
          Makes 1 sandwich

Pinwheel Cheese Quiche

2 tablespoons margarine or butter
2 cups sliced mushrooms
6 green onions, sliced
    (about 2 cups)
1 package (8 ounces) refrigerated
    crescent rolls, separated into
    8 triangles
1 envelope LIPTON® Recipe
    Secrets® Golden Herb with
    Lemon Soup Mix

½ cup half-and-half
4 eggs, beaten
1 cup (about 4 ounces) shredded
    Monterey Jack or mozzarella
    cheese

Preheat oven to 375°F.

In 12-inch skillet, melt margarine over medium heat and cook mushrooms and green onions, stirring occasionally, 5 minutes or until tender. Remove from heat and set aside.

In 9-inch pie plate sprayed with nonstick cooking spray, arrange crescent roll triangles in a spoke pattern with narrow tips hanging over rim of pie plate about 2 inches. Press dough onto bottom and up side of pie plate forming full crust.

In medium bowl, combine golden herb with lemon soup mix, half-and-half and eggs. Stir in cheese and mushroom mixture. Pour into prepared pie crust. Bring tips of dough over filling towards center. Bake uncovered 30 minutes or until knife inserted in center comes out clean. *Makes about 6 servings*

•Also terrific with Lipton® Recipe Secrets® Savory Herb with Garlic Soup Mix.

Double Onion Quiche

3 cups thinly sliced yellow onions
3 tablespoons butter or margarine
1 cup thinly sliced green onions
3 eggs
1 cup heavy cream
½ cup grated Parmesan cheese
¼ teaspoon hot pepper sauce

1 package (1 ounce) HIDDEN VALLEY RANCH® Milk Recipe Original Ranch® salad dressing mix
1 (9-inch) deep-dish pastry shell, baked, cooled
Fresh oregano sprig for garnish

Preheat oven to 350°F. In medium skillet, cook and stir yellow onions in butter, stirring occasionally, 10 minutes. Add green onions; cook 5 minutes. Remove from heat; cool. In large bowl, whisk eggs until frothy. Whisk in cream, cheese, pepper sauce and salad dressing mix. Stir in cooled onion mixture. Pour egg and onion mixture into cooled pastry shell. Bake until top is browned and knife inserted in center comes out clean, 35 to 40 minutes. Cool on wire rack 10 minutes before slicing. Garnish with oregano.

Makes 8 servings

Scrambled Eggs Piperade

1 tablespoon vegetable oil
1 medium onion, cut in half and sliced
½ green bell pepper, seeded and sliced
½ red bell pepper, seeded and sliced

4 large eggs
1 tablespoon water
½ teaspoon salt
½ teaspoon TABASCO® pepper sauce
1 tablespoon butter or margarine
Whole wheat toast

• In 12-inch skillet over medium heat, heat oil until hot. Cook onion and bell peppers until tender-crisp, about 5 minutes, stirring occasionally. In medium bowl, beat eggs, water, salt and TABASCO® sauce until well blended. In 10-inch nonstick skillet over medium heat, melt butter; add egg mixture. Gently stir egg mixture, lifting it up and over bottom as it thickens. Keep stirring until desired texture and doneness. Serve with pepper mixture and whole wheat toast.

Makes 2 servings

Double Onion Quiche

Asparagus-Swiss Soufflé

¼ cup unsalted butter substitute
½ cup chopped yellow onion
¼ cup all-purpose flour
½ teaspoon salt
¼ teaspoon cayenne pepper
 1 cup 2% low fat milk
 1 cup (4 ounces) shredded
   ALPINE LACE® Reduced Fat
   Swiss Cheese

1 cup egg substitute or 4 large
  eggs
1 cup coarsely chopped fresh
  asparagus pieces, cooked
  or frozen asparagus pieces,
  thawed and drained
3 large egg whites

1. Preheat the oven to 325°F. Spray a 1½-quart soufflé dish with nonstick cooking spray.

2. In a large saucepan, melt the butter over medium heat, add the onion and sauté for 5 minutes or until soft. Stir in the flour, salt and pepper and cook for 2 minutes or until bubbly. Add the milk and cook, stirring constantly, for 5 minutes or until the sauce thickens. Add the cheese and stir until melted.

3. In a small bowl, whisk the egg substitute (or the whole eggs). Whisk in a little of the hot cheese sauce, then return this egg mixture to the saucepan and whisk until well blended. Remove from the heat and fold in the drained asparagus.

4. In a medium-size bowl, using an electric mixer set on high, beat the egg whites until stiff peaks form. Fold the hot cheese sauce into the whites, then spoon into the soufflé dish.

5. Place the soufflé on a baking sheet and bake for 50 minutes or until golden brown and puffy.

Makes 8 servings

Asparagus-Swiss Soufflé

Zucchini Mushroom Frittata

Zucchini Mushroom Frittata

1½ cups EGG BEATERS® Healthy
    Real Egg Product
½ cup (2 ounces) shredded
    reduced-fat Swiss cheese
¼ cup skim milk
½ teaspoon garlic powder
¼ teaspoon seasoned pepper
    Nonstick cooking spray

1 medium zucchini, shredded
    (1 cup)
1 medium tomato, chopped
1 (4-ounce) can sliced mushrooms,
    drained
    Tomato slices and fresh basil
    leaves, for garnish

In medium bowl, combine Egg Beaters®, cheese, milk, garlic powder and seasoned pepper; set aside.

Spray 10-inch ovenproof nonstick skillet lightly with nonstick cooking spray. Over medium-high heat, sauté zucchini, tomato and mushrooms in skillet until tender. Pour egg mixture into skillet, stirring well. Cover; cook over low heat for 15 minutes or until cooked on bottom and almost set on top. Remove lid and place skillet under broiler for 2 to 3 minutes or until desired doneness. Slide onto serving platter; cut into wedges to serve. Garnish with tomato slices and basil. *Makes 6 servings*

Prep Time: 20 minutes   **Cook Time:** 20 minutes

Light Farmhouse Frittata

⅓ cup julienned yellow pepper
⅓ cup julienned green pepper
⅓ cup julienned red pepper
⅓ cup chopped green onions
⅓ cup chopped walnuts

8 egg whites
2 egg yolks
2 tablespoons plain nonfat yogurt
1 tablespoon grated Asiago or
   Parmesan cheese

Preheat oven to 350°F. Cook and stir peppers, green onions and walnuts in ovenproof skillet over medium heat 5 minutes. Beat egg whites and yolks; add yogurt. Pour mixture into skillet. Stir and cook until eggs begin to set. Sprinkle with cheese; bake 8 to 10 minutes or until eggs are well set. Cut into wedges. *Makes 4 servings*

Favorite recipe from **Walnut Marketing Board**

Chile Tortilla Brunch Casserole

2 cans (7 ounces each) ORTEGA®
   Whole Green Chiles, split in
   half, divided
6 corn tortillas, cut into strips,
   divided
4 cups (16 ounces) shredded
   Monterey Jack cheese,
   divided
1 cup (1 medium) chopped tomato

4 tablespoons chopped green
   onions (about 3), divided
8 eggs
½ cup milk
½ teaspoon salt
½ teaspoon ground black pepper
½ teaspoon ground cumin
   ORTEGA® Thick & Chunky
   Salsa, hot, medium or mild

LAYER *1 can* of chiles, *3* tortillas and *2 cups* cheese in greased 9-inch square baking pan. Top with tomato and *2 tablespoons* green onions; layer *remaining 1 can* chiles, *remaining 3* tortillas and *remaining 2 cups* cheese over tomato. Beat eggs, milk, salt, pepper and cumin in medium bowl; pour over chile mixture. Bake in preheated 350°F. oven for 40 to 45 minutes or until center is set. Cool for 10 minutes; sprinkle with *remaining 2 tablespoons* green onions. Serve with salsa. *Makes 8 servings*

Feta Brunch Bake

1 medium red bell pepper
2 bags (10 ounces each) fresh
    spinach, washed and
    stemmed
6 eggs
6 ounces crumbled feta cheese

⅓ cup chopped onion
2 tablespoons chopped fresh
    parsley
¼ teaspoon dried dill weed
    Dash ground black pepper

Preheat broiler. Place bell pepper on foil-lined broiler pan. Broil, 4 inches from heat, 15 to 20 minutes or until blackened on all sides, turning every 5 minutes with tongs. Place pepper in paper bag; close bag and set aside to cool about 15 to 20 minutes. To peel pepper, cut around core, twist and remove. Cut in half and peel off skin with paring knife; rinse under cold water to remove seeds. Cut into ½-inch pieces.

To blanch spinach, heat 1 quart water in 2-quart saucepan over high heat to a boil. Add spinach. Return to a boil; boil 2 to 3 minutes until crisp-tender. Drain and immediately plunge into cold water. Drain; let stand until cool enough to handle. Squeeze spinach to remove excess water. Finely chop with chef's knife.

Preheat oven to 400°F. Grease 1-quart baking dish. Beat eggs in large bowl with electric mixer at medium speed until foamy. Stir in bell pepper, spinach, cheese, onion, parsley, dill weed and black pepper. Pour egg mixture into prepared dish. Bake 20 minutes or until set. Let stand 5 minutes before serving. Garnish as desired. *Makes 4 servings*

Feta Brunch Bake

Tomato and Cheese Strata

1 (14.5-ounce) can FRANK'S or
   SNOWFLOSS Italian Style
   Diced Tomatoes, drained
12 to 16 slices white bread (or as
   needed)
2 cups milk
1 (14-ounce) can tomato paste

¾ teaspoon salt
12 ounces shredded mozzarella
   cheese
8 ounces shredded Cheddar
   cheese
¼ cup grated Parmesan cheese
4 eggs, beaten

1. Preheat oven to 350°F. Butter 2-quart casserole or soufflé dish.

2. In shallow dish, place bread slices in milk until softened but not falling apart. Place layer of bread slices in buttered casserole dish.

3. Mix together diced tomatoes, tomato paste and salt. Place layer of tomato mixture over bread slices. Mix mozzarella and Cheddar cheeses together. Sprinkle thin layer over tomato mixture. Continue layering bread, tomatoes and cheeses, reserving small portion of tomato mixture and cheeses. Top with layer of bread.

4. Poke several holes in casserole. Pour eggs over top, allowing eggs to soak into casserole. Top with remaining tomato mixture and cheeses. Sprinkle with Parmesan cheese.

5. Bake at 350° for 50 to 60 minutes and serve immediately.   *Makes 4 to 6 servings*

Prep Time: 20 minutes   **Bake Time:** 50 to 60 minutes

Chocolate Waffles

2 cups all-purpose flour
¼ cup unsweetened cocoa powder
2 tablespoons sugar
1 tablespoon baking powder
½ teaspoon salt
2 cups milk

2 eggs, beaten
¼ cup vegetable oil
1 teaspoon vanilla
Raspberry Syrup (recipe follows)

1. Preheat waffle iron; grease lightly.

2. Sift flour, cocoa, sugar, baking powder and salt into large bowl. Combine milk, eggs, oil and vanilla in small bowl. Stir liquid ingredients into dry ingredients until moistened.

3. For each waffle, pour about ¾ cup batter into waffle iron. Close lid and bake until steaming stops.* Serve with Raspberry Syrup. *Makes about 6 waffles*

Check manufacturer's directions for recommended amount of batter and baking time.

Raspberry Syrup

1 cup water
1 cup sugar

1 package (10 ounces) frozen raspberries in syrup

1. Combine water and sugar in large saucepan. Cook over medium heat, stirring constantly, until sugar has dissolved. Continue cooking until mixture thickens slightly, about 10 minutes.

2. Stir in frozen raspberries; cook, stirring, until berries are thawed. Bring to a boil; continue cooking until syrup thickens slightly, about 5 to 10 minutes. Serve warm.

Makes about 1⅓ cups

Savory Bread Pudding

8 slices thick-cut, day-old white
    bread, crusts trimmed
2 tablespoons unsalted butter
    substitute, softened
2 cups (8 ounces) shredded
    ALPINE LACE® Reduced Fat
    Swiss Cheese, divided
1 cup grated peeled apple

½ cup egg substitute or 2 large
    eggs
2 large egg whites
2 cups 2% low fat milk
½ teaspoon salt
¼ teaspoon freshly ground black
    pepper

1. Preheat the oven to 400°F. Spray a 13×9×2-inch rectangular or 3-quart oval baking dish with nonstick cooking spray. Thinly spread the bread slices with the butter. Cut each bread slice into 4 triangles, making a total of 32. In a small bowl, toss 1¾ cups of the cheese with the grated apple.

2. In a medium-size bowl, using an electric mixer set on high, beat the egg substitute (or the whole eggs), the egg whites, milk, salt and pepper together until frothy and light yellow.

3. To assemble the pudding: Line the bottom of the dish with 16 of the bread triangles. Cover with the apple-cheese mixture, then pour over half the egg mixture. Arrange the remaining 16 triangles around the edge and down the center of the dish, overlapping slightly as you go.

4. Pour the remaining egg mixture over the top, then sprinkle with the remaining ¼ cup of cheese. Bake, uncovered, for 35 minutes or until crisp and golden brown.

Makes 8 servings

Savory Bread Pudding

Cheese Blintzes

Cheese Blintzes

Basic Crêpes (recipe follows)
1 container (15 ounces) ricotta or
    light ricotta cheese
2 tablespoons powdered sugar
1 teaspoon vanilla
⅛ teaspoon ground nutmeg
1 tablespoon margarine or butter,
    melted

Additional powdered sugar
Sour cream
Applesauce
Strawberry or raspberry
    preserves

Prepare Basic Crêpes. Preheat oven to 350°F. Generously grease 13×9-inch baking dish.

Process ricotta cheese, 2 tablespoons powdered sugar, vanilla and nutmeg in food processor about 30 seconds or until smooth. Place about 3 tablespoons cheese mixture in center of each crêpe. Fold bottom edge of crêpe up to partly cover filling; fold in side edges, then roll up completely to enclose filling.

Place blintzes seam side down in prepared dish; brush tops with melted margarine. Bake uncovered 15 to 20 minutes or until heated through. Sprinkle with additional powdered sugar. Serve with sour cream, applesauce and preserves.   *Makes 4 servings*

Basic Crêpes

1½ cups milk
1 cup all-purpose flour
2 eggs

¼ cup margarine or butter, melted
   and cooled, divided
¼ teaspoon salt

Process milk, flour, eggs, 2 tablespoons margarine and salt in food processor until smooth. Let stand at room temperature 30 minutes.

Heat ½ teaspoon margarine in 7- or 8-inch crêpe pan or nonstick skillet over medium heat. Process crêpe batter until blended. Pour ¼ cup batter into pan; tilt pan to spread batter. Cook 1 to 2 minutes or until crêpe is brown around edge and top is dry. Carefully turn crêpe with spatula; cook 30 seconds. Place crêpes between waxed paper to cool. Repeat with remaining batter, adding remaining margarine only as needed to prevent sticking. Cover and refrigerate up to 1 day or freeze up to 1 month before serving.

Makes about 1 dozen crêpes

Sour Cream and Onion Grits

1 cup 3 MINUTE BRAND® Quick
   Grits
½ cup chopped onion
½ cup sour cream
1 package (3 ounces) cream
   cheese, softened
1 tablespoon margarine or butter

1 tablespoon dried parsley flakes
   or dried chives
½ teaspoon onion powder
   (optional)
½ teaspoon garlic powder
½ teaspoon salt (optional)
⅛ teaspoon ground black pepper

Preheat oven to 350°F. Grease 2-quart baking dish. Combine grits, onion, sour cream, cream cheese, margarine, parsley, onion powder, garlic powder, salt and black pepper; mix well. Pour into prepared dish. Bake 30 minutes. Serve immediately.

Makes 8 servings

Silver Dollar Pancakes with Mixed Berry Topping

1¼ cups all-purpose flour
2 tablespoons sugar
2 teaspoons baking soda
1½ cups buttermilk
½ cup EGG BEATERS® Healthy
    Real Egg Product

3 tablespoons margarine, melted,
    divided
Mixed Berry Topping (recipe
    follows)

In large bowl, combine flour, sugar and baking soda. Stir in buttermilk, Egg Beaters®
and 2 tablespoons margarine just until blended.

Brush large nonstick griddle or skillet with some of remaining margarine; heat over
medium-high heat. Using 1 heaping tablespoon batter for each pancake, spoon batter
onto griddle. Cook until bubbly; turn and cook until lightly browned. Repeat with
remaining batter using remaining margarine as needed to make 28 pancakes. Serve hot
with Mixed Berry Topping.

Makes 28 (2-inch) pancakes

Mixed Berry Topping: In medium saucepan, over medium-low heat, combine 1 (12-ounce)
package frozen mixed berries,* thawed, ¼ cup honey and ½ teaspoon grated gingerroot
(or ⅛ teaspoon ground ginger). Cook and stir just until hot and well blended. Serve over
pancakes.

Three cups mixed fresh berries may be substituted.

Prep Time: 20 minutes   **Cook Time:** 20 minutes

Silver Dollar Pancakes with Mixed Berry Topping

Waffles with Strawberry Sauce

2¼ cups all-purpose flour
2 tablespoons sugar
1 tablespoon baking powder
½ teaspoon salt
2 eggs, beaten

¼ cup vegetable oil
2 cups milk
Strawberry Sauce (recipe follows)

1. Preheat waffle iron; grease lightly.

2. Sift flour, sugar, baking powder and salt into large bowl. Combine eggs, oil and milk in medium bowl. Stir liquid ingredients into dry ingredients until moistened.

3. For each waffle, pour about ¾ cup of batter into waffle iron. Close lid and bake until steaming stops.* Serve with Strawberry Sauce.   *Makes about 6 round waffles*

*Check the manufacturer's directions for recommended amount of batter and baking time.

Strawberry Sauce

1 pint strawberries, hulled
2 to 3 tablespoons sugar

1 tablespoon strawberry- or orange-flavored liqueur (optional)

Combine strawberries, sugar and liqueur in blender or food processor. Cover; process until strawberries are puréed.   *Makes 1½ cups*

Waffles with Strawberry Sauce

Strawberry & Banana Stuffed French Toast

1 loaf (12 inches) French bread
2 tablespoons strawberry jam
4 ounces cream cheese, softened
¼ cup chopped strawberries
¼ cup chopped banana

6 eggs, lightly beaten
¾ cup milk
3 tablespoons butter or
   margarine, divided
Strawberry Sauce (page 190)

1. Cut French bread into eight 1½-inch slices. Make pocket in each slice by cutting slit from top of bread almost to bottom.

2. Combine jam, cream cheese, strawberries and banana in small bowl to make filling.

3. Place heaping tablespoon of strawberry filling into each pocket. Press back together.

4. Beat eggs and milk in wide shallow bowl. Add bread; let stand to coat, then turn to coat other side.

5. Heat 2 tablespoons butter in large skillet over medium-low heat. Add as many bread slices as will fit; cook until brown. Turn and cook other side. Remove and keep warm. Repeat with remaining butter and bread slices. Serve with Strawberry Sauce.

Makes 8 slices

Strawberry & Banana Stuffed French Toast

Sunrise French Toast

2 cups cholesterol-free egg
    substitute
½ cup evaporated skimmed milk
1 teaspoon grated orange peel
1 teaspoon vanilla
¼ teaspoon ground cinnamon
1 jar (10 ounces) no-sugar-added
    orange marmalade

1 loaf (1 pound) Italian bread,
    cut into ½-inch-thick slices
    (about 20 slices)
Nonstick cooking spray
Powdered sugar
Maple-flavored syrup (optional)

1. Preheat oven to 400°F. Combine egg substitute, milk, orange peel, vanilla and cinnamon in medium bowl. Set aside.

2. Spread 1 tablespoon marmalade over 1 bread slice to within ½ inch of edge. Top with another bread slice. Repeat with remaining marmalade and bread.

3. Spray griddle or large skillet with cooking spray; heat over medium heat until hot. Dip sandwiches in egg substitute mixture. Do not soak. Cook sandwiches in batches 2 to 3 minutes on each side or until golden brown.

4. Transfer sandwiches to 15×10-inch jelly-roll pan. Bake 10 to 12 minutes or until sides are sealed. Dust with powdered sugar and serve with syrup. *Makes 5 servings*

Harvest Apple Oatmeal

Harvest Apple Oatmeal

1 cup apple juice
1 cup water
1 medium apple, cored and
  chopped
1 cup uncooked old-fashioned
  rolled oats

¼ cup raisins
⅛ teaspoon ground cinnamon
⅛ teaspoon salt

Microwave Directions: Combine apple juice, water and apple in 2-quart microwavable bowl. Microwave at HIGH 3 minutes, stirring halfway through cooking time.

Add oats, raisins, cinnamon and salt; stir until well blended.

Microwave at MEDIUM (50%) 4 to 5 minutes or until thick; stir before serving. Garnish with apple slices, if desired.   *Makes 2 servings*

Conventional Directions: Bring apple juice, water and apple to a boil in medium saucepan over medium-high heat. Stir in oats, raisins, cinnamon and salt until well blended. Cook, uncovered, over medium heat 5 to 6 minutes or until thick, stirring occasionally.

Triple Berry Breakfast Parfaits

Triple Berry Breakfast Parfaits

2 cups vanilla sugar-free nonfat
    yogurt
¼ teaspoon ground cinnamon
1 cup sliced strawberries

½ cup blueberries
½ cup raspberries
1 cup low-fat granola without
    raisins

1. Combine yogurt and cinnamon in small bowl. Combine strawberries, blueberries and raspberries in medium bowl.

2. For each parfait, layer ¼ cup fruit mixture, 2 tablespoons granola and ¼ cup yogurt mixture in parfait glass. Repeat layers. Garnish with mint leaves, if desired.

Makes 4 servings

Date-Nut Granola

2 cups uncooked rolled oats
2 cups barley flakes
1 cup sliced almonds
⅓ cup vegetable oil

⅓ cup honey
1 teaspoon vanilla
1 cup chopped dates

1. Preheat oven to 350°F. Grease 13×9-inch baking pan.

2. Combine oats, barley flakes and almonds in large bowl; set aside.

3. Combine oil, honey and vanilla in small bowl. Pour honey mixture over oat mixture; stir well. Pour into prepared pan.

4. Bake about 25 minutes or until toasted, stirring frequently after the first 10 minutes. Stir in dates while mixture is still hot. Cool. Store tightly covered.   *Makes 6 cups*

Microwaved Oats Cereal

1¾ cups water
⅓ cup old-fashioned rolled oats
⅓ cup oat bran

1 tablespoon brown sugar
¼ teaspoon ground cinnamon
⅛ teaspoon salt

Microwave Directions: Combine water, oats, oat bran, sugar, cinnamon and salt in large microwavable bowl (cereal expands rapidly when it cooks). Cover with plastic wrap; vent.

Microwave on HIGH about 6 minutes or until thickened. Stir well. Let stand 2 minutes before serving.   *Makes 2 servings*

Savory Summertime Oat Bread

Nonstick cooking spray
½ cup finely chopped onion
4¼ to 4½ cups all-purpose flour, divided
2 cups whole wheat flour
2 cups uncooked rolled oats
¼ cup sugar
2 packages quick-rising active dry yeast

1½ teaspoons salt
1½ cups water
1¼ cups skim milk
¼ cup margarine
1 cup finely shredded carrots
3 tablespoons dried parsley leaves
1 tablespoon margarine, melted

1. Spray small nonstick skillet with cooking spray; heat over medium heat until hot. Cook and stir onion 3 minutes or until tender. Set aside.

2. Stir together 1 cup all-purpose flour, whole wheat flour, oats, sugar, yeast and salt in large mixer bowl. Heat water, milk and ¼ cup margarine in medium saucepan over low heat until mixture reaches 120° to 130°F. Add to flour mixture. Blend at low speed just until dry ingredients are moistened; beat 3 minutes at medium speed. Stir in carrots, onion, parsley and remaining 3¼ to 3½ cups all-purpose flour until dough is no longer sticky.

3. Knead dough on lightly floured surface 5 to 8 minutes or until smooth and elastic. Place in large bowl lightly sprayed with cooking spray. Cover and let rise in warm place about 30 minutes or until doubled in bulk.

4. Spray two 8×4-inch loaf pans with cooking spray. Punch dough down. Cover and let rest 10 minutes. Shape into 2 loaves; place in pans. Brush with melted margarine. Cover; let rise in warm place 30 minutes or until doubled in bulk. Meanwhile, preheat oven to 350°F.

5. Bake 40 to 45 minutes or until bread sounds hollow when tapped. Remove from pans; cool on wire racks.

Makes 2 loaves (24 slices)

Savory Summertime Oat Bread

Lemon Poppy Seed Tea Loaf

TEA LOAF

2½ cups all-purpose flour
¼ cup poppy seeds
1 tablespoon grated lemon peel
2 teaspoons baking powder
½ teaspoon baking soda
½ teaspoon salt
1 cup sugar

⅔ cup MOTT'S® Natural Apple
 Sauce
1 whole egg
2 egg whites, lightly beaten
2 tablespoons vegetable oil
1 teaspoon vanilla extract
⅓ cup skim milk

LEMON SYRUP

¼ cup lemon juice

¼ cup sugar

1. Preheat oven to 350°F. Spray 9×5-inch loaf pan with nonstick cooking spray.

2. To prepare Tea Loaf, in large bowl, combine flour, poppy seeds, lemon peel, baking powder, baking soda and salt.

3. In medium bowl, combine 1 cup sugar, apple sauce, whole egg, egg whites, oil and vanilla.

4. Stir apple sauce mixture into flour mixture alternately with milk. Mix until thoroughly moistened. Spread batter into prepared pan.

5. Bake 40 to 45 minutes or until toothpick inserted in center comes out clean. Cool in pan 10 minutes. Invert onto wire rack; turn right side up.

6. To prepare Lemon Syrup, in small saucepan, combine lemon juice and ¼ cup sugar. Cook, stirring frequently, until sugar dissolves. Cool slightly.

7. Pierce top of loaf with metal skewer. Brush lemon syrup over loaf. Let stand until cool. Cut into 16 slices. *Makes 16 servings*

Left to right: **Lemon Poppy Seed Tea Loaf and Morning Glory Bread** *(page 202)*

Morning Glory Bread

2½ cups all-purpose flour
2 teaspoons baking powder
1 teaspoon baking soda
½ teaspoon salt
½ teaspoon ground cinnamon
¼ teaspoon ground nutmeg
¼ teaspoon ground allspice
¾ cup granulated sugar
¾ cup firmly packed light brown sugar
½ cup MOTT'S® Chunky Apple Sauce

3 egg whites
1 tablespoon vegetable oil
1 tablespoon GRANDMA'S® Molasses
¾ cup finely shredded carrots
½ cup raisins
⅓ cup drained, crushed pineapple in juice
¼ cup shredded coconut

1. Preheat oven to 375°F. Spray 8½×4½-inch loaf pan with nonstick cooking spray.

2. In large bowl, combine flour, baking powder, baking soda, salt, cinnamon, nutmeg and allspice.

3. In medium bowl, combine granulated sugar, brown sugar, apple sauce, egg whites, oil and molasses.

4. Stir apple sauce mixture into flour mixture just until moistened. Fold in carrots, raisins, pineapple and coconut. Spread into prepared pan.

5. Bake 45 to 50 minutes or until toothpick inserted in center comes out clean. Cool in pan 10 minutes. Invert onto wire rack; turn right side up. Cool completely. Cut into 16 slices.

Makes 16 servings

The Original Kellogg's® All-Bran® Muffin™

1¼ cups all-purpose flour
½ cup sugar
 1 tablespoon baking powder
¼ teaspoon salt
 2 cups KELLOGG'S®
  ALL-BRAN® Cereal

1¼ cups milk
1 egg
¼ cup vegetable oil
 Vegetable cooking spray

1. Stir together flour, sugar, baking powder and salt. Set aside.

2. In large mixing bowl, combine Kellogg's® All-Bran® cereal and milk. Let stand about 5 minutes or until cereal softens. Add egg and oil. Beat well. Add flour mixture, stirring only until combined. Portion batter evenly into twelve 2½-inch muffin-pan cups coated with cooking spray.

3. Bake at 400°F about 20 minutes or until lightly browned. Serve warm.

Makes 12 muffins

For muffins with reduced calories, fat and cholesterol: Use 2 tablespoons sugar, 2 tablespoons oil, replace milk with 1¼ cups skim milk, and substitute 2 egg whites for 1 egg. Prepare and bake as directed.

Cranberry Oat Bread

Cranberry Oat Bread

¾ cup honey
⅓ cup vegetable oil
2 eggs
½ cup milk
2½ cups all-purpose flour
1 cup quick-cooking rolled oats

1 teaspoon baking soda
1 teaspoon baking powder
½ teaspoon salt
½ teaspoon ground cinnamon
2 cups fresh or frozen cranberries
1 cup chopped nuts

Combine honey, oil, eggs and milk in large bowl; mix well. Combine flour, oats, baking soda, baking powder, salt and cinnamon in medium bowl; mix well. Stir into honey mixture. Fold in cranberries and nuts. Spoon into two 8½×4½×2½-inch greased and floured loaf pans.

Bake in preheated 350°F oven 40 to 45 minutes or until wooden toothpick inserted near center comes out clean. Cool in pans on wire racks 15 minutes. Remove from pans; cool completely on wire racks. *Makes 2 loaves*

Favorite recipe from **National Honey Board**

Many Grains Bread

2¾ to 3¼ cups all-purpose flour, divided
3 cups graham flour, divided
2 packages RED STAR® Active Dry Yeast or Quick•Rise Yeast
4 teaspoons salt
3 cups water
½ cup dark molasses

¼ cup vegetable oil
½ cup buckwheat flour
½ cup rye flour
½ cup soy flour
½ cup yellow cornmeal
½ cup quick rolled oats
Butter

Combine 1½ cups all-purpose flour and 2 cups graham flour, yeast and salt in large bowl; mix well. Heat water, molasses and oil in large saucepan over medium heat until very warm (120° to 130°F). Add to flour mixture. Blend at low speed until moistened; beat 3 minutes at medium speed. By hand, gradually stir in buckwheat, rye and soy flours, cornmeal, oats, remaining graham flour and enough remaining all-purpose flour to make a firm dough. Knead on floured surface 5 to 8 minutes. Place in large greased bowl, turning to grease top. Cover with clean kitchen towel; let rise in warm place about 1 hour or until double in bulk (about 30 minutes for Quick•Rise Yeast).

Punch down dough. Divide into 2 parts. On lightly floured surface, shape each half into round loaf.

Place loaves on large greased baking sheet. Cover; let rise in warm place about 30 minutes or until double in bulk (15 minutes for Quick•Rise Yeast).

Preheat oven to 375°F. With sharp knife, make cross slash across top of each loaf. Bake 35 to 40 minutes until bread sounds hollow when tapped. If bread starts to become too dark, cover loosely with foil during last 5 to 10 minutes of baking. Remove from baking sheet. Brush with butter; cool on wire racks. *Makes 2 round loaves*

Grilled Vegetable Kabobs

1 large red or green bell pepper
1 large zucchini
1 large yellow squash or
   additional zucchini
12 ounces large mushrooms
2 tablespoons olive oil

2 tablespoons red wine vinegar
1 package (7.2 ounces) RICE-
   A-RONI® Herb & Butter
1 large tomato, chopped
¼ cup grated Parmesan cheese

1. Cut red pepper into twelve 1-inch pieces. Cut zucchini and yellow squash crosswise into twelve ½-inch slices. Marinate red pepper, zucchini, yellow squash and mushrooms in combined oil and vinegar 15 minutes.

2. Alternately thread marinated vegetables onto 4 large skewers. Brush with any remaining oil mixture; set aside.

3. Prepare Rice-A-Roni® Mix as package directs.

4. While Rice-A-Roni® is simmering, grill kabobs over medium-low coals *or* broil 4 to 5 inches from heat 12 to 14 minutes or until tender and browned, turning once.

5. Stir tomato into rice. Serve rice topped with kabobs. Sprinkle with cheese.

Makes 4 servings

Serving Suggestion: Serve with ¾ cup nonfat or low-fat yogurt per serving.

Grilled Vegetable Kabobs

Cabbage-Cheese Strudel

1 tablespoon vegetable oil
1 cup chopped onions
½ cup sliced leeks
½ cup sliced button mushrooms
½ cup seeded and chopped tomato
¼ head green cabbage, shredded
1 cup broccoli flowerets, steamed
1½ teaspoons caraway seeds, crushed, divided
1 teaspoon dried dill weed
½ teaspoon salt

¼ teaspoon ground black pepper
1 package (8 ounces) cream cheese, softened
1 egg, beaten
¾ cup cooked brown rice
¾ cup (3 ounces) shredded Cheddar cheese
6 sheets frozen phyllo pastry, thawed
6 to 8 tablespoons margarine or butter, melted

Heat oil in large saucepan over medium heat until hot. Add onions and leeks; cook and stir 3 minutes. Add mushrooms and tomato; cook and stir 5 minutes. Add cabbage, broccoli, 1 teaspoon caraway seeds, dill weed, salt and pepper. Cover; cook over medium heat 8 to 10 minutes or until cabbage wilts. Remove cover; cook 10 minutes more or until cabbage is soft and beginning to brown.

Combine cream cheese, egg, rice and Cheddar cheese in medium bowl. Stir into cabbage mixture until blended.

Preheat oven to 375°F. Unroll phyllo dough. Cover with plastic wrap and damp, clean kitchen towel. Brush 1 phyllo dough sheet with margarine. Top with 2 more sheets, brushing each with margarine. Spoon half of cabbage mixture 2 inches from short end of phyllo. Spread mixture to cover about half of phyllo. Roll up dough from short end with filling. Place, seam side down, on greased cookie sheet. Flatten roll slightly with hands and brush with margarine. Repeat with remaining phyllo, margarine and cabbage mixture. Sprinkle tops of rolls with remaining ½ teaspoon caraway seeds.

Bake 45 to 50 minutes or until golden brown. Cool 10 minutes. Cut each roll diagonally into 3 pieces with serrated knife.

Makes 6 servings

Cabbage-Cheese Strudel

Louisiana Red Beans & Rice

Louisiana Red Beans & Rice

1 package (7.2 ounces) RICE-A-RONI® Herb & Butter
1 cup chopped green or yellow bell pepper
¾ cup chopped onion
2 cloves garlic, minced
2 tablespoons vegetable oil or olive oil
1 can (15 or 16 ounces) red beans or kidney beans, rinsed and drained

1 can (14½ or 16 ounces) tomatoes or stewed tomatoes, undrained
1 teaspoon dried thyme leaves or dried oregano leaves
⅛ teaspoon hot pepper sauce or black pepper
2 tablespoons chopped parsley (optional)

1. Prepare Rice-A-Roni® Mix as package directs.

2. While Rice-A-Roni® is simmering, in second large skillet, sauté green pepper, onion and garlic in oil 5 minutes.

3. Stir in beans, tomatoes, thyme and hot pepper sauce. Simmer, uncovered, 10 minutes, stirring occasionally. Stir in parsley. Serve over rice.   *Makes 5 servings*

Serving Suggestion: Serve with one 8-ounce glass of milk per serving.

Fresh Vegetables over Couscous

3 tablespoons olive or vegetable oil
2 pounds assorted fresh
  vegetables*
1 can (15 to 19 ounces) chick-peas
  or garbanzos, rinsed and
  drained
¼ cup golden raisins (optional)
1 envelope LIPTON® Recipe
  Secrets® Savory Herb with
  Garlic Soup Mix

1½ cups water
2 tablespoons lemon juice**
½ teaspoon ground cumin
  (optional)
1 box (10 ounces) couscous,
  prepared according to
  package directions

In 12-inch skillet, heat oil over medium heat and cook vegetables, stirring occasionally, 5 minutes or until tender. Add chick-peas, raisins and Savory Herb with Garlic Soup Mix blended with water, lemon juice and cumin. Cook, stirring occasionally, 3 minutes. Serve over hot couscous.   *Makes about 4 servings*

*Use any combination of the following, sliced: zucchini, yellow squash, red onions, carrots, mushrooms or red or green bell peppers.

**If using Lipton® Recipe Secrets® Golden Herb with Lemon Soup Mix, omit lemon juice.

•Also terrific with Lipton® Recipe Secrets® Golden Herb with Lemon Soup Mix.

Spaghetti Squash Primavera

2 teaspoons vegetable oil
½ teaspoon finely chopped garlic
¼ cup finely chopped red onion
¼ cup thinly sliced carrot
¼ cup thinly sliced red bell pepper
¼ cup thinly sliced green bell pepper
1 can (14½ ounces) Italian-style stewed tomatoes
½ cup thinly sliced yellow squash
½ cup thinly sliced zucchini

½ cup frozen whole kernel corn, thawed
½ teaspoon dried oregano leaves
⅛ teaspoon dried thyme leaves
1 spaghetti squash (about 2 pounds)
4 teaspoons grated Parmesan cheese (optional)
2 tablespoons finely chopped fresh parsley

1. Heat oil in large skillet over medium-high heat until hot. Add garlic. Cook and stir 3 minutes. Add onion, carrot and peppers. Cook and stir 3 minutes. Add tomatoes, yellow squash, zucchini, corn, oregano and thyme. Cook 5 minutes or until heated through, stirring occasionally.

2. Cut spaghetti squash lengthwise in half. Remove seeds. Cover with plastic wrap. Microwave at HIGH 9 minutes or until spaghetti squash separates easily into strands when tested with fork.

3. Cut each spaghetti squash half lengthwise in half; separate strands with fork. Spoon vegetables evenly over spaghetti squash. Top servings evenly with cheese, if desired, and parsley before serving.

Makes 4 servings

Spaghetti Squash Primavera

Encore Salad

1½ cups white vinegar
1 cup olive oil
¼ cup sugar
2 teaspoons salt
¾ teaspoon black pepper
1 clove garlic, minced
12 pearl onions or very small
    onions
1 cup water
1 small cauliflower, cut into
    flowerets

2 cups canned black-eyed peas,
    rinsed and drained
1 can beets, drained, cut into
    quarters
1 green bell pepper, cut into
    ½-inch strips
1 (6-ounce) can ripe olives,
    drained, halved

Combine vinegar, oil, sugar, salt, black pepper and garlic in medium saucepan. Bring to a boil over high heat, stirring constantly; cool 5 minutes. Add onions and water; bring to a boil. Cover and reduce heat; simmer 2 minutes or until onions are tender. Drain. Add cauliflower, black-eyed peas, beets, green pepper and olives; refrigerate 8 hours, stirring occasionally.

Makes 6 servings

Favorite recipe from **Black-Eyed Pea Jamboree—Athens, Texas**

Apple-Potato Pancakes

1¼ cups unpeeled, finely chopped
    apples
1 cup peeled, grated potatoes
½ cup MOTT'S® Natural Apple
    Sauce
½ cup all-purpose flour

2 egg whites
1 teaspoon salt
    Additional MOTT'S® Natural
    Apple Sauce or apple slices
    (optional)

1. Preheat oven to 475°F. Spray cookie sheet with nonstick cooking spray.

Apple-Potato Pancakes

2. In medium bowl, combine apples, potatoes, ½ cup apple sauce, flour, egg whites and salt.

3. Spray large nonstick skillet with nonstick cooking spray; heat over medium heat until hot. Drop rounded tablespoonfuls of batter 2 inches apart into skillet. Cook 2 to 3 minutes on each side or until lightly browned. Place pancakes on prepared cookie sheet.

4. Bake 10 to 15 minutes or until crisp. Serve with additional apple sauce or apple slices, if desired. Refrigerate leftovers.   *Makes 12 servings*

Spinach Cheese Roulade

4 teaspoons margarine, divided
2 tablespoons all-purpose flour
1 cup skim milk
2 cups EGG BEATERS® Healthy
　　Real Egg Product
1 medium onion, chopped
1 (10-ounce) package fresh
　　spinach, coarsely chopped

½ cup low-fat cottage cheese
　　(1% milkfat)
1 (8-ounce) can no-salt-added
　　tomato sauce
½ teaspoon dried basil leaves
½ teaspoon garlic powder

In small saucepan, over medium heat, melt 3 teaspoons margarine; blend in flour. Cook, stirring until smooth and bubbly; remove from heat. Gradually blend in milk; return to heat. Heat to a boil, stirring constantly until thickened; cool slightly. Stir in Egg Beaters®. Spread mixture in bottom of 15½×10½×1-inch baking pan that has been greased, lined with foil and greased again. Bake at 350°F for 20 minutes or until set.

In medium skillet, sauté onion in remaining 1 teaspoon margarine until tender. Add spinach and cook until wilted, about 3 minutes; stir in cottage cheese. Keep warm.

Invert egg mixture onto large piece of foil. Spread with spinach mixture; roll up from short end. In small saucepan, combine tomato sauce, basil and garlic; heat until warm. To serve, slice roll into 8 pieces; top with warm sauce.　　*Makes 8 servings*

Prep Time: 30 minutes　**Cook Time:** 25 minutes

Warm Winter Walnut Salad

2 cups water
1 teaspoon salt
1 cup bulgur or long-grain white
rice
1 (1-pound) bag mixed frozen
vegetables, such as a mixture
of broccoli, corn and red
peppers

½ cup chopped California walnuts
½ cup chopped green onions
3 tablespoons lemon juice
3 tablespoons chopped fresh
parsley or chives
Freshly ground pepper
4 cups shredded iceberg lettuce
(half a head)

DRESSING

1 cup nonfat yogurt
1 tablespoon lemon juice

1 tablespoon chopped fresh
parsley or chives

In large saucepan, bring water and salt to a boil over high heat. Add bulgur and vegetables; stir to combine. When mixture returns to a boil, reduce heat to low. Cover pan and simmer 15 minutes. Remove from heat and let stand, covered, for 5 minutes.

Place bulgur mixture in large bowl. Add walnuts, onions, 3 tablespoons lemon juice and 3 tablespoons parsley; stir to combine. Season with pepper to taste. Spread lettuce around rim of large platter.

To make dressing, in small bowl stir together yogurt, 1 tablespoon lemon juice and 1 tablespoon parsley.

Mound salad in center of lettuce and spoon some of dressing over salad. Serve with remaining dressing. *Makes 4 servings*

Favorite recipe from **Walnut Marketing Board**

Eggplant Crêpes with Roasted Tomato Sauce

Eggplant Crêpes with Roasted Tomato Sauce

Roasted Tomato Sauce (recipe
  follows)
2 eggplants (about 8 to 9 inches
  long)
Nonstick olive oil cooking spray
1 package (10 ounces) frozen
  chopped spinach, thawed and
  pressed dry

1 cup ricotta cheese
½ cup grated Parmesan cheese
1¼ cups (5 ounces) shredded
  Gruyère* cheese
Fresh oregano leaves for garnish

*Gruyère cheese is a Swiss cheese that has been aged for 10 to 12 months. Any Swiss cheese
may be substituted.*

Prepare Roasted Tomato Sauce; set aside. Cut eggplants lengthwise into ¼-inch-thick
slices. Arrange 18 of largest slices on nonstick baking sheets in single layer. Spray both
sides of eggplant slices with cooking spray. (Reserve any remaining slices for other uses.)

Bake eggplant at 425°F 10 minutes; turn and bake 5 to 10 minutes more or until tender. Cool. *Reduce oven temperature to 350°F.*

Combine spinach, ricotta and Parmesan cheese; mix well. Spray 12×8-inch baking pan with cooking spray. Spread spinach mixture evenly on eggplant slices; roll up slices, beginning at short ends. Place rolls, seam side down, in baking dish. Cover dish with foil and bake 25 minutes. Uncover; sprinkle rolls with Gruyère cheese. Bake, uncovered, 5 minutes more or until cheese is melted. Serve with Roasted Tomato Sauce. Garnish, if desired.

Makes 4 to 6 servings

Roasted Tomato Sauce

**20 ripe plum tomatoes (about
2⅔ pounds), cut in half and
seeded
3 tablespoons olive oil, divided**

**½ teaspoon salt
⅓ cup minced fresh basil
½ teaspoon ground black pepper**

Preheat oven to 450°F. Toss tomatoes with 1 tablespoon oil and salt. Place, cut sides down, on nonstick baking sheet. Bake 20 to 25 minutes or until skins are blistered. Cool. Process tomatoes, remaining 2 tablespoons oil, basil and pepper in food processor until smooth. *Reduce oven temperature to 425°F.*

Makes about 1 cup

Rice Salad with Bel Paese® Cheese

**5 cups cooked rice
2 carrots, thinly sliced
1 (8½-ounce) can artichoke
hearts, drained and sliced
into halves**

**4 ounces pitted olives, drained and
cut into halves
6 to 8 sprigs fresh parsley, minced
6 ounces BEL PAESE® semi-soft
cheese, cubed**

Mix all ingredients together in large serving dish. Toss lightly.

Makes 4 to 6 servings

Cheese Polenta with Vegetable Medley

Cheese Polenta (recipe follows)
1 tablespoon margarine or butter
2 teaspoons olive oil
1 medium fennel bulb with stalks,
    cored and cut into thin
    wedges
1 cup chopped onions
2 tablespoons snipped chives
½ teaspoon sugar
2 carrots, cut into julienne strips
4 ounces medium brussels sprouts
    (6 to 8), cut into halves
½ to 1 cup canned vegetable broth
Salt
Black pepper

Prepare Cheese Polenta; set aside. Heat margarine and oil in large skillet over medium heat until margarine melts. Add fennel. Cook 6 to 8 minutes or until lightly browned on both sides. Place in medium bowl. Add onions, chives and sugar to skillet. Cook and stir 5 minutes or until onions are tender. Return fennel to skillet. Add carrots, brussels sprouts and ½ cup broth. Bring to a boil; reduce heat to low. Cover and simmer 15 to 20 minutes or until brussels sprouts are tender, adding more broth if necessary to keep mixture moist. Season to taste with salt and pepper.

Spray large nonstick skillet with cooking spray. Heat over medium heat until hot. Cut Cheese Polenta into wedges. Cook 3 minutes per side or until browned. Place on serving plates; top with vegetable mixture. Garnish, if desired. *Makes 4 to 6 servings*

Cheese Polenta

1 cup cold water
1 cup yellow cornmeal
1½ cups boiling water
2 to 4 tablespoons crumbled
    Gorgonzola cheese
1 clove garlic, minced
1 teaspoon salt

Stir water into cornmeal in large saucepan. Heat over medium heat until warm. Slowly stir in boiling water. Bring to a boil over medium-high heat. Reduce heat to low. Cook 15 minutes or until mixture is thick, stirring constantly. Stir in cheese, garlic and salt. Pour into greased 8-inch round pan; let stand 10 minutes or until firm.

Makes 4 to 6 servings

Cheese Polenta with Vegetable Medley

Mediterranean Vegetable Salad

2 cups instant couscous
8 cups coarsely chopped
    vegetables, such as
    cucumbers, tomatoes,
    radishes, celery, green bell
    peppers and/or red onions
1 cup olive oil
¼ cup FRENCH'S® Dijon Mustard
¼ cup lemon juice

2 tablespoons minced fresh basil
    leaves *or* 2 teaspoons dried
    basil leaves
2 teaspoons minced fresh thyme
    leaves *or* 1 teaspoon dried
    thyme leaves
2 cloves garlic, minced
1 teaspoon salt
4 ounces goat cheese, crumbled

Prepare couscous according to package directions; fluff with fork. Spread couscous on large serving platter.

Place vegetables in large bowl. Place oil, mustard, lemon juice, herbs, garlic and salt in blender or food processor. Cover and process until well blended. Pour dressing over vegetables; toss well to coat evenly. To serve, arrange vegetables over couscous; sprinkle with cheese.
Makes 4 to 6 servings

Prep Time: 20 minutes   **Cook Time:** 5 minutes

Tortellini Asparagus Salad

Tortellini Asparagus Salad

1 pound fresh asparagus, cut into
  ½-inch pieces
2 cups tightly packed fresh
  spinach leaves, torn into bite-
  sized pieces
1 cup diced red bell pepper
2 packages (9 ounces each)
  small cheese-filled tortellini,
  cooked, drained, cooled

¼ cup red wine vinegar
2 tablespoons olive or vegetable
  oil
1½ teaspoons lemon juice
1 teaspoon sugar
1 teaspoon LAWRY'S® Garlic Salt

Place asparagus on steamer rack; place in deep pot with 1-inch boiling water. Cover and steam 10 minutes. Remove and set aside. Steam spinach on steamer rack in same pot about 45 seconds or until just wilted. In large bowl, combine asparagus, spinach, red pepper and tortellini; blend well. In small bowl, combine vinegar, oil, lemon juice, sugar and Garlic Salt; blend well. Pour over tortellini mixture; toss well.

Makes 4 servings

Hints: Substitute 1½ cups broccoli flowerettes for asparagus. Chopped pimientos can be substituted for red bell pepper.

Tabbouleh

¾ cup bulgur, rinsed, drained
  Boiling water
2 cups chopped seeded cucumber
1 large tomato, seeded, chopped
1 cup snipped parsley
⅓ cup CRISCO® Oil or CRISCO®
  PURITAN® Canola Oil
⅓ cup chopped green onions

2 tablespoons lemon juice
1 teaspoon dried mint leaves,
  crumbled
2 cloves garlic, minced
½ teaspoon salt
⅛ teaspoon white pepper
⅛ teaspoon ground red pepper

Place bulgur in medium mixing bowl. Add enough boiling water to just cover bulgur. Let stand about 1 hour or until bulgur is rehydrated. Drain.

Combine bulgur, cucumber, tomato and parsley in large serving bowl; set aside. Blend remaining ingredients in small mixing bowl. Pour over bulgur mixture; toss to coat. Cover; refrigerate at least 3 hours. Stir before serving.   *Makes 10 to 12 servings*

Artichoke and Olive Salad

1 pound dry rotini pasta, cooked,
  drained, chilled
3½ cups (two 14.5-ounce cans)
  CONTADINA® Pasta Ready
  Chunky Tomatoes Primavera,
  undrained
½ cup (6-ounce jar) artichoke
  hearts, packed in water,
  drained, sliced

½ cup (2.25-ounce can) sliced
  pitted ripe olives, drained
½ cup Italian dressing
¼ cup chopped fresh parsley *or*
  2 teaspoons dried parsley
  flakes, crushed
¼ cup sliced green onions
½ cup sliced almonds, toasted

In large bowl, combine pasta, tomatoes and juice, artichoke hearts, olives, dressing, parsley and green onions; toss well. Cover. Chill before serving. Sprinkle with almonds just before serving.   *Makes 10 servings*

Tabbouleh

Vegetables as a Main Dish with Brown Rice

1 eggplant
2 tablespoons Chef Paul
    Prudhomme's VEGETABLE
    MAGIC®
½ cup apple juice
2 cups chopped onions
1½ cups chopped green bell peppers
1 cup chopped celery
2 cups vegetable stock
1 teaspoon minced fresh garlic

4 cups peeled, diced fresh
    tomatoes *or* 2 (14½-ounce)
    cans diced tomatoes
3 bay leaves
3 cups sliced fresh mushrooms
1 cup medium diced zucchini
1 cup medium diced yellow
    squash
Brown Rice (recipe follows)

Peel eggplant and slice into quarters lengthwise. Sprinkle all surfaces of eggplant with 1 tablespoon of seasoning mix.

Preheat heavy 12-inch nonstick skillet, over high heat, about 4 minutes. Cook seasoned eggplant in skillet until browned, about 2 minutes on each side. Add apple juice and cook for about 6 minutes, turning occasionally, until surfaces of eggplant are sticky and caramelized. Remove eggplant; set aside.

Combine onions, bell peppers, celery and 1½ teaspoons of seasoning mix in skillet; cook, stirring once or twice, until crust forms on bottom of skillet, about 12 minutes. Add 1 cup of stock and scrape bottom of skillet to clear it of all brown bits. Add garlic and cook until vegetables are evenly browned and sweet, about 5 minutes. When liquid has evaporated and new crust has formed, add tomatoes and scrape bottom of skillet. Add bay leaves, mushrooms, zucchini, yellow squash, remaining 1½ teaspoons seasoning mix and 1 cup stock. Mix together, then return eggplant to skillet, submerging it completely in sauce. Reduce heat to medium and simmer until eggplant is tender, about 12 to 15 minutes. Serve with Brown Rice. *Makes 6 to 8 servings*

Brown Rice

1½ cups long-grain brown rice   3 cups vegetable stock
2 bay leaves   ½ teaspoon salt

Place heavy 2-quart pot over high heat. Add rice and bay leaves; brown for 2 minutes. Stir in stock and salt. Bring to a boil; cover and reduce heat to low. Simmer until rice is tender and stock is absorbed, about 20 minutes.

Low-Fat Chimichangas

1 (16-ounce) can black beans,   22 to 24 corn tortillas (6 inches)
    rinsed and drained   1 cup finely chopped green onions,
1 (8-ounce) can stewed tomatoes   including tops
2 to 3 teaspoons chili powder   1½ cups (6 ounces) shredded
1 teaspoon dried oregano   JARLSBERG LITE™ Cheese

Mix beans, tomatoes, chili powder and oregano in medium saucepan. Cover and simmer 5 minutes. Uncover and simmer, stirring and crushing some of beans with wooden spoon, 5 minutes longer. Set aside. Warm tortillas according to package directions; keep warm. Place 1 tablespoon bean mixture on center of each tortilla. Sprinkle with rounded teaspoon onions, then rounded tablespoon cheese. Fold opposite sides of tortillas over mixture, forming square packets. Place folded side down on nonstick skillet. Repeat until all ingredients are used. Cook, covered, over low heat 3 to 5 minutes until heated through and bottoms are crispy. Serve at once or keep warm on covered warming tray.

Makes 6 to 8 servings

Caribbean Pasta Salad with Tropical Island Dressing

1 can black beans, drained and
    rinsed
½ cup thawed orange juice
    concentrate
½ teaspoon ground allspice
6 ounces mafalda pasta
1 teaspoon vegetable oil
4 cups washed and torn romaine
    lettuce leaves
1½ cups fresh pineapple chunks

1 mango, peeled and sliced
1 cup shredded cabbage
⅓ cup chopped onion
⅓ cup chopped red bell pepper
8 ounces piña colada-flavored
    yogurt
½ cup orange juice
1 teaspoon grated fresh ginger
2 oranges

1. Combine beans, juice concentrate and allspice in medium bowl. Cover and refrigerate 1 hour; drain and discard liquid from bean mixture.

2. Cook pasta according to package directions. Drain. Rinse under cold water until cool; drain again. Return to pan; toss with oil.

3. To assemble salad, divide lettuce, pasta, pineapple, beans, mango, cabbage, onion and bell pepper among 6 plates.

4. To prepare dressing, combine yogurt, ½ cup orange juice and ginger in small bowl. Remove colored portion of peel of 1 orange using vegetable peeler. Finely chop peel to measure 1 tablespoon; stir into dressing. Remove white portion of peel from orange and peel remaining orange. Separate oranges into sections; arrange on salads. Serve with dressing.

Makes 6 servings

Caribbean Pasta Salad with Tropical Island Dressing

Mu Shu Vegetables

Mu Shu Vegetables

Peanut Sauce (recipe follows)
3 tablespoons reduced-sodium soy
    sauce
2 tablespoons dry sherry
1½ tablespoons minced fresh ginger
2 teaspoons cornstarch
1½ teaspoons dark sesame oil
3 cloves garlic, minced
1 tablespoon peanut oil
3 leeks, washed and cut into
    2-inch slivers
3 carrots, peeled and julienned

1 cup thinly sliced fresh shiitake
    mushrooms
1 small head Napa or Savoy
    cabbage, shredded (about
    4 cups)
2 cups mung bean sprouts, rinsed
    and drained
8 ounces firm tofu, drained and
    cut into 2½×¼-inch strips
12 (8-inch) flour tortillas, warmed
¾ cup finely chopped honey
    roasted peanuts

Prepare Peanut Sauce; set aside. Combine soy sauce, sherry, ginger, cornstarch, sesame oil and garlic in small bowl until smooth; set aside.

Heat wok over medium-high heat 1 minute or until hot. Drizzle peanut oil into wok and heat 30 seconds. Add leeks, carrots and mushrooms; stir-fry 2 minutes. Add cabbage; stir-fry 3 minutes or until just tender. Add bean sprouts and tofu; stir-fry 1 minute or until hot. Stir soy sauce mixture and add to wok. Cook and stir 1 minute or until thickened.

Spread each tortilla with about 1 teaspoon Peanut Sauce. Spoon ½ cup vegetable mixture on bottom half of tortilla; sprinkle with 1 tablespoon peanuts.

Fold bottom edge of tortilla over filling; fold in side edges. Roll up to completely enclose filling. Or, spoon ½ cup vegetable mixture on one half of tortilla. Fold bottom edge over filling. Fold in one side edge. Serve with Peanut Sauce.   *Makes 6 servings*

Peanut Sauce

3 tablespoons sugar
3 tablespoons dry sherry
3 tablespoons reduced-sodium
    soy sauce

3 tablespoons water
2 teaspoons white wine vinegar
⅓ cup creamy peanut butter

Combine all ingredients except peanut butter in small saucepan. Bring to a boil over medium-high heat, stirring constantly. Boil 1 minute or until sugar melts. Stir in peanut butter until smooth; cool to room temperature.   *Makes ⅔ cup*

Tip: Tortillas can be softened and warmed in microwave oven just before using. Stack tortillas and wrap in plastic wrap. Microwave on HIGH ½ to 1 minute, turning over and rotating ¼ turn once during heating.

Farmers' Market Bowl

4 eggs
½ cup milk
⅔ cup all-purpose flour
½ teaspoon salt, divided
3 tablespoons olive oil, divided
2 red or green bell peppers,
    seeded and thinly sliced
1 medium onion, sliced
2 cloves garlic, minced
2 medium zucchini or yellow
    squash, thinly sliced

1 cup thinly sliced carrots
8 cherry tomatoes, cut into halves
2 tablespoons minced fresh dill
½ teaspoon ground black pepper
    Nonstick cooking spray
1 cup (4 ounces) shredded
    Monterey Jack cheese
    Celery leaves for garnish

Process eggs, milk, flour and ¼ teaspoon salt in food processor or blender until smooth. Let stand 15 minutes.

Preheat oven to 450°F. Heat 1 tablespoon oil in large skillet over medium heat until hot. Add bell peppers, onion and garlic; cook and stir 5 minutes or until just tender. Place in medium bowl. Heat 1 tablespoon oil over medium heat in same skillet. Add zucchini and carrots; cook and stir 8 to 10 minutes or until just tender. Remove from heat. Add bell pepper mixture to skillet; stir in tomatoes, dill, remaining ¼ teaspoon salt and black pepper. Keep warm.

Spray 9-inch ovenproof skillet with cooking spray; brush with remaining 1 tablespoon oil. Place skillet in oven 2 minutes or until hot. Pour batter into skillet. Bake 12 to 14 minutes or until lightly browned and cooked through.

Spoon vegetable mixture into bowl; sprinkle with cheese. Bake 2 minutes more or until cheese is melted. Cut into wedges. Garnish, if desired. *Makes 4 to 6 servings*

Farmers' Market Bowl

Tangy Garlic Tortellini Salad

Tangy Garlic Tortellini Salad

¼ cup mayonnaise
¼ cup plain yogurt
1 tablespoon plus 1½ teaspoons
   lemon juice
1 tablespoon olive oil
2 teaspoons chopped fresh chives
   or ¼ cup chopped green
   onions
1 to 1¼ teaspoons LAWRY'S®
   Garlic Salt
1 teaspoon LAWRY'S® Seasoned
   Pepper

9 ounces fresh cheese-filled
   tortellini *or* 8 ounces spiral
   pasta, cooked and drained
1 medium-sized red bell pepper,
   cut into thin strips
1 medium zucchini, cut into
   julienne strips
2 medium carrots, cut into
   julienne strips

In small bowl, combine all ingredients except pasta and vegetables. In medium bowl, combine pasta and vegetables; mix lightly. Add dressing; toss lightly to coat. Refrigerate at least 30 minutes. Garnish as desired.   *Makes 4 to 6 servings*

Presentation: Serve with crusty French or sourdough bread.

Brown Rice Black Bean Burrito

1 tablespoon vegetable oil
1 medium onion, chopped
2 cloves garlic, minced
1½ teaspoons chili powder
½ teaspoon ground cumin
3 cups cooked brown rice
1 (15- to 16-ounce) can black
    beans, drained and rinsed

1 (11-ounce) can corn, drained
6 (8-inch) flour tortillas
¾ cup (6 ounces) shredded
    reduced-fat Cheddar cheese
2 green onions, thinly sliced
¼ cup plain low-fat yogurt
¼ cup prepared salsa

Heat oil in large skillet over medium-high heat until hot. Add onion, garlic, chili powder and cumin. Sauté 3 to 5 minutes until onion is tender. Add rice, beans and corn; cook, stirring 2 to 3 minutes until mixture is thoroughly heated. Remove from heat.

Spoon ½ cup rice mixture down center of each tortilla. Top each evenly with cheese, green onions and yogurt. Roll up and top evenly with salsa.   *Makes 6 servings*

Favorite recipe from **USA Rice Council**

Texas Onion Pepper Tart

1 prepared crust for single-layer
   pie
1 large (14 to 16 ounces) Texas
   SPRINGSWEET® or Texas
   1015 SUPERSWEET® Onion,
   thinly sliced
1 tablespoon butter or margarine
½ cup chopped red bell pepper

¼ cup (2 ounces) diced green chiles
1 cup (4 ounces) shredded hot
   pepper Monterey Jack cheese
1 cup half-and-half
2 eggs
½ teaspoon salt
¼ teaspoon black pepper
¼ teaspoon hot pepper sauce

Press pie crust onto bottom and sides of 9-inch tart pan with removable bottom *or* into 9-inch pie plate; set aside. Sauté onion in butter over medium heat until very soft and golden brown, about 15 minutes. Add red pepper and green chiles; sauté 2 minutes longer. Refrigerate onion mixture 15 to 20 minutes. Spread onion mixture evenly over bottom of tart crust; top with cheese. Combine half-and-half, eggs, salt, black pepper and hot pepper sauce in small bowl. Pour over cheese. Bake at 375°F 45 minutes or until filling is golden brown and set.

Makes about 6 servings

Individual Tarts: Cut 8 (4-inch) circles from pie crusts. Press pie crusts onto bottoms and sides of 8 (4-inch) tart pans; set aside. Follow directions for single tart, dividing mixtures evenly over each tart crust. Bake at 375°F 30 to 35 minutes or until filling is golden brown and set.

Makes 8 (4-inch) tarts

Lentils, Olives and Feta

3 cups vegetable broth
1¾ cups (12 ounces) lentils, rinsed
and drained
1 clove garlic, minced
½ teaspoon dried basil
Mint Dressing (recipe follows)
4 cups spinach leaves, rinsed and
crisped, divided

1 cup California ripe olives, sliced
⅓ cup thinly sliced green onions
½ cup crumbled feta cheese
Mint sprigs (optional)

Bring broth to a boil. Stir in lentils, garlic and basil. Reduce heat to low; cover and simmer until lentils are tender to bite, about 30 minutes. While lentils are cooking, prepare Mint Dressing and set aside. Finely shred 2 cups spinach leaves; cover and set aside. Remove pan from heat and drain lentils, if necessary. Gently stir in olives, shredded spinach and onions. Spoon lentil mixture over remaining 2 cups spinach leaves on platter and sprinkle with cheese. Drizzle with Mint Dressing and garnish with mint sprigs, if desired.

Makes about 8 cups

Mint Dressing: Beat to blend ⅓ cup lemon juice, 3 tablespoons olive oil, 2 teaspoons honey and ⅛ teaspoon *each* salt and pepper. Just before serving, stir in 3 tablespoons chopped fresh mint.

Prep Time: About 20 minutes   **Cook Time:** About 35 minutes

Favorite recipe from **California Olive Industry**

Fresh Pepper Pasta Salad

5 tablespoons olive oil, divided
4 large red or yellow bell peppers, thinly sliced, divided
2 cloves garlic, cut crosswise into thin slices
3 tablespoons balsamic vinegar
½ teaspoon salt
½ teaspoon ground black pepper
8 ounces rotelle or armoniche pasta

¾ cup fresh basil leaves, stemmed and washed
1½ cups canned chick-peas, drained and rinsed
½ cup shredded Parmesan cheese
⅓ cup chopped walnuts
¼ cup sliced green olives (optional)

Heat 2 tablespoons oil in large nonstick skillet over medium heat. Add half of bell pepper strips and garlic; cook and stir 2 minutes. Cover; cook 10 minutes or until very soft, stirring occasionally. Place cooked peppers in food processor or blender. Add remaining 3 tablespoons oil, vinegar, salt and black pepper; process until smooth. Cool.

Cook pasta according to package directions. Drain and place in large bowl. Add remaining bell pepper strips and dressing; toss to coat. Cool slightly.

Stack some basil leaves; roll up. Slice roll into ¼-inch-thick slices; separate into strips. Repeat with remaining leaves. Add basil, chick-peas, cheese, walnuts and olives, if desired, to pasta mixture; toss to blend. Serve at room temperature or chilled.

Makes 8 cups

Fresh Pepper Pasta Salad

Black-Eyed Pea, Artichoke and Mozzarella Salad

4 medium artichokes
Juice of 2 lemons
Water
1 tablespoon olive oil
2 cups canned black-eyed peas,
    drained and rinsed
6 ounces part-skim mozzarella
    cheese, cut into $\frac{1}{2}$-inch cubes

1 cup celery slices
$\frac{3}{4}$ cup finely diced red onion
$\frac{1}{2}$ jar (4 ounces) whole pimiento,
    juice reserved and cut into
    $\frac{1}{4}$-inch squares
Herbed Vinaigrette (recipe
    follows)
Bibb lettuce leaves

Remove dark outer leaves of artichokes until leaves are pale green. Cut $1\frac{1}{2}$ inches off tops and trim stems. Cut artichokes lengthwise into quarters. Combine lemon juice and water in medium bowl. Place quarters in lemon water. Remove small heart leaves from centers; discard. Scoop out fuzzy chokes; discard. Cut artichoke quarters lengthwise into thin slices.

Heat olive oil in large skillet over medium heat until hot. Add artichokes; discard lemon water. Cook 5 to 7 minutes or until tender and lightly browned. Cool and place in large bowl. Add peas, cheese, celery, onion, pimiento and 1 tablespoon pimiento liquid.

Prepare Herbed Vinaigrette. Pour vinaigrette over artichoke mixture; toss gently. Cover; refrigerate 4 hours, tossing twice. Serve chilled or at room temperature over lettuce leaves.   *Makes about 4 (2-cup) servings*

Herbed Vinaigrette

$\frac{1}{3}$ cup olive oil
2 tablespoons minced fresh basil
2 tablespoons minced fresh
    oregano

2 tablespoons lemon juice
1 tablespoon balsamic vinegar
1 teaspoon Dijon mustard
$\frac{1}{2}$ teaspoon ground black pepper

Whisk all ingredients in small bowl until blended.   *Makes about 1 cup*

Black-Eyed Pea, Artichoke and Mozzarella Salad

Rice Cakes with Mushroom Walnut Ragoût

Rice Cakes with Mushroom Walnut Ragoût

⅔ cup arborio rice
1 egg
1 egg white
½ cup grated Parmesan cheese
3 tablespoons minced green
    onions
1 ounce dried porcini mushrooms
1 cup boiling water
1 tablespoon olive oil
1 medium onion, sliced
2 cloves garlic, minced

8 ounces button mushrooms,
    sliced
1 teaspoon dried oregano
1 can (14½ ounces) tomato
    wedges, undrained
2 teaspoons lemon juice
¼ teaspoon salt
½ teaspoon ground black pepper
⅓ cup chopped toasted walnuts
    Asiago or Parmesan cheese
    shavings

Cook rice according to package directions. Cool.

Preheat oven to 350°F. Spray 8-inch square baking pan with nonstick cooking spray. Beat egg and egg white in medium bowl until blended. Add rice, grated Parmesan and green onions; mix well. Press into prepared pan. Bake 20 to 25 minutes or until set.

Soak dried mushrooms in boiling water in small bowl 15 to 20 minutes or until soft. Drain, reserving liquid. Chop mushrooms. Heat oil in large nonstick skillet over medium heat until hot. Add onion and garlic; cook and stir 5 minutes. Add fresh mushrooms, dried mushrooms and oregano; cook and stir 5 minutes or until fresh mushrooms are tender.

Drain tomatoes, reserving ¼ cup juice. Add tomatoes, reserved juice, reserved mushroom liquid, lemon juice, salt and pepper to skillet. Bring to a boil. Reduce heat to low. Simmer, uncovered, 15 minutes or until sauce thickens. Stir in walnuts.

Cut rice cakes into 8 rectangles. Top with ragoût; sprinkle cheese over ragoût.

Makes 4 servings

Three-Bean Pasta

- 1 pound medium or wide egg noodles
- 1 (15-ounce) can kidney beans, rinsed and drained
- 1 (15-ounce) can chick-peas, rinsed and drained
- 1 cup frozen green beans, thawed
- 1 small red onion, chopped
- 1 red bell pepper, seeds and ribs removed, chopped
- 3 tablespoons chopped fresh parsley
- 3 tablespoons Dijon mustard
- 3 tablespoons red wine vinegar
- 2 tablespoons vegetable oil

Prepare pasta according to package directions; drain. Rinse under cold water and drain again. In large bowl, stir together pasta, kidney beans, chick-peas, green beans, onion and bell pepper. In small bowl, stir together remaining ingredients. Toss pasta with dressing and serve.

Makes 4 servings

Favorite recipe from **National Pasta Association**

Grilled Portobello & Pepper Wraps

1 container (8 ounces) sour cream
1 teaspoon dried dill weed
1 teaspoon onion powder
2 tablespoons vegetable oil
1 large clove garlic, minced
2 portobello mushrooms, stems removed

1 large green bell pepper, quartered
1 large red bell pepper, quartered
Salt and black pepper
6 (6-inch) flour tortillas, warmed

1. Prepare barbecue grill for direct cooking.

2. Combine sour cream, dill and onion powder in small bowl; set aside. Combine oil and garlic in another small bowl; set aside.

3. Spray barbecue grid with nonstick cooking spray. Place mushrooms and bell peppers on prepared grid. Brush lightly with oil mixture; season with salt and black pepper to taste.

4. Grill on covered grill over medium-hot coals 10 minutes or until bell peppers are crisp-tender, turning halfway through grilling time. Remove mushrooms and peppers to cutting board; cut into 1-inch slices.

5. Place on serving platter. Serve with sour cream mixture and tortillas.

Makes 4 to 6 servings

Prep and Cook Time: 18 minutes

Serving Suggestion: Serve with spicy refried beans and salsa.

Grilled Portobello & Pepper Wraps

Dilled Ranch Wild Rice Salad

3½ cups cooked wild rice
1 package (1 pound) frozen
    broccoli, cauliflower, pea pods
    and yellow peppers, thawed
    and drained
1 cup chopped green onions
½ cup pine nuts or slivered
    almonds, toasted
½ cup grated Parmesan cheese

½ cup olive oil
¼ cup chopped fresh dill or to
    taste
¼ cup chopped red bell pepper
3 tablespoons minced fresh chives
1 package (1 ounce) ranch salad
    dressing mix
Freshly ground black pepper
Radicchio or red cabbage leaves

Chop vegetables into small pieces. In large bowl, mix wild rice, vegetables, onions, nuts, cheese, oil, dill, red pepper, chives, ranch mix and black pepper; combine well. Chill 1 hour. Serve on radicchio or cabbage leaves.   *Makes 8 to 10 servings*

Variation: Add 4-ounce package crumbled blue cheese.

Favorite recipe from **Minnesota Cultivated Wild Rice Council**

Penne Pasta and Roasted Vegetable Salad

6 carrots (about ⅔ pound), cut
    diagonally in ¼-inch pieces
⅓ cup olive oil, divided
1 teaspoon sugar
3 cups small cauliflowerets
8 ounces uncooked penne pasta
2 tablespoons white wine vinegar

½ teaspoon curry powder
¼ teaspoon salt
⅛ teaspoon ground red pepper
¼ cup chopped fresh chives
3 tablespoons slivered almonds,
    toasted
4 ounces goat cheese, crumbled

Penne Pasta and Roasted Vegetable Salad

Preheat oven to 400°F. Place carrots in large bowl. Add 2 teaspoons oil and sugar; toss until carrots are coated with oil. Spread in single layer on nonstick baking sheet. Toss cauliflower with 2 teaspoons oil in same bowl; spread cauliflower in single layer on second nonstick baking sheet. Bake 20 minutes or just until vegetables are tender and beginning to brown, rotating baking sheets after 10 minutes. Place vegetables in large bowl.

Meanwhile, cook penne according to package directions. Drain and add to vegetables in bowl.

Combine remaining ¼ cup oil, vinegar, curry powder, salt and red pepper in small bowl. Pour over penne mixture. Add chives and almonds; toss gently. Let cool to room temperature. Sprinkle with cheese. *Makes 4 (2-cup) servings*

Brown Rice Primavera

1¼ cups water
½ cup long-grain brown rice, uncooked
½ teaspoon salt
¼ teaspoon dried basil leaves, crumbled
⅛ teaspoon black pepper
1 tablespoon CRISCO® Oil
1 carrot, peeled, diced (about ½ cup)

1 small zucchini, diced (about ½ cup)
1 small yellow squash, diced (about ½ cup)
1 small red bell pepper, seeded, diced (about ½ cup)
2 green onions, thinly sliced (about ¼ cup)

1. Bring water to a boil in medium saucepan on medium heat. Add rice, salt, basil and black pepper. Reduce heat to low. Cover; simmer 40 to 45 minutes or until water is absorbed and rice is tender.

2. Heat Crisco® Oil in large skillet on medium-high heat. Add carrot, zucchini, yellow squash, red pepper and green onions. Cook and stir 5 to 7 minutes or until tender.

3. Transfer rice to serving bowl. Add vegetables; toss to combine. Serve immediately.

Makes 4 servings

Curried Vegetables

1 package (7.2 ounces) RICE-A-RONI® Herb & Butter
⅓ cup raisins
2 tablespoons margarine or butter
1 medium onion, chopped
2 cloves garlic, minced
1 tablespoon all-purpose flour
2 teaspoons curry powder

1 package (16 ounces) frozen mixed carrot, broccoli and red pepper vegetable medley
1 cup water
½ teaspoon salt (optional)
¼ cup slivered almonds, toasted (optional)

1. Prepare Rice-A-Roni® Mix as package directs, adding raisins with contents of seasoning packet.

2. In 3-quart saucepan, melt margarine over medium heat. Add onion and garlic; sauté 3 to 4 minutes. Add flour and curry powder; cook 30 seconds, stirring frequently.

3. Add frozen vegetables, water and salt. Cover; bring to a boil over high heat. Reduce heat and continue cooking 10 minutes, stirring occasionally.

4. Serve rice topped with vegetable mixture; sprinkle with almonds.

Makes 4 servings

Serving Suggestion: Serve with 1 cup nonfat or low-fat yogurt per serving.

Baja Style Chili Pepper Penne Salad

1 (12-ounce) package PASTA
    LABELLA® Chili Pepper
    Penne Rigate
¾ cup julienned carrots
¾ cup julienned red onion
¾ cup diced seeded peeled
    cucumber
¾ cup chopped avocado
¼ cup chopped cilantro

⅓ cup extra-virgin olive oil
¼ cup white wine vinegar
¼ cup fresh lime juice
1 teaspoon dried oregano leaves
½ teaspoon onion powder
½ teaspoon garlic powder
    Salt and pepper, to taste
⅓ cup shredded Romano cheese

Cook pasta according to package directions. When pasta is al dente, put in colander and rinse with cold water until cool to touch. Drain pasta well and put in large mixing bowl. Add carrots, onion, cucumber, avocado and cilantro to pasta. In small mixing bowl, whisk together olive oil, vinegar, lime juice and all remaining spices. Pour dressing over pasta mixture. Toss well. Sprinkle with Romano cheese and serve.

Makes 4 servings

Pasta Pesto Salad

PASTA SALAD

8 ounces three-color rotini pasta (corkscrews)

3 small bell peppers (1 green, 1 red and 1 yellow), seeded and cut into thin strips

1 pint cherry tomatoes, stemmed and halved (2 cups)

6 ounces (1 block) ALPINE LACE® Fat Free Pasteurized Process Skim Milk Cheese Product—For Mozzarella Lovers, cut into ½-inch cubes (1½ cups)

1 cup thin carrot circles

1 cup thin strips red onion

1 cup slivered fresh basil leaves

SPICY DRESSING

½ cup (2 ounces) shredded ALPINE LACE® Fat Free Pasteurized Process Skim Milk Cheese Product—For Parmesan Lovers

⅓ cup firmly packed fresh parsley

⅓ cup extra virgin olive oil

⅓ cup red wine vinegar

2 large cloves garlic

1 tablespoon whole-grain Dijon mustard

¾ teaspoon freshly ground black pepper

½ teaspoon salt

1. To make the Pasta Salad: Cook the pasta according to package directions until al dente. Drain in a colander, rinse under cold water and drain again. Place the pasta in a large shallow pasta bowl and toss with the remaining salad ingredients.

2. To make the Spicy Dressing: In a food processor or blender, process all of the dressing ingredients for 30 seconds or until well blended.

3. Drizzle the dressing on the salad and toss to mix thoroughly. Cover with plastic wrap and refrigerate for 1 hour so that the flavors can blend, or let stand at room temperature for 1 hour.

Makes 6 main-dish servings

Pasta Pesto Salad

Casseroles & One–Dish Meals

Broccoli Lasagna Bianca

1 (15- to 16-ounce) container
    fat-free ricotta cheese
1 cup EGG BEATERS® Healthy
    Real Egg Product
1 tablespoon minced basil *or*
    1 teaspoon dried basil leaves
½ cup chopped onion
1 clove garlic, minced
2 tablespoons margarine
¼ cup all-purpose flour
2 cups skim milk

2 (10-ounce) packages frozen
    chopped broccoli, thawed and
    well drained
1 cup (4 ounces) shredded part-
    skim mozzarella cheese
9 lasagna noodles, cooked and
    drained
1 small tomato, chopped
2 tablespoons grated Parmesan
    cheese
Fresh basil leaves, for garnish

In medium bowl, combine ricotta cheese, Egg Beaters® and minced basil; set aside. In large saucepan, over medium heat, sauté onion and garlic in margarine until tender-crisp. Stir in flour; cook for 1 minute. Gradually stir in milk; cook, stirring until mixture thickens and begins to boil. Remove from heat; stir in broccoli and mozzarella cheese.

In lightly greased 13×9×2-inch baking dish, place 3 lasagna noodles; top with ⅓ each ricotta and broccoli mixtures. Repeat layers 2 more times. Top with tomato; sprinkle with Parmesan cheese. Bake at 350°F for 1 hour or until set. Let stand 10 minutes before serving. Garnish with basil leaves. *Makes 8 servings*

Prep Time: 20 minutes   **Cook Time:** 90 minutes

Broccoli Lasagna Bianca

Bean and Vegetable Burrito

Bean and Vegetable Burritos

1 tablespoon olive oil
1 medium onion, thinly sliced
1 jalapeño pepper, seeded, minced
1 tablespoon chili powder
3 cloves garlic, minced
2 teaspoons dried oregano leaves, crushed
1 teaspoon ground cumin
1 large sweet potato, baked, cooled, peeled and diced *or* 1 can (16 ounces) yams in syrup, drained, rinsed and diced

1 can (15 ounces) black beans or pinto beans, drained, rinsed
1 cup frozen whole kernel corn, thawed, drained
1 green bell pepper, chopped
2 tablespoons lime juice
¾ cup (3 ounces) shredded reduced-fat Monterey Jack cheese
4 flour tortillas (10 inches)
Sour cream (optional)

Preheat oven to 350°F. Heat oil over medium-high heat in large saucepan or Dutch oven. Add onion and cook 10 minutes or until golden, stirring often. Add jalapeño, chili powder, garlic, oregano and cumin; stir 1 minute more. Add 1 tablespoon water and stir; remove from heat. Stir in sweet potato, beans, corn, pepper and lime juice.

Spoon 2 tablespoons cheese in center of each tortilla. Top with 1 cup filling. Fold bottom edge of tortilla up over filling; fold in sides, then roll up to completely enclose filling. Place burritos seam side down on baking sheet. Cover with foil and bake 30 minutes or until heated through. Serve with sour cream, if desired.   *Makes 4 servings*

Viking Vegetable Cassoulet

4 cups sliced mushrooms
2 tablespoons olive oil
2 large onions, thickly sliced
1 large clove garlic, minced
2 medium zucchini, cut into
    1-inch pieces
1½ cups sliced yellow squash
2 cans (16 ounces each) white
    beans, drained

1 can (14½ ounces) plum
    tomatoes, cut up, with juice
⅓ cup chopped parsley
1 teaspoon dried basil, crushed
½ teaspoon dried oregano, crushed
½ cup bread crumbs
1 teaspoon butter, melted
2 cups (8 ounces) shredded
    JARLSBERG Cheese

Preheat oven to 350°F. In large, deep skillet, brown mushrooms in oil. Add onions and garlic; sauté 5 minutes. Add zucchini and squash; sauté until vegetables are crisp-tender. Stir in beans, tomatoes, parsley, basil and oregano.

Spoon into 2-quart baking dish. Combine bread crumbs and butter in small bowl. Sprinkle bread crumbs around edge. Bake at 350°F 20 minutes. Top with cheese and bake 20 minutes longer.   *Makes 6 to 8 servings*

Barley, Bean and Corn Frittata

2 cups water
½ cup barley
¾ teaspoon salt, divided
2 teaspoons olive oil
1 can (15 ounces) black beans,
    drained and rinsed
2 cups (8 ounces) shredded
    Cheddar cheese, divided
¾ cup fresh cut corn*

½ cup chopped green bell pepper
¼ cup chopped cilantro
7 eggs *or* 1¾ cups egg substitute
1 cup cottage cheese
½ teaspoon ground red pepper
1 cup medium fresh or prepared
    salsa
Sour cream for garnish

Bring water to a boil in medium saucepan over high heat. Add barley and ¼ teaspoon salt. Reduce heat to low. Cover and simmer 40 to 45 minutes or until tender. Let stand, covered, 5 minutes. Drain.

Preheat oven to 400°F. Brush 10-inch cast iron or ovenproof skillet with olive oil. Layer barley, beans, 1 cup Cheddar cheese, corn, bell pepper and cilantro in skillet. Process eggs, cottage cheese, remaining ½ teaspoon salt and ground red pepper in blender or food processor just until smooth. Carefully pour egg mixture over layers.

Bake 30 minutes or until egg mixture is set. Sprinkle with remaining 1 cup Cheddar cheese. Bake 5 minutes or until cheese is melted. Spoon salsa evenly over top. Let stand 5 minutes before cutting into wedges. Garnish, if desired.   *Makes 6 to 8 servings*

*Frozen corn can be substituted for fresh; thaw before using.

Barley, Bean and Corn Frittata

Eggplant Bulgur Casserole

1 cup bulgur wheat
½ cup chopped green pepper
¼ cup chopped onion
¼ cup butter
4 cups cubed peeled eggplant
1 (15-ounce) can tomato sauce
1 (14½-ounce) can tomatoes,
    undrained, cut up
½ cup cold water
½ teaspoon dried oregano leaves,
    crushed
1 (8-ounce) package
    PHILADELPHIA BRAND®
    Cream Cheese, softened
1 egg
    KRAFT® 100% Grated
    Parmesan Cheese

• Preheat oven to 350°F.

• Sauté bulgur wheat, pepper and onion in butter in large skillet until vegetables are tender.

• Stir in eggplant, tomato sauce, tomatoes, water and oregano. Cover; simmer 15 to 20 minutes or until eggplant is tender, stirring occasionally.

• Beat cream cheese and egg in small mixing bowl at medium speed with electric mixer until well blended.

• Place half of vegetable mixture in 1½-quart baking dish or casserole; top with cream cheese mixture and remaining vegetable mixture. Cover.

• Bake 15 minutes. Remove cover; sprinkle with Parmesan cheese. Continue baking 10 minutes or until thoroughly heated.   *Makes 8 to 10 servings*

Prep Time: 30 minutes   **Cook Time:** 25 minutes

Tex-Mex Barley Bake

1 small onion, chopped
1 small green bell pepper, diced
1 tablespoon vegetable oil
1 clove garlic, chopped
2 cups medium pearled barley,
    cooked
3 cups cooked pinto beans
1 can (15 ounces) Mexican-style
    stewed tomatoes, drained,
    chopped

1 cup sliced pitted ripe olives
1½ teaspoons chili powder
½ teaspoon salt
½ teaspoon ground cumin
1 cup (4 ounces) shredded
    Cheddar cheese

Cook and stir onion and green pepper in oil over medium-low heat 10 minutes. Add garlic. Cook and stir 1 minute. Add remaining ingredients except cheese. Pour into 6 lightly greased individual casseroles. Bake in preheated 350°F oven 35 to 40 minutes or until hot and bubbly. Stir in cheese. Bake 10 minutes or until cheese is melted.

Makes 6 servings

Favorite recipe from **North Dakota Barley Council**

Onion and Roasted Pepper Tamale Pie with Salsa Colorado

Onion and Roasted Pepper Tamale Pie with Salsa Colorado

....

2½ cups all-purpose flour
  1 cup masa harina de maiz*
  ½ teaspoon salt
  ½ pound butter, chilled and cut
     into small pieces
8 to 10 tablespoons ice water
3 medium onions, thinly sliced
1 tablespoon olive oil
2 (4-ounce) cans whole green
    chiles, dried and sliced
2 whole roasted red peppers,
    dried and cut into strips

1 cup (4 ounces) shredded
    Monterey Jack cheese
1 teaspoon ground cumin
1 teaspoon ground coriander
½ teaspoon dry mustard
¼ teaspoon salt
¼ teaspoon black pepper
4 eggs
1 cup sour cream
  Salsa Colorado (recipe follows)

Cornmeal may be substituted for masa harina de maiz.

260

Preheat oven to 400°F. Combine flour, masa harina de maiz and salt in food processor fitted with knife blade; cover and process until blended. Sprinkle butter evenly over flour mixture; cover and process until mixture resembles coarse meal. Pour ice water evenly over mixture; cover and pulse until dough holds together. Form dough into a ball; press evenly on bottom and halfway up sides of 10×3-inch springform pan. Bake 15 minutes. Let cool. *Reduce oven temperature to 325°.*

Sauté onions in oil until lightly browned and tender. Arrange chiles and red peppers on bottom of crust. Sprinkle with cheese. Combine cumin, coriander, mustard, salt and black pepper; sprinkle half of cumin mixture evenly over cheese. Arrange onions on top; sprinkle with remaining cumin mixture. Beat eggs and sour cream; pour evenly over onions. Bake 45 to 50 minutes or until set. Let cool 15 minutes before cutting. Serve with Salsa Colorado.

Makes 8 to 10 servings

Salsa Colorado

1 (16-ounce) can tomato purée
½ cup water
½ (7-ounce) can chipotle peppers
   in adobo sauce

2 medium onions, chopped
4 cloves garlic, crushed
¼ teaspoon salt

Combine all ingredients in medium saucepan; bring to a boil. Cover; reduce heat and simmer 20 minutes. Purée in blender or food processor bowl. Serve with Tamale Pie.

Makes about 3 cups

Favorite recipe from **National Onion Association**

Three Cheese Vegetable Lasagna

1 teaspoon olive oil
1 large onion, chopped
3 cloves garlic, minced
1 can (28 ounces) no-salt-added
   tomato purée
1 can (14½ ounces) no-salt-added
   tomatoes, undrained and
   chopped
2 cups sliced fresh mushrooms
1 medium zucchini, finely
   chopped
1 large green bell pepper, chopped
2 teaspoons dried basil leaves,
   crushed
1 teaspoon *each* salt and sugar
   (optional)
½ teaspoon red pepper flakes
½ teaspoon dried oregano leaves,
   crushed
2 cups (15 ounces) SARGENTO®
   Light Ricotta Cheese
1 package (10 ounces) frozen
   chopped spinach, thawed and
   squeezed dry
2 egg whites
2 tablespoons (½ ounce)
   SARGENTO® Fancy
   Shredded Parmesan Cheese
8 ounces lasagna noodles, cooked
   without oil or salt
¾ cup (3 ounces) *each*
   SARGENTO® Light Fancy
   Shredded Mozzarella and
   Mild Cheddar Cheese,
   divided

Preheat oven to 375°F. Spray large skillet with nonstick vegetable spray. Heat oil in large skillet over medium heat; add onion and garlic. Cook until tender, stirring occasionally. Add tomato purée, tomatoes and liquid, mushrooms, zucchini, bell pepper, basil, salt, sugar, pepper flakes and oregano. Bring to a boil; reduce heat to low. Cover and simmer 10 minutes or until vegetables are crisp-tender. Combine ricotta cheese, spinach, egg whites and Parmesan cheese in medium bowl; mix well. Spread 1 cup sauce in bottom of 13×9-inch baking dish. Layer 3 lasagna noodles over sauce. Top with half the ricotta cheese mixture and 2 cups remaining sauce. Repeat layering with 3 more lasagna noodles, remaining ricotta mixture and 2 cups sauce. Combine mozzarella and Cheddar cheeses. Sprinkle ¾ cup mozzarella cheese mixture over sauce. Top with remaining lasagna noodles and sauce. Cover with foil; bake 30 minutes. Uncover; bake 15 minutes more. Sprinkle with remaining ¾ cup cheese mixture. Let stand 10 minutes before serving. *Makes 10 servings*

Three Cheese Vegetable Lasagna

Torta Rustica

1 package active dry yeast
1 teaspoon sugar
1 cup warm water (105° to 115°F)
3 cups plus 2 tablespoons
    all-purpose flour, divided
1½ teaspoons salt, divided
3 tablespoons vegetable oil,
    divided
1½ teaspoons dried basil leaves,
    divided
1½ cups chopped onions
1 cup chopped carrots
2 cloves garlic, minced
2 medium zucchini, cubed

½ pound button mushrooms, sliced
1 can (16 ounces) whole tomatoes,
    undrained and chopped
1 can (15 ounces) artichoke
    hearts, drained and cut into
    halves
1 medium red bell pepper, seeded
    and cut into 1-inch squares
½ teaspoon dried oregano leaves
¼ teaspoon ground black pepper
2 cups (8 ounces) shredded
    provolone or mozzarella
    cheese

Sprinkle yeast and sugar over warm water in small bowl; stir until yeast is dissolved. Let stand 5 minutes or until mixture is bubbly. Combine 3 cups flour and 1 teaspoon salt in food processor. With food processor running, add yeast mixture, 2 tablespoons oil and ½ teaspoon basil. Process until mixture forms dough that leaves side of bowl, adding additional water or flour 1 tablespoon at a time if necessary. *Dough will be sticky.* Place dough in large greased bowl; turn dough over. Cover with towel; let rise in warm place about 1 hour or until doubled in bulk.

Heat remaining 1 tablespoon oil in large saucepan over medium heat until hot. Add onions, carrots and garlic; cook and stir 5 minutes or until onions are tender. Stir in zucchini, mushrooms, tomatoes, artichoke hearts, bell pepper, remaining 1 teaspoon basil, oregano, remaining ½ teaspoon salt and black pepper. Bring to a boil over high heat. Reduce heat to low. Cover and simmer 10 minutes.

Punch down dough. Knead dough on lightly floured surface 1 minute. Cover with towel; let rest 10 minutes.

Torta Rustica

Preheat oven to 400°F. Grease 2-quart casserole or soufflé dish. Roll two thirds of dough on lightly floured surface to ½-inch thickness. Ease dough into casserole, allowing dough to extend 1 inch over edge. Spoon half of vegetable mixture into casserole. Sprinkle with 1 cup cheese. Repeat layers. Roll remaining dough on lightly floured surface into circle 2 inches larger than top of casserole; cut decorative designs in top of dough with paring knife. Place dough over filling. Fold edges of top dough over bottom dough; pinch with fingertips to seal edges.

Bake 30 to 35 minutes or until crust is golden brown, covering edge of dough with foil if necessary to prevent overbrowning. *Makes 6 servings*

Veggie Jack Burrito

1 tablespoon vegetable oil
2 cups sliced mushrooms
2 cups broccoli florets
1 red onion, sliced
1 medium carrot, shredded
1 medium zucchini, shredded
¼ cup sliced green onions
1 clove garlic, minced

1 cup green salsa
3 cups (12 ounces) shredded
    Wisconsin Monterey Jack
    Cheese or Mexican cheese
    blend, divided
8 flour tortillas
    Additional green or red salsa

In 10-inch skillet heat oil until hot; add vegetables and garlic. Cook over medium-high heat until slightly tender, 5 to 7 minutes. Stir in 1 cup salsa. Place vegetable mixture and 2 cups cheese on tortillas. Fold burrito- or taco-style; place in 12×8-inch baking dish. Cover with foil. Bake at 400°F for 15 to 20 minutes or until heated through. Top with salsa and remaining 1 cup cheese. Continue baking 5 to 7 minutes or until cheese is melted.

Makes 8 burritos

Favorite recipe from **Wisconsin Milk Marketing Board**

Wild Rice Pesto Tart

1 package (6½ ounces) pizza
    crust mix
1¾ cups cooked wild rice, divided
1 tablespoon cornmeal
1 tablespoon butter
1 tablespoon vegetable oil
2 medium onions, thinly sliced
½ cup prepared pesto sauce

1 jar (4½ ounces) sliced
    mushrooms, drained
1 cup sugar snap peas, halved
    horizontally
2 cups mozzarella cheese, divided
1 small tomato, thinly sliced
½ teaspoon seasoned salt

Preheat oven to 375°F. Prepare crust mix according to package directions; blend in 1¼ cups wild rice. Let stand 5 minutes. Sprinkle cornmeal on greased 15×10-inch jelly-roll pan; press dough in pan. Bake 12 minutes; set aside.

Meanwhile, in large skillet melt butter; add oil and onions. Cook over medium-low heat until golden brown, stirring often. Spread pesto on crust; layer mushrooms, remaining ½ cup wild rice, peas, 1 cup cheese, tomato and onions. Sprinkle with seasoned salt and remaining 1 cup cheese. Bake 12 to 15 minutes, until cheese is lightly browned.

Makes 4 main-dish servings

Favorite recipe from **Minnesota Cultivated Wild Rice Council**

Mexicali Wild Rice Casserole

2 cups cooked wild rice
1 can (about 17 ounces) whole kernel corn, drained
1 can (about 4 ounces) chopped or diced green chilies, drained

2 cups (16 ounces) chunky, mild salsa (use medium for hotter flavor)
1 cup grated Cheddar or Monterey Jack cheese
Corn or tortilla chips

Combine wild rice with corn and chilies; spread in lightly oiled 11×7-inch casserole. Spread salsa over mixture and sprinkle with cheese. Cover and heat at 350°F about 30 minutes. Serve with a basket of corn or tortilla chips. *Makes 4 servings*

Serving Suggestion: To serve individual servings, heat casserole ingredients without cheese and spoon over corn or tortilla chips on individual plates; sprinkle cheese on top and, if desired, heat either under a broiler or in a microwave to melt cheese.

Favorite recipe from **Minnesota Cultivated Wild Rice Council**

Vegetable-Enchilada Casserole

1 small eggplant, peeled and
   quartered
1 medium zucchini
½ pound fresh mushrooms
   Nonstick cooking spray
½ cup chopped green onions,
   divided
2 cloves garlic, minced
1 cup GUILTLESS GOURMET®
   Salsa (mild, medium or hot)

6 ounces GUILTLESS
   GOURMET® Baked Tortilla
   Chips (yellow or white corn),
   divided
¾ cup GUILTLESS GOURMET®
   Nacho Dip (mild or spicy)
2½ cups shredded lettuce
1 medium tomato, chopped
3 tablespoons low fat sour cream

Slice eggplant, zucchini and mushrooms; set aside. Coat large nonstick skillet with cooking spray. Heat over medium-high heat until hot. Add reserved vegetables, ¼ cup onions and garlic; cover and cook 5 minutes or until tender, stirring occasionally. Stir in salsa. Reduce heat to low; cover and simmer 30 minutes.

Preheat oven to 350°F. To assemble casserole, coat 12×8-inch baking dish with cooking spray. Arrange half the tortilla chips in dish and top with vegetable mixture. Cover; bake 20 to 30 minutes or until heated through. Coarsely crush remaining tortilla chips; sprinkle over vegetable mixture. Spoon nacho dip over crushed chips. Bake, uncovered, 5 minutes more or until chips are crisp and lightly browned.

To serve, divide lettuce among 8 individual serving plates or spread on serving platter. Spoon casserole over lettuce. Sprinkle with chopped tomato and remaining ¼ cup onions. Dollop with sour cream. *Makes 8 servings*

Vegetable-Enchilada Casserole

Stuffed Jumbo Shells with Garlic Vegetables

Stuffed Jumbo Shells with Garlic Vegetables

Garlic Vegetables (recipe follows)
12 jumbo pasta shells
2 cups ricotta cheese
1 package (10 ounces) frozen
    chopped spinach, thawed and
    squeezed dry
¼ cup plus 2 tablespoons grated
    Parmesan cheese, divided

2 cloves garlic, minced
¾ teaspoon dried marjoram leaves
½ to 1 teaspoon salt
½ teaspoon dried basil leaves
½ teaspoon ground black pepper
¼ teaspoon dried thyme leaves

Prepare Garlic Vegetables. Spoon into 10-inch round baking dish.

Preheat oven to 350°F. Cook shells according to package directions. Drain and cool.

Combine ricotta, spinach, ¼ cup Parmesan cheese, garlic, marjoram, salt, basil, pepper and thyme in medium bowl. Spoon cheese mixture into shells. Arrange shells on top of Garlic Vegetables. Carefully spoon sauce from vegetables over shells.

Bake, loosely covered with foil, 35 to 40 minutes or until stuffed shells are heated through. Sprinkle remaining 2 tablespoons Parmesan cheese over shells.

Makes 4 servings

Garlic Vegetables

2 tablespoons olive oil, divided	1 medium yellow summer squash
1 large head garlic, peeled and coarsely chopped	2 large carrots, cut diagonally into ¼-inch slices
⅓ cup sun-dried tomatoes (not packed in oil)	2 tablespoons minced fresh parsley
2 tablespoons all-purpose flour	Salt
1¼ cups canned vegetable broth	Ground black pepper
1 medium zucchini	

Heat 1 tablespoon oil in small skillet over medium heat until hot. Add garlic; cook and stir 2 to 3 minutes. Reduce heat to low and cook about 15 minutes or until garlic is golden brown, stirring frequently. Add tomatoes; cook over medium heat 2 minutes. Stir in flour. Cook and stir 2 minutes. Gradually stir in broth. Cook 1 to 2 minutes or until sauce thickens, stirring constantly.

Cut zucchini and squash lengthwise into halves. Cut each half into crosswise slices.

Heat remaining 1 tablespoon oil in medium skillet over medium heat until hot. Add carrots; cook and stir 2 minutes. Add zucchini and squash; cook and stir 3 minutes or until crisp-tender. Remove from heat. Stir garlic mixture and parsley into carrot mixture in skillet. Season to taste with salt and pepper.

Makes 2 cups

Roasted Vegetable Lasagna

12 pieces lasagna, uncooked
8 ounces mushrooms, halved
2 zucchini or yellow squash, halved lengthwise and cut crosswise into $\frac{1}{2}$-inch pieces
2 yellow or red bell peppers, cut into 1-inch pieces
1 small red onion, cut into 1-inch pieces
2 tablespoons balsamic vinegar
1 teaspoon olive or vegetable oil
2 cloves garlic, minced
$\frac{1}{2}$ teaspoon dried rosemary, crushed
1 (26-ounce) jar fat-free spaghetti sauce
1 (15-ounce) container part-skim ricotta cheese
1 (10-ounce) package frozen chopped spinach, thawed, squeezed dry
1 large egg white
$\frac{1}{4}$ teaspoon red pepper flakes
1 cup shredded part-skim mozzarella cheese
$\frac{1}{4}$ cup grated Parmesan cheese

Prepare lasagna according to package directions. Preheat oven to 425°F. Coat shallow roasting pan with nonstick cooking spray. Add mushrooms, squash, bell peppers and onion. In small dish, combine vinegar, oil, garlic and rosemary; brush evenly over vegetables. Bake vegetables 15 minutes; stir. Continue baking 8 to 10 minutes or until vegetables are browned and tender. *Reduce oven temperature to 375°F.* Spoon 1 cup spaghetti sauce over bottom of 13×9-inch baking dish. Arrange 4 pieces of lasagna (3 lengthwise, 1 crosswise) over sauce. Cover lasagna with 1 cup sauce. In medium bowl, combine ricotta cheese, spinach, egg white and hot red pepper flakes. Drop half of cheese mixture by spoonfuls over sauce; arrange half of roasted vegetables between spoonfuls of cheese mixture. Arrange another 4 pieces of lasagna over cheese and vegetables, pressing lightly; top with 1 cup sauce. Repeat layering with remaining cheese, roasted vegetables, 4 pieces of lasagna and remaining sauce.

Cover lasagna with foil; bake 45 minutes. Uncover; sprinkle with mozzarella and Parmesan cheeses; continue baking, uncovered, 5 minutes or until cheeses are melted. Let stand 10 minutes before serving.

Makes 8 servings

Favorite recipe from **National Pasta Association**

Fiesta Burrito Bake

Fiesta Burrito Bake

....

1 envelope LIPTON® Recipe
   Secrets® Fiesta Herb with
   Red Pepper Soup Mix
1 can (15 ounces) refried beans
½ cup sour cream
¼ cup water

10 (6-inch) flour tortillas
1 medium tomato, coarsely
   chopped
1 cup (4 ounces) shredded
   Cheddar cheese

Preheat oven to 375°F.

In small bowl, combine Fiesta Herb with Red Pepper Soup Mix, beans, sour cream and
water. Evenly spoon bean mixture onto tortillas, then roll. In 13×9-inch baking dish
sprayed with nonstick cooking spray, arrange rolled tortillas; top with tomato, then
cheese. Bake covered 15 minutes. Remove cover and continue baking 10 minutes or
until cheese is melted and tortillas are heated through. Serve, if desired, with shredded
lettuce, sour cream and guacamole.

Makes 10 tortillas

Chile-Cheese Casserole

1½ cups light ricotta cheese
1 cup (4 ounces) shredded
    HEALTHY CHOICE® Fat
    Free Cheddar Shreds
1 (4-ounce) can chopped green
    chiles, drained
½ cup cholesterol free egg product
¼ cup chopped green onions
4 (6-inch) corn tortillas
    Vegetable cooking spray
¼ cup chopped green pepper
1 clove garlic, minced
2 (16-ounce) cans red kidney
    beans, drained and rinsed

1 (14½-ounce) can no-salt-added
    whole tomatoes, undrained
    and coarsely chopped
1 (8-ounce) can no-salt-added
    tomato sauce
2 teaspoons chili powder
½ cup (2 ounces) shredded
    HEALTHY CHOICE® Fat
    Free Cheddar Shreds
2 tablespoons chopped green
    onions

Combine first 5 ingredients in medium bowl; stir well and set aside.

Cut each tortilla into 8 wedges; place on ungreased baking sheet. Bake at 350° for 10 minutes or until crisp. Set aside.

Coat nonstick skillet with cooking spray; place over medium-high heat until hot. Add green pepper and garlic; sauté until tender. Stir in beans and next 3 ingredients; bring to a boil. Reduce heat; simmer, uncovered, 15 minutes, stirring occasionally.

Spread half of ricotta cheese mixture in 2-quart casserole coated with cooking spray; arrange 8 tortilla wedges over cheese mixture. Spread half of bean mixture evenly over wedges. Repeat layers with remaining cheese mixture, 8 tortilla wedges and remaining bean mixture.

Cover and bake at 350° for 30 minutes. Sprinkle with Cheddar shreds; bake, uncovered, additional 5 minutes or until cheese melts. Top with 2 tablespoons green onions. Serve with remaining tortilla wedges.

Makes 8 servings

Basque-Style Eggplant Casserole

6 tablespoons oil, divided
1 onion, cut into strips
2 green bell peppers, seeded and
    cut into strips
5 large mushrooms, sliced
1 rib celery, sliced diagonally
5 cloves CHRISTOPHER
    RANCH Garlic, minced
6 tomatoes, peeled and diced

Salt to taste
1 tablespoon fines herbes
2 eggs
1 tablespoon water
1 large eggplant
½ cup freshly grated Parmesan
    cheese
1 cup shredded Swiss cheese

Heat 3 tablespoons oil in large skillet; add onion, green peppers, mushrooms, celery and garlic. Sauté until tender. Add tomatoes. Bring to a boil. Add salt and fines herbes. Turn heat to low and simmer sauce for 30 minutes. Beat eggs, water and pinch of salt. Peel eggplant and slice into large slices. Dip in egg mixture and fry eggplant in skillet with remaining 3 tablespoons oil until tender. Arrange eggplant slices in large baking dish. Sprinkle with Parmesan cheese. Pour tomato sauce over top and sprinkle with Swiss cheese. Heat in 350° oven until cheese is melted. *Makes 4 servings*

Vegetable Frittata

2 tablespoons butter or margarine
1 bag (16 ounces) BIRDS EYE®
    frozen Farm Fresh Mixtures
    Broccoli, Corn and Red
    Peppers

8 eggs
½ cup water
1 tablespoon TABASCO®
    pepper sauce
¾ teaspoon salt

• Melt butter in 12-inch nonstick skillet over medium heat. Add vegetables; cook and stir 3 minutes.

• Lightly beat eggs, water, TABASCO® sauce and salt.

• Pour egg mixture over vegetables in skillet. Cover and cook 10 to 15 minutes or until eggs are set.

• To serve, cut into wedges.

Makes about 4 servings

Prep Time: 5 minutes   **Cook Time:** 20 minutes

Serving Suggestion: Serve with warm crusty bread and a green salad.

Vegetable Frittata

Wisconsin Asiago Corn Risotto

2 cans (15 ounces each) vegetable
    broth
1 cup (8 ounces) carrot juice
2 tablespoons olive oil
1 onion, coarsely chopped
1 tablespoon coarsely chopped
    garlic
1 cup arborio or short-grain rice
1 bag (16 ounces) frozen corn,
    thawed and drained
¼ cup chopped fresh Italian
    parsley

2 teaspoons chopped fresh thyme
    or rosemary *or* 1 teaspoon
    dried herbs
½ cup (2 ounces) grated Wisconsin
    Parmesan cheese
½ cup (2 ounces) grated Wisconsin
    Romano cheese
1 teaspoon chopped chives
½ teaspoon black pepper
1 cup (4 ounces) Wisconsin Asiago
    cheese shavings

In 2-quart saucepan heat broth and carrot juice until simmering. In Dutch oven, heat olive oil until hot; add onion, garlic and rice. Cook over medium heat, adding 1 cup simmering broth mixture. Stir rice constantly; gradually add remaining broth mixture, allowing liquid to be absorbed, 25 to 30 minutes. Add corn, parsley and thyme; stir in Parmesan and Romano. Sprinkle with chives and pepper; top with shavings of Asiago.

Makes 6 servings

Favorite recipe from **Wisconsin Milk Marketing Board**

Old Mexico Black Beans & Rice

2 tablespoons vegetable oil
1 package (6.8 ounces) RICE-
    A-RONI Spanish Rice
½ cup chopped green bell pepper
½ cup chopped onion
2 cloves garlic, minced
1 can (14½ ounces) tomatoes,
    undrained, chopped
¼ to ½ teaspoon hot pepper sauce

1 can (16 ounces) black beans,
    rinsed, drained
1 can (16 ounces) pinto beans,
    rinsed, drained
½ cup (2 ounces) shredded
    Cheddar cheese or Monterey
    Jack cheese
2 tablespoons chopped parsley or
    cilantro (optional)

1. In large skillet, heat oil over medium heat. Add rice-vermicelli mix, green pepper, onion and garlic; sauté, stirring frequently, until vermicelli is golden brown.

2. Stir in 2 cups water, tomatoes, hot pepper sauce and contents of seasoning packet; bring to a boil over high heat.

3. Cover; reduce heat. Simmer 15 minutes.

4. Stir in black and pinto beans.

5. Cover; continue to simmer 5 minutes or until liquid is absorbed and rice is tender. Serve topped with cheese; sprinkle with parsley, if desired. *Makes 4 servings*

Pinto Bean & Zucchini Burritos

6 (6-inch) flour tortillas
¾ cup GUILTLESS GOURMET®
    Pinto Bean Dip (mild or
    spicy)
2 teaspoons water
1 teaspoon olive oil
1 medium zucchini, chopped
¼ cup chopped green onions

¼ cup GUILTLESS GOURMET®
    Green Tomatillo Salsa
1 cup GUILTLESS GOURMET®
    Salsa (mild, medium or hot),
    divided
1½ cups shredded lettuce
    Fresh cilantro leaves (optional)

Preheat oven to 300°F. Wrap tortillas in foil. Bake 10 minutes or until softened and heated through. Meanwhile, combine bean dip and water in small bowl. Heat oil in large skillet over medium-high heat until hot. Add zucchini and onions. Cook and stir until zucchini is crisp-tender; stir in bean dip mixture and tomatillo salsa.

Fill each tortilla with zucchini mixture, dividing evenly. Roll up tortillas; place on 6 individual serving plates. Top with salsa. Serve hot with lettuce. Garnish with cilantro, if desired.

Makes 6 servings

Pinto Bean & Zucchini Burrito

Indian Vegetable Curry

2 to 3 teaspoons curry powder
1 can (16 ounces) sliced potatoes,
  drained
1 bag (16 ounces) BIRDS EYE®
  frozen Farm Fresh Mixtures
  Broccoli, Cauliflower and
  Carrots

1 can (15 ounces) chick-peas,
  drained
1 can (14½ ounces) stewed
  tomatoes
1 can (13¾ ounces) vegetable
  broth
2 tablespoons cornstarch

• Stir curry powder in large skillet over high heat until fragrant, about 30 seconds.

• Stir in potatoes, vegetables, chick-peas and tomatoes; bring to boil. Reduce heat to medium-high; cover and cook 8 minutes.

• Blend broth with cornstarch; stir into vegetables. Cook until thickened.

Makes about 6 servings

Prep Time: 5 minutes   **Cook Time:** 15 minutes

Serving Suggestion: Serve with white or brown rice.

Indian Vegetable Curry

Risotto with Vegetables and Cheese

3 large cloves garlic, sliced
1 medium onion, sliced
8 ounces sliced mushrooms (mixed
    varieties if possible, such as
    portobello, cremini, shiitake
    and oyster)
4½ cups vegetable stock
1½ cups basmati rice
1½ cups chopped green onions,
    including green stems

½ cup *each* diced red, green and
    yellow bell peppers
1 cup (4 ounces) shredded
    JARLSBERG Cheese
Chopped chives or green onions
    and additional JARLSBERG,
    for garnish

Heat nonstick saucepan over medium-high heat; reduce to medium-low and steam garlic, sliced onion and mushrooms, tightly covered, until onion has softened, about 6 minutes. In another saucepan, bring stock to a boil and add rice. Simmer, covered, 20 minutes or until liquid is absorbed. Stir in garlic mixture, green onions, peppers and cheese. Garnish with chives or additional onions and cheese.   *Makes 6 to 8 servings*

Three-Pepper Risotto

2 tablespoons olive or vegetable
    oil
3 medium red, green and/or
    yellow bell peppers, diced
1½ cups arborio, regular or
    converted rice
½ cup dry white wine, vermouth
    or water

1 envelope LIPTON® Recipe
    Secrets® Savory Herb with
    Garlic Soup Mix
3½ cups boiling water, divided
½ cup grated Parmesan cheese

In heavy-duty 3-quart saucepan, heat oil over medium-high heat and cook peppers, stirring occasionally, 5 minutes. Add rice and cook, stirring constantly, 3 minutes. Slowly add wine and cook, stirring constantly, until liquid is absorbed. Stir in Savory Herb with Garlic Soup Mix blended with 1 cup boiling water. Reduce heat to low and simmer uncovered, stirring frequently, until liquid is absorbed. Continue adding remaining 2½ cups boiling water, ½ cup at a time, stirring frequently, until rice is slightly creamy and just tender. Stir in cheese.   *Makes about 4 servings*

Note: Arborio rice is found in specialty food stores. This high-starch, short, fat grain rice is used in risotto for its creamy texture.

•Also terrific with Lipton® Recipe Secrets® Golden Herb with Lemon, Onion, Golden Onion or Onion-Mushroom Soup Mix.

Mediterranean Rice

1 tablespoon olive or vegetable oil
⅓ cup chopped onion
1¾ cups (14.5-ounce can) CONTADINA® Stewed Tomatoes, undrained
1 cup uncooked long-grain white rice

⅓ cup water
¼ cup canned diced green chiles, drained
¾ teaspoon seasoned salt
½ teaspoon chili powder

In medium saucepan with cover, heat oil. Add onion; sauté for 2 to 3 minutes or until tender. Stir in tomatoes and juice, rice, water, chiles, seasoned salt and chili powder. Bring to a boil; cover. Reduce heat to low. Cook for 20 minutes or until rice is tender and liquid is absorbed, stirring occasionally throughout cooking time to prevent sticking. Fluff rice before serving.   *Makes 4 servings*

Vegetable Risotto

2 tablespoons olive oil, divided
1 medium zucchini, cubed
1 medium yellow summer squash, cubed
1 cup shiitake mushroom slices
1 cup chopped onions
1 clove garlic, minced
6 plum tomatoes, stemmed, seeded and quartered
1 teaspoon dried oregano leaves
3 cups Vegetable Stock (page 74)
¾ cup arborio rice
¼ cup grated Parmesan cheese
Salt
Black pepper
½ cup frozen peas, thawed
Fresh oregano for garnish

Heat 1 tablespoon oil in large saucepan over medium heat until hot. Add zucchini and squash; cook and stir 5 minutes or until crisp-tender. Place in medium bowl; set aside. Add mushrooms, onions and garlic to saucepan; cook and stir 5 minutes or until tender. Add tomatoes and oregano; cook and stir 2 to 3 minutes or until tomatoes are soft. Place in bowl with zucchini mixture. Wipe saucepan clean with paper towels.

Place stock in small saucepan; bring to a boil over medium heat. Reduce heat to medium-low to keep stock hot, but not boiling.

Meanwhile, heat remaining 1 tablespoon oil in saucepan over medium heat until hot. Add rice; cook and stir 2 minutes. Add ¾ cup stock to rice. Reduce heat to medium-low, maintaining a simmer. Cook and stir until rice has absorbed stock. Repeat, adding stock 3 more times, cooking and stirring until rice has absorbed stock, about 20 to 25 minutes.

Stir cheese into rice mixture. Season to taste with salt and pepper. Stir in reserved vegetables and peas; cook until heated through. Serve immediately. Garnish, if desired.

Makes 4 to 6 servings

Vegetable Risotto

Olive and Bean Burritos

1 teaspoon cornstarch
2 teaspoons water
2 tablespoons lime juice
1 teaspoon honey
½ teaspoon ground coriander
¼ teaspoon ground cumin
2 teaspoons vegetable oil
1 (15-ounce) can kidney beans,
 drained
1½ cups fresh corn kernels *or*
 1 (10-ounce) package frozen
 corn

¾ cup chopped California ripe
 olives
⅓ cup thinly sliced green onions
8 flour tortillas (7 or 9 inches)
1 cup (4 ounces) shredded
 jalapeño Jack or Monterey
 Jack cheese
Sour cream

Combine cornstarch with water. Add lime juice, honey, coriander and cumin; blend well and set aside. Heat oil over medium-high heat; add beans, corn and olives. Cook, stirring gently, just until hot, about 3 minutes. Add lime mixture. Cook, stirring gently, until mixture boils and thickens slightly, 1 to 2 minutes. Remove pan from heat and stir in green onions. Divide bean mixture equally among tortillas; sprinkle with cheese. Top with sour cream to taste. Roll tortilla to enclose filling. *Makes 4 servings*

Prep Time: About 10 minutes **Cook Time:** About 5 minutes

Favorite recipe from **California Olive Industry**

Dragon Tofu

Dragon Tofu

¼ cup soy sauce
1 tablespoon creamy peanut
butter
1 package (about 12 ounces)
firm tofu, drained
1 medium zucchini
1 medium yellow squash

2 teaspoons peanut or
vegetable oil
½ teaspoon hot chili oil
2 cloves garlic, minced
2 cups packed torn fresh spinach
leaves
¼ cup coarsely chopped cashews
or peanuts (optional)

Whisk soy sauce into peanut butter in small bowl. Press tofu lightly between paper towels; cut into ¾-inch squares or triangles. Place in single layer in shallow dish. Pour soy sauce mixture over tofu; stir gently to coat all surfaces. Let stand at room temperature 20 minutes. Cut zucchini and yellow squash lengthwise into ¼-inch-thick slices; cut each slice into 2×¼-inch strips. Heat nonstick skillet over medium-high heat. Add peanut and chili oils; heat until hot. Add garlic, zucchini and yellow squash; stir-fry 3 minutes. Add tofu mixture; cook 2 minutes or until tofu is heated through and sauce is slightly thickened, stirring occasionally. Stir in spinach; remove from heat. Sprinkle with cashews, if desired.

Makes 2 servings

Vegetable Stir-Fry in Spicy Black Bean Sauce

1 teaspoon vegetable oil
1 medium onion, chopped
1 medium green bell pepper, cut
   into strips
3 carrots, cut into julienne strips
   (matchstick size)

3 cups shredded cabbage (green,
   red or napa)
1 cup tofu, crumbled
4 cups cooked rice, kept warm
   Fresh chives and radishes
   (optional)

BLACK BEAN SAUCE

1 cup GUILTLESS GOURMET®
   Spicy Black Bean Dip
2 teaspoons water
¼ cup low sodium soy sauce

¼ cup cooking sherry
1 tablespoon minced peeled
   gingerroot
1 clove garlic, minced

Heat oil in wok or large skillet over medium-high heat until hot. Add onion, pepper, carrots, cabbage and tofu; stir-fry until crisp-tender.

To prepare Black Bean Sauce, combine bean dip and water in small bowl; mix well. Stir in remaining Black Bean Sauce ingredients; pour over stir-fried vegetables. Stir-fry over high heat 2 minutes more. Reduce heat to low; cook 2 to 4 minutes more or until heated through, stirring often. Serve over hot rice. Garnish with chives and radishes, if desired.

Makes 6 servings

Vegetable Stir-Fry in Spicy Black Bean Sauce

Cheesy Vegetarian Stir-Fry

2 teaspoons olive oil
1 cup thinly sliced onion
3 cloves garlic, minced
4 cups zucchini, cubed
1 to 2 teaspoons dried Italian
    seasoning

1 (9-ounce) package frozen
    artichoke hearts, thawed,
    cooked and drained (optional)
½ cup marinara sauce
½ cup shredded JARLSBERG
    LITE™ Cheese

Heat oil in wok over high heat; stir-fry onion and garlic 3 minutes or until lightly browned. Add zucchini and Italian seasoning; stir-fry 3 minutes or until crisp-tender. Remove from heat and stir in artichoke hearts, marinara sauce and cheese. Serve with cannellini beans or over pasta such as linguine. *Makes 4 to 6 servings*

Stir-Fry Rice and Vegetables

3 tablespoons vegetable oil
1 bunch green onions, white
    and green parts chopped
    separately
1 medium sweet potato, peeled,
    halved lengthwise and thinly
    sliced
1 small green bell pepper, cut into
    thin strips

2 carrots, thinly sliced
1 zucchini, thinly sliced
2 cups cooked brown rice
1 cup bean sprouts
1 cup sliced fresh mushrooms
¼ cup honey
¼ cup soy sauce

Heat oil in wok or large, heavy skillet over medium-high heat. Stir-fry white parts of onions, sweet potato, bell pepper, carrots and zucchini until barely tender. Add rice, sprouts, mushrooms and green onion tops. Cook quickly until heated through. If necessary, add more oil. Combine honey and soy sauce in cup. Pour over mixture and stir. Serve immediately. *Makes 6 to 8 servings*

Favorite recipe from **National Honey Board**

Vegetable Lo Mein

Vegetable Lo Mein

8 ounces uncooked vermicelli or
    thin spaghetti, cooked and
    drained
¾ teaspoon dark sesame oil
½ teaspoon vegetable oil
3 cloves garlic, minced
1 teaspoon grated fresh ginger
2 cups sliced bok choy
½ cup sliced green onions

2 cups shredded carrots
6 ounces firm tofu, drained and
    cubed
6 tablespoons rice wine vinegar
¼ cup plum preserves
¼ cup water
1 teaspoon reduced-sodium soy
    sauce
½ teaspoon red pepper flakes

Toss vermicelli with sesame oil in large bowl until well coated. Heat vegetable oil in large nonstick skillet or wok over medium heat. Stir in garlic and ginger; stir-fry 10 seconds. Add bok choy and onions; stir-fry 3 to 4 minutes until crisp-tender. Add carrots and tofu; stir-fry 2 to 3 minutes until carrots are crisp-tender.

Combine vinegar, preserves, water, soy sauce and crushed red pepper in small saucepan. Heat over medium heat until preserves are melted, stirring constantly. Combine noodles, vegetable mixture and sauce in large bowl; mix well. *Makes 6 servings*

Oriental Fried Rice

1 tablespoon vegetable oil
1 egg, beaten
1 box (10 ounces) BIRDS EYE®
    frozen Chinese or Japanese
    Stir-Fry Vegetables

2 cups cooked rice*
2 tablespoons soy sauce

• Heat 1 teaspoon oil in large skillet over high heat. Add egg; let spread in pan to form flat pancake shape.

• Cook 30 seconds. Turn egg over (egg pancake may break apart); cook 30 seconds more. Remove from skillet; cut into thin strips.

• Remove seasoning pouch from vegetables. Add remaining 2 teaspoons oil to skillet; stir in rice and vegetables.

• Reduce heat to medium-high; cover and cook 5 minutes, stirring twice.

• Add contents of seasoning pouch, soy sauce and cooked egg to skillet; mix well.

• Cook, uncovered, 2 minutes or until heated through.	*Makes 2 servings*

*Need cooked rice in a hurry? Prepare instant white or brown rice, then proceed with recipe.

Prep Time: 5 minutes   **Cook Time:** 10 minutes

Oriental Fried Rice

Vegetarian Rice Noodles

Vegetarian Rice Noodles

½ pound firm tofu cakes, rinsed
    and drained
1 (½-pound) jicama *or* 1 can
    (8 ounces) sliced water
    chestnuts, drained
2 large leeks
1 cup vegetable oil
2 medium sweet potatoes, peeled
    and sliced (1 pound)
8 ounces very thin dried rice
    vermicelli
½ cup low-sodium soy sauce

⅓ cup sugar
¼ cup lime juice
2 fresh red Thai chili peppers *or*
    1 large red jalapeño pepper,*
    halved, seeded and finely
    chopped
¼ cup chopped unsalted dry
    roasted peanuts
2 tablespoons chopped fresh mint
2 tablespoons chopped fresh
    cilantro
Mint leaves for garnish

*Chili peppers can sting and irritate the skin; wear rubber gloves when handling peppers and do not touch eyes. Wash hands after handling.

• Dry tofu on paper towels. Cut cakes into 4 squares; cut each square diagonally into 2 triangles. Set aside.

• Cut top and bottom ends from jicama. Peel with paring knife. Cut jicama into ¼-inch-thick slices. Cut slices into 1-inch squares; set aside. (Omit step if using water chestnuts.)

• Cut off and discard root tips and green tops from leeks. Cut leeks lengthwise in half. Rinse under cold water several times to remove all grit. Place leeks, cut sides down, on cutting board. Cut leeks crosswise into ¼-inch-thick slices; set aside.

• Heat oil in wok over medium-high heat about 4 minutes or until hot. Add tofu; fry about 4 minutes per side or until golden brown. Remove tofu with slotted spatula to baking sheet lined with paper towels; drain. Reheat oil. Add jicama; fry about 5 minutes or until lightly browned, stirring occasionally. Remove with slotted spatula to same baking sheet; drain. Repeat with sweet potatoes in 2 batches, reheating oil each time. Add leeks; fry 1 minute. Pour leeks into large strainer over heatproof bowl to drain; set aside. Reserve 1 tablespoon oil.

• Place 4 cups water in wok; bring to a boil over high heat. Add vermicelli and cook 3 minutes or *just* until tender but still firm, stirring frequently. Drain in colander; rinse under cold running water to stop cooking. Drain again; place vermicelli in large bowl. Add 1 tablespoon reserved oil; toss lightly to coat. Cut noodles into 10-inch lengths.

• Combine soy sauce, sugar, lime juice and peppers in wok; heat over medium heat just until sugar dissolves. Add noodles; toss until coated with soy mixture. Gently stir in tofu, vegetables, peanuts, chopped mint and cilantro. Transfer to serving plate or place wok on table over wok ring stand or trivet. Garnish, if desired. *Makes 4 servings*

Eggplant Italiano

1¼ pounds eggplant
2 medium onions
2 ribs celery
½ cup pitted ripe olives
2 tablespoons olive oil, divided
1 can (16 ounces) diced tomatoes, drained
2 tablespoons balsamic vinegar

1 tablespoon sugar
1 tablespoon capers, drained
1 teaspoon dried oregano or basil leaves, crushed
Salt and black pepper to taste
Fresh basil leaves, leaf lettuce and red jalapeño pepper for garnish

• Cut eggplant into 1-inch cubes. Thinly slice onions. Cut celery into 1-inch pieces. Cut olives crosswise in half; set aside.

• Heat wok over medium-high heat 1 minute or until hot. Drizzle 1 tablespoon oil into wok and heat 30 seconds. Add onions and celery; stir-fry about 2 minutes or until tender. Move onions and celery up side of wok. Reduce heat to medium.

• Add remaining 1 tablespoon oil to bottom of wok and heat 30 seconds. Add eggplant; stir-fry about 4 minutes or until tender. Add tomatoes; mix well. Cover and cook 10 minutes.

• Stir olives, vinegar, sugar, capers and oregano into eggplant mixture. Season with salt and black pepper. Transfer to serving dish. Garnish, if desired.   *Makes 6 servings*

Eggplant Italiano

Stir-Fried Tofu and Vegetables

½ pound firm tofu cakes, rinsed
   and drained
1 medium yellow onion
1 medium zucchini
1 medium yellow squash
1 small red bell pepper
1 cup vegetable oil
½ cup sliced fresh mushrooms

1 package (6 ounces) frozen snow
   peas, thawed
¼ cup water
2 tablespoons soy sauce
2 tablespoons tomato paste*
¼ teaspoon salt
⅛ teaspoon black pepper

• Dry tofu on paper towels. Cut crosswise into ¼-inch-thick slices; set aside.

• Cut onion into 8 wedges. Scrub zucchini and yellow squash; cut off ends. Cut zucchini and yellow squash into 1-inch pieces. Cut red pepper lengthwise in half. Remove stem and seeds. Rinse, dry and cut into ¼-inch strips. Set aside.

• Heat oil in wok over medium-high heat about 5 minutes or until hot. Add tofu; fry about 8 minutes per side or until golden brown, turning once. Remove tofu with slotted spatula to baking sheet lined with paper towels. Drain all but 2 tablespoons oil from wok.

• Add onion to wok; stir-fry 1 minute. Add zucchini, yellow squash and mushrooms; stir-fry 6 to 7 minutes until zucchini and yellow squash are crisp-tender.

• Add red pepper, snow peas and water to wok; cook 2 to 3 minutes or until crisp-tender, stirring occasionally. Stir in soy sauce, tomato paste, salt and black pepper until well mixed. Add tofu; stir-fry until heated through and coated with sauce. Transfer to serving dish. *Makes 4 servings*

Remaining tomato paste may be transferred to small resealable plastic food storage bag and frozen.

Stir-Fried Tofu and Vegetables

FLAVOR–PACKED PASTAS

Roma Artichoke and Tomato Ragu

1¾ cups (14.5-ounce can) CONTADINA® Recipe Ready Diced Tomatoes, drained
1 cup (6-ounce jar) marinated artichoke hearts, sliced, undrained
¼ cup sliced ripe olives, drained
2 tablespoons chopped fresh parsley *or* 2 teaspoons dried parsley flakes
2 tablespoons chopped fresh basil *or* 2 teaspoons dried basil leaves, crushed
1 clove garlic, minced
¼ teaspoon salt
⅛ teaspoon ground black pepper

COMBINE tomatoes, artichoke hearts and juice, olives, parsley, basil, garlic, salt and pepper in large bowl.

COVER; chill for several hours to blend flavors.

TOSS with pasta or serve at room temperature on toasted Italian bread slices or pizza.

Makes 4 servings

Roma Artichoke and Tomato Ragu

Fettuccine with Olive Pesto

10 ounces dried fettuccine
1½ cups whole pitted California
    ripe olives
3 tablespoons drained capers
4 teaspoons lemon juice
1 tablespoon olive oil

2 teaspoons Dijon mustard
2 to 3 cloves garlic, peeled
¼ cup finely chopped fresh basil
¼ cup grated Parmesan cheese
    Basil sprigs

Cook fettuccine according to package directions. While pasta cooks, combine olives, capers, lemon juice, oil, mustard and garlic in food processor or blender. Process until coarsely puréed. Stir in chopped basil and cheese; set aside. Drain pasta well and transfer to large warm serving bowl. Spoon pesto over pasta and mix gently. Garnish with basil sprigs. *Makes 4 servings*

Cook Time: About 15 minutes   **Prep Time:** About 15 minutes

Favorite recipe from **California Olive Industry**

Classic Macaroni and Cheese

2 cups elbow macaroni
3 tablespoons butter or margarine
¼ cup chopped onion (optional)
2 tablespoons all-purpose flour
½ teaspoon salt
⅛ teaspoon pepper

2 cups milk
2 cups (8 ounces) SARGENTO®
    Classic or Fancy Shredded
    Mild Cheddar Cheese,
    divided

Cook macaroni according to package directions; drain. In medium saucepan, melt butter and cook onion about 5 minutes or until tender. Stir in flour, salt and pepper. Gradually add milk and cook, stirring occasionally, until thickened. Remove from heat. Add 1½ cups Cheddar cheese and stir until cheese melts. Combine cheese sauce with cooked macaroni. Place in 1½-quart casserole; top with remaining ½ cup Cheddar cheese. Bake at 350°F, 30 minutes or until bubbly and cheese is golden brown. *Makes 6 servings*

Lemon-Tossed Linguine

Lemon-Tossed Linguine

8 ounces uncooked linguine
    noodles
3 tablespoons fresh lemon juice
2 teaspoons reduced-calorie
    margarine
2 tablespoons minced chives
⅓ cup skim milk
1 teaspoon cornstarch
1 tablespoon minced fresh dill *or*
    1 teaspoon dried dill weed

1 tablespoon minced fresh parsley
    or 1 teaspoon dried parsley
    flakes
2 teaspoons grated lemon peel
¼ teaspoon ground white pepper
3 tablespoons grated Romano or
    Parmesan cheese

Cook linguine according to package directions, omitting salt. Drain well. Place in medium bowl; sprinkle lemon juice over noodles.

Meanwhile, melt margarine in small saucepan over medium heat. Add chives; cook until chives are soft. Combine milk and cornstarch in small bowl; stir into saucepan. Cook and stir until thickened. Stir in dill, parsley, lemon peel and pepper.

Pour milk mixture over noodles. Sprinkle with cheese; toss to coat evenly. Garnish with lemon slices and dill sprigs, if desired. Serve immediately. *Makes 3 servings*

Rigatoni with Four Cheeses

3 cups milk
1 tablespoon chopped carrot
1 tablespoon chopped celery
1 tablespoon chopped onion
1 tablespoon parsley sprigs
½ bay leaf
¼ teaspoon black peppercorns
¼ teaspoon hot pepper sauce
  Dash ground nutmeg
¼ cup butter
¼ cup all-purpose flour

½ cup grated Wisconsin Parmesan
  cheese
¼ cup grated Wisconsin Romano
  cheese
12 ounces uncooked rigatoni,
  cooked and drained
1½ cups (6 ounces) shredded
  Wisconsin Cheddar cheese
1½ cups (6 ounces) shredded
  Wisconsin mozzarella cheese
¼ teaspoon chili powder

Combine milk, carrot, celery, onion, parsley, bay leaf, peppercorns, hot pepper sauce and nutmeg in large saucepan. Bring to a boil. Reduce heat to low; simmer 10 minutes. Strain; reserve liquid.

Preheat oven to 350°F. Melt butter in medium saucepan over medium heat. Stir in flour. Gradually stir in reserved liquid. Cook, stirring constantly, until thickened. Remove from heat. Add Parmesan and Romano cheeses; stir until blended. Pour into large bowl. Add rigatoni; toss gently to coat. Combine Cheddar and mozzarella cheeses in medium bowl. Place half the rigatoni mixture in greased 2-quart casserole; sprinkle with cheese mixture. Top with remaining rotini mixture. Sprinkle with chili powder. Bake 25 minutes or until bubbly. Garnish as desired. *Makes 6 servings*

Favorite recipe from **Wisconsin Milk Marketing Board**

Rigatoni with Four Cheeses

Fettuccine with Sun-Dried Tomato Cream

⅔ cup sun-dried tomatoes
3 to 4 cloves garlic
1 (8-ounce) container
    PHILADELPHIA BRAND®
    Soft Cream Cheese
½ teaspoon dried oregano leaves,
    crushed
¼ cup butter or margarine

¼ cup BREAKSTONE'S®
    Sour Cream
1 pound fettuccine, cooked,
    drained, kept warm
¼ cup olive oil
    Salt and pepper
2 tablespoons chopped fresh
    parsley

• Cover tomatoes with boiling water; let stand 10 minutes. Drain.

• Place tomatoes and garlic in food processor or blender container; process until coarsely chopped. Add cream cheese and oregano; process until well blended.

• Melt butter in medium saucepan; stir in cream cheese mixture and sour cream. Cook until thoroughly heated.

• Toss warm fettuccine with oil.

• Add cream cheese mixture. Season to taste with salt and pepper. Sprinkle with chopped parsley. Serve immediately. *Makes 8 to 10 servings*

Prep Time: 30 minutes

Fettuccine with Sun-Dried Tomato Cream

Penne with Creamy Tomato Sauce

Penne with Creamy Tomato Sauce

1 tablespoon olive or vegetable oil
½ cup diced onion
2 tablespoons dry vermouth, white wine or chicken broth
1¾ cups (14.5-ounce can) CONTADINA® Pasta Ready Chunky Tomatoes Primavera, undrained

½ cup heavy whipping cream
8 ounces dry penne or rigatoni, cooked, drained, kept warm
1 cup pitted ripe olives, drained, sliced
½ cup (2 ounces) grated Parmesan cheese
¼ cup sliced green onions

In large skillet, heat oil. Add diced onion; sauté for 2 to 3 minutes or until onion is tender. Add vermouth; cook for 1 minute. Stir in tomatoes and juice, cream, pasta, olives and Parmesan cheese; heat thoroughly, stirring occasionally. Sprinkle with green onions.

Makes 4 servings

Pasta with Spinach-Cheese Sauce

¼ cup FILIPPO BERIO® Extra-
 Virgin Flavorful Olive Oil,
 divided
1 medium onion, chopped
1 clove garlic, chopped
3 cups chopped fresh spinach,
 washed and well drained
1 cup low-fat ricotta or cottage
 cheese

½ cup chopped fresh parsley
1 teaspoon dried basil leaves,
 crushed
1 teaspoon lemon juice
¼ teaspoon black pepper
¼ teaspoon ground nutmeg
¾ pound uncooked spaghetti

1. Heat 3 tablespoons olive oil in large skillet over medium heat. Add onion and garlic; cook and stir until onion is tender.

2. Add spinach to skillet; cook 3 to 5 minutes or until spinach wilts.

3. Place spinach mixture, cheese, parsley, basil, lemon juice, pepper and nutmeg in covered blender container. Blend until smooth. Leave in blender, covered, to keep sauce warm.

4. Cook pasta according to package directions until tender. *Do not overcook.* Drain pasta, reserving ¼ cup water. Toss pasta with remaining 1 tablespoon olive oil in large bowl.

5. Add reserved ¼ cup water to sauce in blender. Blend; serve sauce over pasta.

Makes 4 servings

Roasted Vegetables Provençal

8 ounces medium or large
 mushrooms, halved
1 large zucchini, cut into 1-inch
 pieces, halved
1 large yellow squash or
 additional zucchini, cut into
 1-inch pieces, quartered
1 large red or green bell pepper,
 cut into 1-inch pieces
1 small red onion, cut into ¼-inch
 slices, separated into rings
3 tablespoons olive oil

2 cloves garlic, minced
1 teaspoon dried basil
1 teaspoon dried thyme leaves
½ teaspoon salt (optional)
¼ teaspoon freshly ground black
 pepper
4 large plum tomatoes, quartered
⅔ cup milk
2 tablespoons margarine or butter
1 package (5.1 ounces) PASTA
 RONI™ Parmesan Sauce with
 Angel Hair Pasta

1. Heat oven to 425°F. In 15×10-inch jelly-roll pan combine mushrooms, zucchini, yellow squash, bell pepper and onion; add combined oil, garlic, basil, thyme, salt and black pepper. Toss to coat. Bake 15 minutes; stir in tomatoes. Continue baking 5 to 10 minutes or until vegetables are tender.

2. While vegetables are roasting, combine 1⅓ cups water, milk and margarine in medium saucepan; bring just to a boil. Gradually add pasta while stirring. Stir in contents of seasoning packet. Reduce heat to medium.

3. Boil, uncovered, stirring frequently, 4 minutes. Sauce will be very thin, but will thicken upon standing. Remove from heat.

4. Let stand 3 minutes or until desired consistency. Stir before serving. Serve pasta topped with vegetables.

Makes 4 servings

Roasted Vegetables Provençal

Linguine with Paprikash Sauce

12 ounces linguine
2 medium red bell peppers
2 tablespoons olive oil
1 medium onion, thinly sliced
1 clove garlic, minced
2 tablespoons all-purpose flour
4 teaspoons sweet Hungarian
    paprika

½ teaspoon salt
¼ teaspoon ground black pepper
1 can (8 ounces) tomato sauce
1 cup canned vegetable broth
½ cup sour cream

Cook linguine according to package directions. Drain in colander. Place in large warm bowl; keep warm.

Meanwhile, cut red peppers lengthwise into thin strips; cut strips crosswise into halves.

Heat oil in large skillet over medium heat until hot. Add bell peppers, onion and garlic; cook and stir 8 to 10 minutes or until peppers are very soft.

Combine flour, paprika, salt and black pepper in small bowl. Stir into bell pepper mixture. Cook over medium heat 3 minutes, stirring occasionally. Combine tomato sauce and broth; stir into skillet. Bring to a boil, stirring constantly. Reduce heat to low and simmer, uncovered, until sauce thickens.

Remove skillet from heat; place sour cream in small bowl. Stir in several spoonfuls hot mixture. Stir sour cream mixture into sauce in skillet. Cook over low heat 1 minute or until heated through. *Do not boil.* Pour over linguine; toss.   *Makes 5 to 6 servings*

Thai Noodles with Peanut Sauce

2 packages (3 ounces each)
    Oriental flavor instant ramen
    noodles
2 cups BIRDS EYE® frozen Farm
    Fresh Mixtures Broccoli,
    Carrots and Water Chestnuts

⅓ cup hot water
¼ cup creamy peanut butter
1 teaspoon sugar
⅛ to ¼ teaspoon crushed red
    pepper flakes

• Reserve seasoning packets from noodles.

• Bring 4 cups water to boil in large saucepan. Add noodles and vegetables. Cook 3 minutes, stirring occasionally; drain.

• Meanwhile, whisk together hot water, peanut butter, sugar, red pepper flakes and reserved seasoning packets in large bowl until blended.

• Add noodles and vegetables; toss to coat. Serve warm.   *Makes about 4 servings*

Prep Time: 5 minutes   **Cook Time:** 10 minutes

Serving Suggestion: Add shredded carrot, thinly sliced cucumber or green onion for additional flavor and color.

Cheesy Herb-Stuffed Mushrooms with Spinach Fettuccine

2 packages (9 ounces each) fresh
    spinach fettuccine
⅓ cup extra-virgin olive oil
1 tablespoon dried basil leaves
2 cloves garlic, minced

1 package (6½ ounces) garlic and
    herb soft spreadable cheese
16 large mushrooms, rinsed and
    stems removed

1. Prepare barbecue grill for direct cooking.

2. Cook fettuccine according to package directions. Drain; return to saucepan.

3. Meanwhile, combine oil, basil and garlic in small bowl; pour over cooked pasta. Toss well; set aside.

4. Cut aluminum foil into 4 large squares. Spoon about 1 tablespoon cheese into each mushroom cap. Place four mushroom caps, cheese sides up, in center of each square. Fold aluminum foil to close, leaving small air pocket directly above cheese.

5. Place packets on grid. Grill, on covered grill, over hot coals 5 minutes or until mushroom caps are fork-tender. Remove from grill.

6. Transfer fettuccine to serving bowl. Remove mushroom caps from packets; arrange over fettuccine. Serve immediately. *Makes 4 to 6 servings*

Prep and Cook Time: 30 minutes

Cheesy Herb-Stuffed Mushrooms with Spinach Fettuccine

Springtime Vegetable Pasta

8 ounces fusilli or rotini, uncooked
1 can (14½ ounces) diced
   tomatoes with roasted garlic,
   liquid reserved
4 ounces fresh green beans, cut
   into 1-inch pieces
¼ teaspoon dried oregano leaves,
   crushed

1½ cups zucchini and/or yellow
   squash, thinly sliced
1 cup frozen peas
1 cup marinated artichoke hearts,
   quartered, liquid reserved
½ teaspoon salt
¼ teaspoon ground black pepper
¼ cup shredded Parmesan cheese

Prepare pasta according to package directions. Drain well; place in serving bowl. Cover and keep warm. Place tomatoes and liquid, green beans and oregano in large skillet. Bring to a boil over high heat; reduce heat to medium-low. Cover; simmer until green beans are just tender, about 3 minutes. Stir in zucchini and squash; simmer until crisp-tender. Add peas, artichokes and liquid, salt and pepper; simmer until heated through. Pour over pasta; stir until well coated. Sprinkle Parmesan over each serving. Garnish, if desired.

Makes about 6 servings

Linguine with Spinach Pesto

1 (10-ounce) package frozen
   chopped spinach, thawed and
   well drained
1 cup EGG BEATERS® Healthy
   Real Egg Product
⅓ cup PLANTERS® Walnut Pieces
¼ cup grated Parmesan cheese

2 cloves garlic, crushed
1 pound thin linguine, cooked in
   unsalted water and drained
½ cup diced red bell pepper
   Additional grated Parmesan
   cheese, optional

In electric blender container or food processor, blend spinach, Egg Beaters®, walnuts, ¼ cup cheese and garlic until smooth. Toss with hot linguine and bell pepper. Top with additional cheese if desired.

Makes 8 servings

Garden Primavera Pasta

6 ounces bow-tie pasta
1 jar (6 ounces) marinated
artichoke hearts
2 cloves garlic, minced
½ teaspoon dried rosemary, crushed
1 can (14½ ounces) DEL
MONTE® Pasta Style Chunky
Tomatoes

1 green pepper, cut into thin strips
1 large carrot, cut into 3-inch
julienne strips
1 medium zucchini, cut into
3-inch julienne strips
12 small pitted ripe olives
(optional)

Cook pasta according to package directions; drain. Drain artichokes, reserving
marinade. Toss pasta in 3 tablespoons artichoke marinade; set aside. Cut artichoke
hearts into halves. In large skillet, cook garlic and rosemary in 1 tablespoon artichoke
marinade. Add remaining ingredients, except pasta and artichokes. Cook, uncovered,
over medium-high heat 4 to 5 minutes or until vegetables are tender-crisp and sauce is
thickened. Add artichoke hearts. Spoon over pasta. Serve with grated Parmesan cheese,
if desired.

Makes 4 servings

Mushroom-Laced Fettuccine

3 tablespoons margarine or butter
½ pound assorted sliced fresh
mushrooms, such as
portabella, crimini, shiitake,
white, morels, porcini or
enoki

1 envelope LIPTON® Recipe
Secrets® Savory Herb with
Garlic Soup Mix
1¼ cups milk
8 ounces fettuccine or linguine,
cooked and drained

In 10-inch skillet, melt margarine over medium heat and cook mushrooms, stirring
occasionally, 6 minutes or until tender. Add savory herb with garlic soup mix blended
with milk. Bring to a boil over high heat, stirring frequently. Toss with hot fettuccine.
Serve immediately.

Makes about 2 main-dish servings

Spicy Ravioli and Cheese

Spicy Ravioli and Cheese

1 medium red bell pepper, thinly
  sliced
1 medium green bell pepper,
  thinly sliced
1 medium yellow bell pepper,
  thinly sliced
1 tablespoon olive or vegetable oil
½ teaspoon LAWRY'S® Seasoned
  Salt

¼ teaspoon LAWRY'S® Garlic
  Powder with Parsley
¼ teaspoon sugar
1 package (8 or 9 ounces) fresh or
  frozen ravioli
1½ cups chunky salsa, divided
4 ounces mozzarella cheese, thinly
  sliced
2 green onions, sliced

Place bell peppers in broilerproof baking dish; sprinkle with oil, Seasoned Salt, Garlic Powder with Parsley and sugar. Broil 15 minutes or until tender and browned, turning once. Prepare ravioli according to package directions. Pour ¾ cup salsa in bottom of 8-inch square baking dish. Alternate layers of bell peppers, ravioli, cheese and green onions. Pour remaining ¾ cup salsa over layers. Cover with foil; bake in 350°F oven 15 to 20 minutes or until heated through and cheese melts. *Makes 4 to 6 servings*

Vegetable Pasta

2 cups chopped onions
1 cup chopped celery
2 tablespoons Chef Paul
    Prudhomme's VEGETABLE
    MAGIC®
1½ cups apple juice
5 tablespoons all-purpose flour,
    browned*
3 tablespoons tamari**
2 teaspoons balsamic vinegar
5 cups vegetable stock

1 cup freshly cut corn kernels
1 cup peeled matchstick-size
    carrots
1 cup peeled matchstick-size
    turnip
1 cup matchstick-size zucchini
1 cup matchstick-size yellow
    squash
1 cup broccoli florets
1 cup cauliflower florets
4 cups cooked pasta

Preheat heavy nonstick 5-quart stockpot over high heat to 350°, about 4 minutes.

Add onions, celery, and seasoning mix; stir and cook for 4 minutes, checking bottom of stockpot occasionally for sticking. Add apple juice; scrape brown bits from bottom of stockpot and cook until almost all of liquid evaporates, about 5 to 6 minutes.

Add browned flour, tamari, and vinegar and stir until the flour is completely absorbed, forming a thick paste. Spread this mixture evenly over bottom of stockpot and cook, scraping bottom frequently, for 1 minute. Add stock; stir until all the ingredients are well mixed, and bring to a boil. Add corn and carrots and cook for 2 minutes. Add turnip and cook for 2 more minutes. Add remaining vegetables and cook for 2 minutes. Fold in pasta and cook just until pasta is heated through, about 3 to 4 minutes.

Makes 4 servings

To brown flour, preheat small skillet over medium-high heat for 2 minutes. Add flour and whisk constantly to break up all the lumps, shaking skillet until flour is light tan. Reduce heat to medium and whisk constantly until flour is medium tan. Sift and set aside.

**Tamari is a very rich, flavorful soy sauce available in specialty markets and international or ethnic food sections of many supermarkets. If you cannot find tamari where you shop, use any good quality soy sauce.*

Alpine Fettuccine

½ pound white fettuccine, preferably fresh
½ pound green fettuccine, preferably fresh
1½ teaspoons extra virgin olive oil
1 cup sliced fresh mushrooms
1 cup chopped red bell pepper
½ cup skim milk
6 ounces (1 carton) ALPINE LACE® Fat Free Cream Cheese with Garlic & Herbs

1. Cook the fettuccine according to package directions until al dente. Drain well and place in a large shallow pasta bowl. Toss with the oil and keep warm.

2. Meanwhile, spray a medium-size nonstick skillet with nonstick cooking spray. Add the mushrooms and bell pepper and sauté until soft. Toss with the fettuccine.

3. In a small saucepan, bring the milk to a boil over medium heat. Add the cream cheese and stir until melted. Toss with pasta and serve immediately.

Makes 6 main-dish servings (1½ cups each)

Asian Chili Pepper Linguine

1 (12-ounce) package PASTA LABELLA® Chili Pepper Linguine
¼ cup vegetable oil
1 small carrot, julienned
1 small yellow squash, julienned
1 medium Spanish onion, chopped
2 cloves garlic, crushed
2 tablespoons toasted sesame seeds
2 tablespoons soy sauce
Salt and pepper, to taste

Cook pasta according to package directions. In large skillet, heat oil. Add carrot, squash, onion and garlic and sauté for 4 minutes. Add sesame seeds and soy sauce and simmer for 2 minutes. Season with salt and pepper to taste. Serve over hot chili pepper linguine.

Makes 3 servings

Alpine Fettuccine

Penne with Tomatoes, Basil Leaves and Blue Cheese

1 pound penne, mostaccioli or
other medium pasta shape,
uncooked
12 ripe plum tomatoes (about 1½
pounds), quartered *or* 1 pint
cherry tomatoes, cut into
halves
2 cups lightly packed whole fresh
basil leaves

½ cup (2 ounces) finely crumbled
blue cheese
2 tablespoons olive or vegetable
oil
2 tablespoons white wine vinegar
Salt and black pepper to taste

Toss tomatoes, basil, cheese, oil and vinegar in large bowl. Season to taste with salt and pepper. Refrigerate and let marinate 45 minutes to 24 hours. Cook pasta according to package directions.

When pasta is done, drain well. Add pasta to tomato mixture and toss to mix. Let stand at room temperature about 15 minutes before serving.   *Makes 12 servings*

Note: Use smallest basil leaves for recipe. If leaves are longer than an inch long, tear in half crosswise before adding to tomato mixture.

Favorite recipe from **National Pasta Association**

Penne with Tomatoes, Basil Leaves and Blue Cheese

Fresh Tomato Pasta Andrew

Fresh Tomato Pasta Andrew

1 pound fresh tomatoes, cut into
    wedges
1 cup packed fresh basil leaves
2 cloves garlic, chopped
2 tablespoons olive oil
8 ounces Camenzola cheese *or*
    6 ounces ripe Brie plus 2
    ounces Stilton cheese, each
    cut into small pieces

Salt and white pepper to taste
4 ounces uncooked angel hair
    pasta, vermicelli or other thin
    pasta, cooked, drained, kept
    warm
Grated Parmesan cheese

Place tomatoes, basil, garlic and oil in food processor or blender; process using on/off pulsing action until coarsely chopped. Combine tomato mixture and Camenzola cheese in large bowl. Season to taste with salt and white pepper. Add pasta; toss gently until cheese melts. Serve with Parmesan cheese. Garnish as desired.

Makes 2 main-dish servings

Favorite recipe from **California Tomato Commission**

Pasta with Cauliflower, Raisins, Pine Nuts and Romano Cheese

⅓ cup golden raisins
1 small head cauliflower, cut into
    flowerets
3 tablespoons tomato paste
1½ cups hot water
1 medium onion, chopped
3 tablespoons vegetable oil

⅓ cup pine nuts (pignoli)
1 pound uncooked ziti or rigatoni
    pasta
1 cup (about 2 ounces) CUCINA
    CLASSICA ITALIANA®
    grated Pecorino Romano
Fresh parsley sprigs (optional)

Place raisins in small bowl. Add lukewarm water to cover raisins. Let stand until raisins are softened, 10 to 15 minutes. Drain. Set aside.

Meanwhile, in medium saucepan, cook cauliflower in 1-inch boiling salted water until tender-crisp, 4 to 6 minutes. Drain. Rinse with cold water. Set aside. In small mixing bowl, dissolve tomato paste in 1½ cups hot water. Set aside.

In large skillet, sauté onion in vegetable oil until tender. Stir in tomato mixture. Simmer for 15 minutes. Stir in cauliflower, pine nuts and raisins. Simmer for 10 minutes.

In large saucepan of boiling water, cook pasta until tender but still firm. Drain in colander. Place in large serving dish. Pour sauce over pasta. Toss to coat. Sprinkle with cheese. Garnish with parsley.

Makes 4 servings

Wisconsin Cheesy Pasta Primavera

1 cup diagonally sliced carrots
6 tablespoons butter, divided
1 cup sliced yellow squash
2 cups quartered mushrooms
1 cup halved Chinese pea pods
¼ cup sliced green onions
1 tablespoon chopped fresh basil
   leaves *or* 1 teaspoon dried
   basil leaves

8 ounces hot cooked fettuccine
1 cup low-fat or cream-style
   cottage cheese
½ cup grated Wisconsin Parmesan
   cheese
Salt and black pepper

In large skillet, sauté carrots in 4 tablespoons butter for 5 minutes. Add squash; cook 2 minutes. Add mushrooms, pea pods and green onions; cook until vegetables are tender, about 5 minutes. Stir in basil. Combine fettuccine and remaining 2 tablespoons butter; toss until butter is melted. Toss in cottage cheese and Parmesan cheese. Place fettuccine mixture on serving platter; top with vegetable mixture. Season with salt and pepper to taste.   *Makes 4 servings*

Favorite recipe from **Wisconsin Milk Marketing Board**

Linguine with Sun-Dried Tomato Pesto

½ cup sun-dried tomatoes
½ cup loosely packed fresh basil
1 teaspoon dried oregano leaves
1 clove garlic, minced
2 tablespoons olive oil

1½ tablespoons grated Parmesan
   cheese
8 ounces linguine or angel hair
   pasta, cooked and kept warm

Combine sun-dried tomatoes with ½ cup hot water in small bowl; soak 3 to 5 minutes or until tomatoes are soft and pliable. Drain; reserve liquid. Combine tomatoes, basil, oregano, garlic, oil and cheese in food processor or blender. Process, adding enough reserved liquid 1 teaspoon at a time, until mixture is of medium to thick sauce consistency. Spoon over pasta and toss; serve immediately.   *Makes 4 servings*

Wisconsin Cheesy Pasta Primavera

Cheese Ravioli with Pumpkin Sauce

⅓ cup sliced green onions
1 to 2 cloves garlic, finely chopped
½ teaspoon fennel seeds
1 cup evaporated skim milk
1 tablespoon all-purpose flour
¼ teaspoon salt

⅛ teaspoon ground black pepper
½ cup solid pack pumpkin
2 packages (9 ounces *each*)
    refrigerated cheese ravioli
2 tablespoons grated Parmesan
    cheese (optional)

Generously spray medium nonstick saucepan with cooking spray; heat over medium heat until hot. Add onions, garlic and fennel seeds; cook and stir 3 minutes or until onions are tender. Blend milk, flour, salt and pepper in small bowl until smooth; stir into saucepan. Bring to a boil over high heat; boil until thickened, stirring constantly. Stir in pumpkin; reduce heat to low. Meanwhile, cook pasta according to package directions, omitting salt. Drain. Divide ravioli evenly among 6 plates. Top with pumpkin sauce and sprinkle with cheese, if desired. *Makes 6 servings*

Fresca Lemon Pepper Penne Primavera

1 (12-ounce) package PASTA
    LABELLA® Lemon Pepper
    Penne
¼ cup olive oil
½ cup yellow onions, sliced
1 tablespoon garlic, minced
½ cup broccoli florets

½ cup asparagus tips
½ cup sliced mushrooms
½ teaspoon dried dill weed
    Salt and pepper, to taste
¼ cup white Zinfandel wine
¼ cup Parmesan cheese, grated

Cook pasta according to package directions; reserve ¾ cup pasta cooking broth. Meanwhile, heat olive oil in large skillet and sauté onions and garlic for 3 minutes. Add broccoli, asparagus, mushrooms, dill, salt and pepper; cook and stir for 5 minutes. Add reserved broth and wine to skillet. Simmer for 3 minutes. Add hot pasta and blend well with all ingredients. Sprinkle with Parmesan cheese and serve. *Makes 3 servings*

Cheese Ravioli with Pumpkin Sauce

Pasta with Roasted Vegetables

1 (2-pound) butternut squash, peeled, seeded and cut into 1-inch cubes
1 (10-ounce) container fresh Brussel sprouts, each cut into halves
1 small bulb fennel (about 8 ounces), trimmed, halved and thinly sliced
¼ cup olive oil
3 large cloves garlic, peeled and halved lengthwise
¾ teaspoon salt
½ teaspoon dried oregano leaves
8 ounces penne or ziti pasta
¼ cup pumpkin seeds
½ cup grated Parmesan cheese
1½ teaspoons TABASCO® pepper sauce

• Preheat oven to 450°F. In roasting pan, combine squash, Brussel sprouts, fennel, olive oil, garlic, salt and oregano. Bake 20 minutes, stirring occasionally.

• Meanwhile, prepare penne according to package directions. During last 2 minutes of roasting vegetables, add pumpkin seeds to vegetables. Continue cooking until seeds are lightly toasted.

• To serve, toss cooked, drained pasta with roasted vegetables, Parmesan cheese and TABASCO® sauce to mix well. *Makes 4 servings*

Pasta with Onions and Goat Cheese

2 teaspoons olive oil
4 cups thinly sliced sweet onions
¾ cup (3 ounces) goat cheese
¼ cup skim milk
6 ounces uncooked baby bow-tie or other small pasta
1 clove garlic, minced
2 tablespoons dry white wine
1½ teaspoons chopped fresh sage *or* ½ teaspoon dried sage leaves
½ teaspoon salt
¼ teaspoon black pepper
2 tablespoons chopped toasted walnuts

Pasta with Onions and Goat Cheese

Heat oil in large nonstick skillet over medium heat. Add onions; cook slowly until golden and caramelized, about 20 to 25 minutes, stirring occasionally.

Combine goat cheese and milk in small bowl; stir until well blended. Set aside.

Cook pasta according to package directions, omitting salt. Drain and set aside.

Add garlic to onions in skillet; cook until softened, about 3 minutes. Add wine, sage, salt and pepper; cook until moisture is evaporated. Remove from heat; add pasta and goat cheese mixture, stirring to melt cheese. Sprinkle with walnuts. *Makes 4 servings*

Pepperonata

3 tablespoons olive or vegetable
    oil
1 *each*: red, yellow and green bell
    pepper, thinly sliced
3 cups thinly sliced red or yellow
    onion
2 large cloves garlic, minced
3½ cups (two 14.5-ounce cans)
    CONTADINA® Recipe Ready
    Diced Tomatoes, drained
2 tablespoons chopped fresh
    parsley *or* 2 teaspoons dried
    parsley flakes

1 tablespoon plus 1½ teaspoons
    balsamic or red wine vinegar
1 teaspoon salt
½ teaspoon dried thyme leaves,
    crushed
¼ teaspoon ground black pepper
8 ounces dry pasta, cooked,
    drained, kept warm
1 tablespoon chopped parsley
    (optional)

In large skillet, heat oil. Add bell peppers, onion and garlic; sauté for 6 to 8 minutes or until vegetables are tender. Stir in tomatoes, parsley, vinegar, salt, thyme and black pepper; simmer, uncovered, for 12 to 15 minutes or until heated through, stirring occasionally. Serve over pasta. Sprinkle with parsley, if desired.   *Makes 4 servings*

Pasta with Sunflower Kernels

½ cup sunflower oil
3 parsley sprigs, chopped
3 cloves garlic, minced
1 teaspoon grated lemon peel
½ teaspoon salt

½ teaspoon black pepper
8 ounces tomato, spinach or plain
    spaghetti, cooked and drained
⅔ cup grated Parmesan cheese
½ cup roasted sunflower kernels

Heat sunflower oil in small skillet over medium-high heat. Add parsley, garlic and lemon peel; cook and stir 1 minute. Add salt and pepper. Pour over hot pasta. Add Parmesan cheese and sunflower kernels; toss lightly.   *Makes 4 servings*

Favorite recipe from **National Sunflower Association**

Pepperonata

Spicy Thai Noodles

1¼ cups water
2½ teaspoons brown sugar
2 teaspoons soy sauce
1 teaspoon LAWRY'S® Garlic
   Powder with Parsley
¾ teaspoon LAWRY'S®
   Seasoned Salt
½ teaspoon cornstarch

⅛ to ¼ teaspoon hot pepper flakes
¼ cup chunky peanut butter
¼ cup sliced green onions
1 tablespoon chopped fresh
   cilantro
8 ounces linguine, cooked, drained
   and kept hot
1½ cups shredded red cabbage

In large, deep skillet, combine water, brown sugar, soy sauce, Garlic Powder with Parsley, Seasoned Salt, cornstarch and hot pepper flakes. Bring to a boil. Reduce heat to low; simmer, uncovered, 5 minutes. Cool 10 minutes. Stir in peanut butter, green onions and cilantro. Add hot linguine and cabbage; toss lightly to coat. Serve immediately. Garnish as desired. *Makes 4 servings*

Presentation: Great served with a marinated cucumber salad.

Porcini Mushroom Penne Rigate with Garlic Butter Sauce

1 (12-ounce) package PASTA
   LABELLA® Porcini
   Mushroom Penne Rigate
2 tablespoons butter
1 tablespoon extra virgin olive oil
1½ cups chopped mushrooms

2 teaspoons minced garlic
¾ cup white wine
¼ cup minced green onions
2 tablespoons lemon juice
¼ cup grated Parmesan cheese
1½ tablespoons chopped parsley

Cook pasta according to package directions. Heat butter and olive oil in large skillet; sauté mushrooms and garlic over medium heat for 4 minutes. Add wine, green onions and lemon juice to skillet and simmer. Mix in hot porcini mushroom penne rigate; sprinkle with cheese and parsley and serve. *Makes 3 servings*

Spicy Thai Noodles

Cheese Ravioli with Wild Mushroom Sauce

Cheese Ravioli with Wild Mushroom Sauce

2 tablespoons olive oil
1 medium onion, chopped
1 clove garlic, minced
8 ounces firm tofu
1½ cups ricotta cheese
1 cup grated Parmesan cheese,
    divided

½ teaspoon dried rosemary leaves
¼ teaspoon salt
64 plain or colored wonton
    wrappers (about 1⅓ packages)
Wild Mushroom Sauce
  (recipe follows)

Heat oil in small skillet over medium heat until hot. Add onion and garlic; cook and stir 5 minutes or until tender. Place in medium bowl.

Drain tofu on paper towels. Cut into 1-inch cubes. Process tofu, ricotta cheese, ⅓ cup Parmesan cheese, rosemary and salt in food processor until smooth. Stir into onion mixture in bowl.

To make ravioli, work with 8 wonton wrappers at a time, keeping remaining wrappers covered with plastic wrap. Place about 1 tablespoon cheese mixture in center of each wrapper. Brush edges of wrappers with water. Place second wrapper over filling and press edges together to seal. Cover with plastic wrap and set aside. Repeat with remaining wrappers and cheese mixture. Prepare Wild Mushroom Sauce; keep warm.

Bring 3 quarts water to a boil in Dutch oven over high heat. Place 8 ravioli in water. Reduce heat to medium-high and boil gently, uncovered, 3 to 4 minutes or until ravioli float to surface and are just tender. Remove to warm platter with slotted spoon. Repeat with remaining ravioli. Serve ravioli with Wild Mushroom Sauce and sprinkle with remaining ⅔ cup Parmesan cheese.

Makes 8 servings

Wild Mushroom Sauce

3 tablespoons olive oil	1 tablespoon dried basil leaves
12 ounces shiitake or porcini mushrooms, sliced	½ to 1 teaspoon dried thyme leaves
	3 cups vegetable broth, divided
6 ounces cremini or button mushrooms, sliced	1½ tablespoons cornstarch
	2 tablespoons minced parsley
1½ cups sliced green onions and tops	½ teaspoon salt
	4 to 6 dashes hot pepper sauce

Heat oil in large skillet over medium heat until hot. Add mushrooms, green onions, basil and thyme; cook and stir 5 minutes or until mushrooms release liquid. Continue cooking 10 minutes or until mushrooms have darkened and all liquid is evaporated, stirring occasionally. Add 2¾ cups broth; bring to a boil. Reduce heat to medium-low and simmer, uncovered, 10 to 12 minutes or until broth is reduced by one-third. Return liquid to a boil.

Combine cornstarch and remaining ¼ cup broth in small cup. Add to mushroom mixture. Boil, stirring constantly, 1 to 2 minutes or until thickened. Stir in parsley, salt and pepper sauce.

Makes about 3 cups

Vegetables with Spinach Fettuccine

6 solid pack sun-dried tomatoes
3 ounces uncooked spinach
   florentine fettuccine or
   spinach fettuccine
1 tablespoon olive oil
¼ cup chopped onion
¼ cup sliced red bell pepper

1 clove garlic, minced
½ cup sliced mushrooms
½ cup coarsely chopped fresh
   spinach
¼ teaspoon salt
¼ teaspoon ground nutmeg
⅛ teaspoon ground black pepper

Place sun-dried tomatoes in small bowl; pour boiling water over tomatoes to cover. Let stand 10 to 15 minutes or until tomatoes are tender. Drain tomatoes; discard liquid. Cut tomatoes into strips. Cook pasta according to package directions, omitting salt. Drain. Heat oil in large nonstick skillet over medium heat until hot. Add onion, bell pepper and garlic; cook and stir 3 minutes or until vegetables are crisp-tender. Add mushrooms and spinach; cook and stir 1 minute. Add sun-dried tomatoes, pasta, salt, nutmeg and black pepper; cook and stir 1 to 2 minutes or until heated through.   *Makes 6 servings*

Four-Pepper Penne

1 medium onion, sliced
1 small red bell pepper, thinly
   sliced
1 small green bell pepper, thinly
   sliced
1 small yellow bell pepper, thinly
   sliced
1½ teaspoons minced garlic
1 tablespoon vegetable oil

1 (26-ounce) jar HEALTHY
   CHOICE® Traditional
   Pasta Sauce
1 teaspoon dried basil
½ teaspoon dried savory
¼ teaspoon black pepper
½ pound penne, cooked and
   drained

In Dutch oven or large nonstick saucepan, cook and stir onion, bell peppers and garlic in hot oil until vegetables are tender-crisp. Add pasta sauce, basil, savory and black pepper. Heat through over medium heat. Serve over penne.   *Makes 6 servings*

Vegetables with Spinach Fettuccine

VEGETABLES ON THE SIDE

Artichoke-Carrot Sauté

1 tablespoon butter
2 small carrots, diagonally cut
   into thin slices
1 clove garlic, minced
½ teaspoon dried basil leaves, dill
   weed or tarragon leaves
1 small red bell pepper, cut into
   thin strips

1 medium yellow squash, cut into
   matchsticks
4 artichoke hearts, drained, rinsed
   and quartered
1½ teaspoons lemon juice
   Salt and pepper

1. Melt butter in large skillet over medium heat. Add carrots, garlic and basil; cook and stir 2 minutes. Add bell pepper; cook and stir 2 minutes. Add yellow squash and artichokes; cook and stir 3 minutes.

2. Add lemon juice; cook and stir 1 minute. Add salt and pepper to taste.

Makes 2 servings

Prep and Cook Time: 20 minutes

Artichoke-Carrot Sauté

Easy Dilled Succotash

Easy Dilled Succotash

1½ cups frozen lima beans
  1 small onion, finely chopped
1½ cups frozen whole kernel corn,
    thawed

1 teaspoon salt
1 teaspoon sugar
1 teaspoon dried dill weed

1. Bring ½ cup water in medium saucepan to a boil over high heat. Add beans and onion; cover. Reduce heat to low. Simmer 8 minutes.

2. Stir corn into bean mixture; cover. Simmer 5 minutes or until vegetables are tender. Drain bean mixture; discard liquid.

3. Place bean mixture in serving bowl; stir in salt, sugar and dill weed until well blended. Garnish as desired. *Makes 4 servings*

Broccoli-Rice Casserole

3 cups chopped fresh broccoli
2 tablespoons reduced-calorie
  margarine, divided
¼ cup chopped onion
3 tablespoons all-purpose flour
½ teaspoon dry mustard
1¼ cups skim milk
⅛ teaspoon pepper

1¾ cups cooked long-grain rice
  (cooked without salt or fat)
1 cup (4 ounces) HEALTHY
  CHOICE® Fat Free Cheddar
  Shreds
¼ cup nonfat mayonnaise
Vegetable cooking spray
⅓ cup crushed melba toast

Cook broccoli in boiling water 3 minutes or until crisp-tender. Drain; plunge into cold water. Drain again.

Melt 1½ tablespoons margarine in saucepan; add onion and sauté until tender. Add flour and mustard; cook 1 minute, stirring constantly with wire whisk. Gradually add milk, stirring constantly. Cook, stirring constantly, 2 minutes or until thickened and bubbly. Remove from heat; stir in pepper. Combine broccoli, milk mixture, rice, cheese, and mayonnaise. Spoon into shallow 2-quart casserole coated with cooking spray.

Melt remaining 1½ teaspoons margarine; add toast crumbs. Sprinkle over broccoli mixture. Bake at 350° for 25 minutes or until heated.   *Makes 8 side-dish servings*

Hot & Spicy Glazed Carrots

2 tablespoons vegetable oil
2 dried whole red chili peppers
1 pound carrots, peeled and cut
  diagonally into ⅛-inch slices

¼ cup KIKKOMAN® Teriyaki
  Baste & Glaze

Heat oil in hot wok or large skillet over high heat. Add chili peppers and stir-fry until darkened; remove and discard. Add carrots; reduce heat to medium. Stir-fry 4 minutes, or until tender-crisp. Stir in Teriyaki Baste & Glaze and cook until carrots are glazed. Garnish as desired. Serve immediately.   *Makes 4 servings*

Green Beans with Blue Cheese

1 box (9 ounces) BIRDS EYE®
    frozen Cut Green Beans
2 tablespoons walnut pieces
    (toasted, if desired)

1 heaping tablespoon Roquefort
    or other blue cheese
1 tablespoon butter or margarine,
    melted (optional)

• Cook beans according to package directions.

• Combine with remaining ingredients; mix well.

• Serve hot with salt and pepper to taste.

Makes 3 servings

Prep Time: 2 to 3 minutes   **Cook Time:** 4 to 6 minutes

Calico Corn

1 bag (16 ounces) BIRDS EYE®
    frozen Corn

½ cup finely diced green pepper
½ cup chopped tomato

• Cook corn according to package directions.

• Combine corn with green pepper and tomato.

• Add salt and pepper to taste.

Makes 4 to 6 servings

Prep Time: 2 to 3 minutes   **Cook Time:** 6 to 8 minutes

Top to bottom: **Green Beans with Blue Cheese and Calico Corn**

Iowa Corn Pudding

½ cup egg substitute *or* 2 large
    eggs
2 large egg whites
3 tablespoons all-purpose flour
1 tablespoon sugar
½ teaspoon freshly ground black
    pepper
1 can (16½ ounces) cream-style
    corn
2 cups fresh corn kernels or
    frozen corn, thawed and
    drained

1 cup (4 ounces) shredded
    ALPINE LACE® American
    Flavor Pasteurized Process
    Cheese Product
½ cup finely chopped red bell
    pepper
⅓ cup 2% low fat milk
1 tablespoon unsalted butter
    substitute
¼ teaspoon paprika
    Sprigs of fresh parsley

1. Preheat the oven to 350°F. Spray an 8-inch round baking dish with nonstick cooking spray. (A deep-dish pie plate works well.) Place in the oven to heat.

2. Meanwhile, in a large bowl, using an electric mixer set on high, beat the egg substitute (or the whole eggs) and egg whites with the flour, sugar and black pepper until smooth. Stir in the creamed corn, corn kernels, cheese, bell pepper and milk. Pour into the hot baking dish.

3. Dot with the butter and sprinkle with the paprika. Bake, uncovered, for 55 minutes or until set. Let stand for 15 minutes before serving. Garnish with the parsley.

Makes 6 servings

Iowa Corn Pudding

Curried Baked Beans

1 pound small dry white beans
6 cups water
1 teaspoon salt
2 medium apples, cored, pared
    and diced
⅔ cup honey

½ cup golden raisins
1 small onion, minced
⅓ cup sweet pickle relish
1 tablespoon prepared mustard
1 teaspoon curry powder
    (or to taste)

Combine beans, water and salt in large saucepan. Let stand overnight. Bring to a boil over high heat. Reduce heat to low and simmer 2 hours, adding water, if needed. Drain beans, reserving liquid. Combine beans with remaining ingredients. Pour into 2½-quart casserole. Add enough bean liquid to barely cover. Bake, covered, at 300°F 1 hour. Remove cover; bake about 30 minutes, adding more liquid, if needed.

Makes 8 servings

Favorite recipe from **National Honey Board**

Festive Green Beans

1 tablespoon olive oil
1 tablespoon butter or margarine
3 medium leeks, well rinsed and
    sliced
2 large red bell peppers, seeded
    and cut into thin strips
2 pounds green beans, trimmed

1 large clove garlic, minced
1½ teaspoons salt
1 teaspoon TABASCO® pepper
    sauce
1 teaspoon grated lemon peel
¼ cup sliced natural almonds,
    toasted

In 12-inch skillet over medium heat, heat oil and butter; add leeks. Cook 5 minutes, stirring occasionally. Add red pepper strips; cook 5 minutes longer or until vegetables are tender. Meanwhile, steam green beans for 5 minutes or until crisp-tender. Drain. Add beans, garlic, salt, TABASCO® sauce and grated lemon peel to skillet; toss to mix well. Sprinkle with toasted almonds.

Makes 8 servings

"New" Crunchy Green Beans

1 box (9 ounces) BIRDS EYE®
    frozen French Cut Green
    Beans with Toasted Almonds
1 tablespoon vegetable or olive oil
2 teaspoons red wine or cider
    vinegar

1 teaspoon instant minced onions
    or 1 tablespoon fresh diced
    onion
⅓ cup herbed croutons, coarsely
    crushed

• Preheat oven to 375°F. Combine green beans (reserve almonds in packet), oil, vinegar and onions; mix well.

• Place mixture in 1-quart baking dish sprayed with nonstick cooking spray. Combine croutons and almonds from packet. Sprinkle over green bean mixture.

• Bake 15 to 20 minutes or until beans are heated through and almonds are golden brown.

Makes 3 to 4 servings

Prep Time: 5 minutes   **Cook Time:** 15 to 20 minutes

Corn Maque Choux

2 tablespoons butter or margarine
½ cup chopped onion
½ cup chopped green pepper
4 cups whole kernel corn (canned,
    fresh or frozen, thawed)

1 medium tomato, chopped
¼ teaspoon salt
½ teaspoon TABASCO®
    pepper sauce

• In 3-quart saucepan melt butter over medium heat.

• Add onion and green pepper; cook 5 minutes or until tender, stirring frequently.

• Stir in corn, tomato, salt and TABASCO® sauce.

• Reduce heat and simmer 10 to 15 minutes or until corn is tender.

Makes 3 cups

Sweet & Hot Marinated Mushrooms

⅓ cup honey
¼ cup white wine vinegar
¼ cup dry white wine or vegetable
    broth
2 tablespoons vegetable oil
1 tablespoon soy sauce
1 tablespoon dark sesame oil
1 clove garlic, minced

1 small green onion, chopped
1 teaspoon grated fresh gingerroot
½ teaspoon grated orange peel
¼ teaspoon ground red pepper
1 pound fresh small button
    mushrooms
Parsley sprigs and orange
    wedges for garnish (optional)

Combine honey, vinegar, wine, vegetable oil, soy sauce, sesame oil, garlic, green onion, gingerroot, orange peel and red pepper in small saucepan. Cook and stir mixture over low heat until hot. Place mushrooms in heatproof bowl; pour hot marinade over mushrooms. Cover and marinate 3 hours in refrigerator, stirring occasionally. Arrange mushrooms in serving dish; garnish with parsley sprigs and orange wedges, if desired.

Makes 4 to 6 servings

Favorite recipe from **National Honey Board**

Leeks with Bel Paese®

3 leeks
3 tablespoons butter
1 tablespoon olive oil
2 cups milk

4 ounces BEL PAESE® Semi-soft
    Cheese, thinly sliced
Pepper

Remove leek tops to within 2 inches of bulb. Remove outer layer of bulb. Wash leeks thoroughly. Cut into large pieces. In medium saucepan, melt butter over medium-low heat. Add oil, milk and leeks. Cover and cook until tender, 20 to 30 minutes. Drain thoroughly. Preheat oven to 350°F. Butter 1-quart casserole. Place leeks in prepared casserole. Cover with slices of cheese. Bake until cheese is melted, 10 to 15 minutes. Sprinkle with pepper to taste. Serve immediately.

Makes 4 servings

Sweet & Hot Marinated Mushrooms

Spiced Mushroom Pecan Rice Timbales

1 cup finely chopped shiitake or
    other mushrooms
¾ cup apple juice
1 (3-inch) cinnamon stick, broken
    in half
¼ teaspoon salt

3 whole allspice
¾ cup uncooked white basmati
    rice
¼ cup finely toasted pecans
3 tablespoons minced fresh chives
    or green onions

1. Spray 5 (5-ounce) custard cups or molds with nonstick cooking spray; set aside. Spray heavy medium saucepan with cooking spray; heat over medium-high heat until hot. Add mushrooms; cook and stir 5 minutes or until tender.

2. Stir ¾ cup water, apple juice, cinnamon sticks, salt and allspice into saucepan; bring to a boil over high heat. Stir in rice; cover. Reduce heat to medium-low. Simmer 15 to 20 minutes or until liquid is absorbed and rice is tender. Remove saucepan from heat. Remove cinnamon sticks and allspice; discard. Stir pecans and chives into saucepan. Spoon rice mixture evenly into prepared cups; pack down with back of spoon. Let stand 5 minutes; unmold onto serving plates. Serve immediately. *Makes 5 servings*

Savory Apple Sauté

½ cup butter or margarine
2 cups sliced onions
5 Golden Delicious apples
½ teaspoon dried basil, crushed

¼ cup brandy
½ cup water
1 tablespoon red wine vinegar
1 teaspoon cornstarch

In large skillet, melt butter over medium-low heat; add onions and sauté 20 minutes or until soft and golden. Meanwhile, core, peel, and slice apples. Add apples and basil to onion mixture and cook 3 minutes. Stir in brandy and reduce heat to low. In small bowl, blend water, vinegar, and cornstarch; stirring, pour over apple mixture. Increase heat to medium and cook, stirring, until thickened. *Makes 1½ cups*

Favorite recipe from **Washington Apple Commission**

Spiced Mushroom Pecan Rice Timbales

Onions Stuffed with Vegetables and Cheese

1½ cups (6 ounces) shredded
    JARLSBERG LITE™ Cheese
1 cup flavored bread crumbs
1 tablespoon fresh thyme leaves
    or 1 teaspoon dried thyme,
    crushed
6 onions (6 to 7 ounces each)
1 teaspoon olive or vegetable oil
1 teaspoon minced garlic

¾ cup finely chopped green pepper
    (1 medium pepper)
½ cup finely chopped celery with
    leaves
1½ cups vegetable broth or white
    wine (or a mixture), divided
3 teaspoons grated Parmesan
    cheese, optional
½ cup salsa (or gravy), optional

Mix cheese, bread crumbs and thyme; set aside.

Peel onions. Cut about ½ inch off tops and scoop out middles, leaving ½-inch shells. Cut ¼ inch off stem ends so onions will sit and set aside.

Finely chop enough onion center to measure ½ cup and set aside. Reserve remaining onion for another use.

Heat oil in skillet; add garlic and sauté over high heat 1 minute. Add ½ cup chopped onion, pepper and celery and sauté 2 minutes. Add 2 tablespoons broth and cover quickly to steam 2 minutes. Cool. Add onion mixture and ¼ cup broth to bread crumb mixture. Stuff onions with mixture (about ½ cup in each). If desired, top each onion with ½ teaspoon Parmesan cheese.

Place in baking dish. Pour remaining broth around onions. Tent with foil, crimping sides around dish but not touching onion tops. Bake 1 hour at 400° or until onions are tender.

To serve, lift onions out with slotted spoon and, if desired, mix salsa or gravy into pan juices. Spoon over onions.

Makes 6 servings

Note: Onion peels and reserved onion may be added to a vegetable stockpot.

Sautéed Garlic Potatoes

Sautéed Garlic Potatoes

2 pounds boiling potatoes, peeled
   and cut into 1-inch pieces
3 tablespoons FILIPPO BERIO®
   Olive Oil
6 cloves garlic, skins on
1 tablespoon lemon juice

1 tablespoon chopped fresh chives
1 tablespoon chopped fresh
   parsley
Salt and freshly ground black
   pepper

Place potatoes in large colander; rinse under cold running water. Drain well; pat dry.
In large nonstick skillet, heat olive oil over medium heat until hot. Add potatoes in a
single layer. Cook, stirring and turning frequently, 10 minutes or until golden brown.
Add garlic. Cover; reduce heat to low and cook very gently, shaking pan and stirring
mixture occasionally, 15 to 20 minutes or until potatoes are tender when pierced with
fork. Remove garlic; discard skins. In small bowl, crush garlic; stir in lemon juice. Add
to potatoes; mix well. Cook 1 to 2 minutes or until heated through. Transfer to serving
dish; sprinkle with chives and parsley. Season to taste with salt and pepper.

Makes 4 servings

Southwestern Twice-Baked Spuds

2 baking potatoes with skins
(about 6 ounces each)
½ cup GUILTLESS GOURMET®
Nacho Dip (mild or spicy)
¼ cup finely chopped green onions
¼ teaspoon coarsely ground black
pepper

2 tablespoons GUILTLESS
GOURMET® Salsa (mild,
medium or hot)
2 tablespoons chopped fresh
cilantro
Nasturtium flowers (optional)

Preheat oven to 400°F. Scrub potatoes with vegetable brush; pierce in several places with fork. Bake potatoes 45 to 50 minutes or until fork-tender. Remove from oven; cool potatoes until safe enough to handle.

Reduce oven temperature to 300°F. Slice potatoes in half lengthwise. Form 4 shells by scooping out most of potato pulp, being careful not to pierce skin. Place pulp in large bowl; mash with potato masher or whip with electric mixer. Add nacho dip, onions and pepper. Blend until smooth. Add salsa and cilantro; mix until blended. Fill potato shells with equal amount of potato mixture, heaping to form mounds. Wrap skins in foil, leaving tops open. Place on baking sheet.

Bake 25 minutes or until heated through. Serve hot. Garnish with edible flowers, if desired.

Makes 4 servings

Southwestern Twice-Baked Spud

Potatoes Jarlsberg

8 medium new potatoes, peeled
and quartered
2 medium turnips, peeled and cut
into chunks
1 medium onion, finely chopped
¼ cup butter or margarine,
softened

¼ cup chopped fresh parsley
1¼ cups (5 ounces) shredded
JARLSBERG Cheese, divided
½ teaspoon salt
¼ teaspoon grated nutmeg
⅛ teaspoon black pepper

In large saucepan, cook potatoes in lightly salted water for 10 minutes. Add turnips and onion; cook 15 minutes longer or until vegetables are tender. Drain well. Beat with electric mixer until smooth. Beat in butter and parsley. Add ¾ cup Jarlsberg, salt, nutmeg and pepper. Reserve 1 cup mixture.

Spread remaining potato mixture into buttered 1½-quart baking dish. Press reserved potato mixture through pastry bag with star tip around edge of casserole.

Bake at 350° for 40 minutes. Sprinkle remaining ½ cup Jarlsberg in center of casserole. Bake 5 minutes longer. *Makes 8 servings*

Savory Sweet Potato Sticks

3 medium sweet potatoes (about
1½ pounds)
3 cups KELLOGG'S® RICE
KRISPIES® cereal, crushed
to ¾ cup
½ teaspoon garlic salt
¼ teaspoon onion salt

⅛ teaspoon cayenne
½ cup all-purpose flour
2 egg whites
2 tablespoons water
Vegetable cooking spray
Salsa (optional)

1. Wash potatoes and cut lengthwise into ½-inch slices. Cut slices into ½-inch strips. Set aside.

2. In shallow pan or plate, combine Kellogg's® Rice Krispies® cereal and spices. Set aside. Place flour in second shallow pan or plate. Set aside. Beat together egg whites and water. Set aside. Coat potatoes with flour, shaking off excess. Dip coated potatoes in egg mixture, then coat with cereal mixture. Place in single layer on foil-lined baking sheet coated with cooking spray.

3. Bake at 400°F about 30 minutes or until lightly browned. Serve hot with salsa, if desired.

Makes 15 servings

Prep Time: 25 minutes   **Bake Time:** 15 minutes

Ratatouille

1 small eggplant, cut into ½-inch cubes
2 green peppers, diced
1 medium onion, sliced
1 clove garlic, minced
¼ cup olive oil
1 can (14½ ounces) DEL MONTE® FreshCut™ Zucchini with Italian-Style Tomato Sauce
1 can (14½ ounces) DEL MONTE® Original Recipe Stewed Tomatoes
½ teaspoon salt
⅛ teaspoon black pepper

Cook eggplant, green peppers, onion and garlic in oil over medium-high heat, stirring constantly. Add zucchini, tomatoes, salt and black pepper. Cover; simmer 30 minutes.

Makes 6 to 8 servings

Acorn Squash Filled with Savory Spinach

4 small acorn squash
2 tablespoons FILIPPO BERIO®
    Olive Oil
1 (10-ounce) package frozen
    chopped spinach, thawed and
    drained
1 (8-ounce) container ricotta
    cheese

1 tablespoon grated Parmesan
    cheese
¼ teaspoon freshly ground black
    pepper
⅛ teaspoon salt
⅛ teaspoon ground nutmeg

Preheat oven to 325°F. Cut squash crosswise in half. Scoop out seeds and fibers; discard. Brush insides and outsides of squash halves with olive oil. Place in large shallow roasting pan. Bake, uncovered, 35 to 40 minutes or until tender when pierced with fork.

In medium bowl, combine spinach, ricotta cheese, Parmesan cheese, pepper, salt and nutmeg. Spoon equal amounts of spinach mixture into squash halves. Bake, uncovered, an additional 10 to 15 minutes or until heated through.   *Makes 8 servings*

Spinach Pie

1 tablespoon FILIPPO BERIO®
    Olive Oil
1 pound fresh spinach, washed,
    drained and stems removed
1 medium potato, cooked and
    mashed

2 eggs, beaten
¼ cup cottage cheese
2 tablespoons grated Romano
    cheese
Salt

Preheat oven to 350°F. Grease 8-inch round cake pan with olive oil. Tear spinach into bite-size pieces. In large bowl, combine spinach, potato, eggs, cottage cheese and Romano cheese. Spoon mixture into prepared pan. Bake 15 to 20 minutes or until set. Season to taste with salt.   *Makes 6 servings*

Acorn Squash Filled with Savory Spinach

Baked Spiced Squash

Baked Spiced Squash

2 boxes (12 ounces each) BIRDS
   EYE® frozen Cooked Winter
   Squash, thawed
2 egg whites, lightly beaten
¼ cup brown sugar

2 teaspoons butter or margarine,
   melted
1 teaspoon cinnamon
½ cup herbed croutons, coarsely
   crushed

• Preheat oven to 400°F. Combine squash, egg whites, sugar, butter and cinnamon; mix well.

• Pour into 1-quart baking dish sprayed with nonstick cooking spray.

• Bake 20 to 25 minutes or until center is set.

• Remove from oven; sprinkle crushed croutons on top. Bake 5 to 7 minutes longer or until croutons are browned.
Makes 6 to 8 servings

Prep Time: 5 minutes   **Cook Time:** 25 to 35 minutes

Honey-Grilled Vegetables

12 small red potatoes, halved
¼ cup honey
3 tablespoons dry white wine
1 clove garlic, minced
1 teaspoon dried thyme, crushed
½ teaspoon salt
½ teaspoon black pepper
2 zucchini, halved lengthwise and
    cut crosswise into halves

1 medium eggplant, sliced ½ inch
    thick
1 green bell pepper, cut vertically
    in eighths
1 red bell pepper, cut vertically in
    eighths
1 large onion, sliced ½ inch thick

Cover potatoes with water. Bring to a boil and simmer 5 minutes; drain. Combine honey, wine, garlic, thyme, salt and black pepper; mix well. Place vegetables on oiled barbecue grill over hot coals. Grill 20 to 25 minutes, turning and brushing with honey mixture every 7 or 8 minutes.

Makes 4 to 6 servings

Oven Method: Toss vegetables with honey mixture. Bake, uncovered, at 400°F 25 minutes or until tender; stir every 8 to 10 minutes to prevent burning.

Favorite recipe from **National Honey Board**

Vegetable Sauté

2 tablespoons FILIPPO BERIO® Olive Oil
2 yellow squash, trimmed and cut into 1-inch chunks
1 medium onion, sliced
4 baby eggplants, trimmed and halved lengthwise
1 medium yellow bell pepper, cut into ¼-inch strips
8 baby carrots, peeled and trimmed
8 cherry tomatoes, cut in half
1 tablespoon chopped garlic
1 tablespoon chopped fresh thyme*
½ cup coarsely chopped fresh basil*
Salt and freshly ground black pepper
Fresh thyme sprig (optional)

In large heavy skillet, heat olive oil over medium-high heat until hot. Add squash, onion, eggplants, bell pepper and carrots. Cook, stirring constantly, 5 minutes. Add tomatoes, garlic and thyme. Cook, stirring constantly, 3 minutes or until vegetables are tender-crisp. Stir in basil. Season to taste with salt and black pepper. Garnish with thyme sprig, if desired.

Makes 6 servings

Omit herbs if fresh are unavailable. Do not substitute dried herb leaves.

Vegetable Sauté

Grilled Vegetables with Balsamic Vinaigrette

1 medium eggplant	¼ cup balsamic vinegar
(about 1¼ pounds)	1 teaspoon salt
2 medium zucchini	¼ teaspoon black pepper
2 to 3 medium yellow squash	1 clove garlic, minced
2 medium red bell peppers	2 to 3 tablespoons finely chopped
¾ cup olive oil	mixed fresh herbs

Trim, then slice eggplant, zucchini and yellow squash lengthwise into ¼- to ½-inch-thick slices. Core, seed and cut red peppers into 1-inch-wide strips. Place vegetables in a deep serving platter or wide shallow casserole. Combine oil, vinegar, salt, black pepper, garlic and chopped herbs in small bowl. Pour vinaigrette over vegetables; turn to coat. Let stand 30 minutes or longer. Lift vegetables from vinaigrette, leaving vinaigrette that doesn't cling to the vegetables in the dish.

Oil hot grid to help prevent sticking. Grill vegetables, on a covered grill, over medium **KINGSFORD®** briquets, 8 to 16 minutes until fork-tender, turning once or twice. (Time will depend on the vegetable; eggplant takes the longest.) As vegetables are done, return them to the platter, then turn to coat with vinaigrette. (Or, cut eggplant, zucchini and yellow squash into cubes, then toss with red peppers and vinaigrette.) Serve warm or at room temperature.

Makes 6 servings

Grilled Vegetables with Balsamic Vinaigrette

Marinated Vegetables

2 cups broccoli flowerettes
2 cups cauliflower flowerettes
8 ounces fresh green beans, cut
    into 2-inch pieces
2 cups diagonally sliced carrots
1 cup cherry tomatoes, halved
½ cup chopped red onion
⅓ cup GREY POUPON®
    COUNTRY DIJON® Mustard

⅓ cup olive oil
¼ cup REGINA® Red Wine
    Vinegar
1 teaspoon sugar
1 teaspoon dried oregano leaves
¼ teaspoon coarsely ground black
    pepper
⅓ cup oil-packed sun-dried tomato
    strips

In large heavy pot, steam broccoli, cauliflower, green beans and carrots until tender-crisp. Rinse vegetables in cold water and drain well; place in large serving bowl. Stir in cherry tomatoes and onion. In small bowl, whisk mustard, oil, vinegar, sugar, oregano and pepper; stir in sun-dried tomatoes. Pour dressing over vegetables, tossing to coat well. Chill for at least 2 hours before serving, stirring occasionally. Garnish as desired.

Makes 6 servings

Honey Kissed Winter Vegetables

2 to 2½ cups pared seeded ½-inch
    winter squash cubes
1 turnip, pared and cut into
    ½-inch cubes
2 carrots, pared and cut into
    ½-inch slices

1 small onion, cut into quarters
¼ cup honey
2 tablespoons butter or
    margarine, melted
1 teaspoon grated orange peel
¼ teaspoon ground nutmeg

Steam squash, turnip, carrots and onion on rack over 1 inch of boiling water in large covered skillet about 5 minutes or until tender. Drain. Combine honey, butter, orange peel and nutmeg in small bowl. Drizzle over vegetables and toss to coat in heated serving dish.

Makes 4 to 6 servings

Favorite recipe from **National Honey Board**

Marinated Vegetables

Sicilian Caponata

5 tablespoons olive oil, *divided*
8 cups (1½ pounds) unpeeled
    eggplant, cut into ½-inch
    cubes
2½ cups sliced onions (2 small)
1 cup chopped celery (3 stalks)
1¾ cups (14.5-ounce can)
    CONTADINA® Pasta Ready
    Chunky Tomatoes with
    Olive Oil, Garlic and Spices,
    undrained

⅓ cup chopped ripe olives, drained
¼ cup balsamic or red wine
    vinegar
2 tablespoons capers
2 teaspoons granulated sugar
½ teaspoon salt
    Dash ground black pepper

HEAT *3 tablespoons* oil in medium skillet over high heat. Add eggplant; cook for 6 minutes or until eggplant is tender. Remove from skillet; drain on paper towels.

ADD *remaining 2 tablespoons* oil to skillet; heat over medium heat. Sauté onions and celery for 5 minutes or until tender.

STIR in tomatoes and juice and eggplant; bring to a boil. Reduce heat; simmer, covered, for 15 minutes. Stir in olives, vinegar, capers, sugar, salt and pepper. Cook for 5 minutes.

Makes 4½ cups

Sicilian Caponata

Grilled Vegetables al Fresco

2 large red bell peppers
2 medium zucchini

1 large eggplant

SPICY MARINADE

⅔ cup white wine vinegar
½ cup soy sauce
2 tablespoons minced ginger
2 tablespoons olive oil

2 tablespoons dark sesame oil
2 large cloves garlic, minced
2 teaspoons TABASCO® pepper
   sauce

• Seed red peppers; cut each pepper into quarters. Cut each zucchini lengthwise into ¼-inch-thick strips. Slice eggplant into ¼-inch-thick rounds.

• In 13×9-inch baking dish, combine Spicy Marinade ingredients. Place vegetable pieces in mixture; toss to mix well. Cover and refrigerate vegetables at least 2 hours or up to 24 hours, turning occasionally.

• About 30 minutes before serving, preheat grill to medium heat, placing rack 5 to 6 inches above coals. Place red peppers, zucchini and eggplant slices on grill rack. Grill vegetables 4 minutes, turning once and brushing with marinade occasionally.

Makes 4 servings

To Broil: Preheat oven broiler and broil vegetables 5 to 6 inches below broiler flame for 4 minutes on each side.

Acknowledgments

**The publisher would like to thank the companies and organizations
listed below for the use of their recipes and photographs
in this publication.**

Alpine Lace Brands, Inc.
American Italian Pasta Company
Athens Foods®
BC-USA
BelGioioso® Cheese, Inc.
Birds Eye
Black-Eyed Pea Jamboree—Athens, Texas
California Olive Industry
California Tomato Commission
California Tree Fruit Agreement
California Wild Rice
Canned Food Information Council
Chef Paul Prudhomme's® Magic Seasoning
    Blends®
Christopher Ranch Garlic
Cucina Classica Italiana, Inc.
Del Monte Corporation
Dole Food Company, Inc.
Filippo Berio Olive Oil
The Fremont Company, Makers of Frank's
    & SnowFloss Kraut and Tomato Products
Golden Grain/Mission Pasta
Grandma's Molasses, a division of
    Cadbury Beverages Inc.
Guiltless Gourmet, Incorporated
Healthy Choice®
The HVR Company
Kellogg Company
Kikkoman International Inc.
The Kingsford Products Company
Kraft Foods, Inc.
Lawry's® Foods, Inc.

Lipton
McIlhenny Company
Michigan Bean Commission
Minnesota Cultivated Wild Rice Council
MOTT'S® U.S.A., a division of
    Cadbury Beverages Inc.
Mushroom Council
Nabisco, Inc.
National Honey Board
National Onion Association
National Pasta Association
National Sunflower Association
Nestlé Food Company
Norseland, Inc.
North Dakota Barley Council
Northwest Cherry Growers
Pimento Canners of America
The Procter & Gamble Company
The Quaker® Oatmeal Kitchens
Ralston Foods, Inc.
Reckitt & Colman Inc.
RED STAR® Yeast & Products,
    A Division of Universal Foods
    Corporation
Sargento Foods Inc.®
South Texas Onion Committee
The Sugar Association, Inc.
Sunkist Growers
USA Rice Council
Walnut Marketing Board
Washington Apple Commission
Wisconsin Milk Marketing Board

VOLUME MEASUREMENTS (dry)

$\frac{1}{8}$ teaspoon = 0.5 mL
$\frac{1}{4}$ teaspoon = 1 mL
$\frac{1}{2}$ teaspoon = 2 mL
$\frac{3}{4}$ teaspoon = 4 mL
1 teaspoon = 5 mL
1 tablespoon = 15 mL
2 tablespoons = 30 mL
$\frac{1}{4}$ cup = 60 mL
$\frac{1}{3}$ cup = 75 mL
$\frac{1}{2}$ cup = 125 mL
$\frac{2}{3}$ cup = 150 mL
$\frac{3}{4}$ cup = 175 mL
1 cup = 250 mL
2 cups = 1 pint = 500 mL
3 cups = 750 mL
4 cups = 1 quart = 1 L

VOLUME MEASUREMENTS (fluid)

1 fluid ounce (2 tablespoons) = 30 mL
4 fluid ounces ($\frac{1}{2}$ cup) = 125 mL
8 fluid ounces (1 cup) = 250 mL
12 fluid ounces (1$\frac{1}{2}$ cups) = 375 mL
16 fluid ounces (2 cups) = 500 mL

WEIGHTS (mass)

$\frac{1}{2}$ ounce = 15 g
1 ounce = 30 g
3 ounces = 90 g
4 ounces = 120 g
8 ounces = 225 g
10 ounces = 285 g
12 ounces = 360 g
16 ounces = 1 pound = 450 g

DIMENSIONS

$\frac{1}{16}$ inch = 2 mm
$\frac{1}{8}$ inch = 3 mm
$\frac{1}{4}$ inch = 6 mm
$\frac{1}{2}$ inch = 1.5 cm
$\frac{3}{4}$ inch = 2 cm
1 inch = 2.5 cm

OVEN TEMPERATURES

250°F = 120°C
275°F = 140°C
300°F = 150°C
325°F = 160°C
350°F = 180°C
375°F = 190°C
400°F = 200°C
425°F = 220°C
450°F = 230°C

BAKING PAN SIZES

Utensil	Size in Inches/Quarts	Metric Volume	Size in Centimeters
Baking or Cake Pan (square or rectangular)	8×8×2	2 L	20×20×5
	9×9×2	2.5 L	22×22×5
	12×8×2	3 L	30×20×5
	13×9×2	3.5 L	33×23×5
Loaf Pan	8×4×3	1.5 L	20×10×7
	9×5×3	2 L	23×13×7
Round Layer Cake Pan	8×1½	1.2 L	20×4
	9×1½	1.5 L	23×4
Pie Plate	8×1¼	750 mL	20×3
	9×1¼	1 L	23×3
Baking Dish or Casserole	1 quart	1 L	—
	1½ quart	1.5 L	—
	2 quart	2 L	—